JOURNAL FOR THE STUDY OF THE NEW TESTAMENT SUPPLEMENT SERIES
44

Executive Editor, Supplement Series
David Hill

Publishing Editor
David E. Orton

JSOT Press
Sheffield

To my parents, Wilfried and Elise Heinzel,
who sponsored and supported my lengthy scholarly journey;

To the memory of L. Benjamin Busch,
who helped me to start it at the right place;

and to Mary Chilton Callaway,
who—as a mother and scholar—
inspired me to finish it against all odds.

The
NEW COVENANT
in
HEBREWS

Susanne Lehne

Journal for the Study of the New Testament
Supplement Series 44

Copyright © 1990 Sheffield Academic Press

Published by JSOT Press
JSOT Press is an imprint of
Sheffield Academic Press Ltd
The University of Sheffield
343 Fulwood Road
Sheffield S10 3BP
England

Typeset by Sheffield Academic Press
and
Printed in Great Britain
by Billing & Sons Ltd
Worcester

British Library Cataloguing in Publication Data

Lehne, Susanne
The new covenant in Hebrews.
1. Bible. N.T. Hebrews—Critical studies
I. Title II. Series
227.8706

ISSN 0143-5108
ISBN 1-85075-238-9

CONTENTS

ABBREVIATIONS

AB	Anchor Bible
ALGHJ	Arbeiten zur Literatur und Geschichte des hellenistischen Judentums
AnBib	Analecta biblica
ATR	*Anglican Theological Review*
AUSS	*Andrews University Seminary Studies*
Bib	*Biblica*
BSac	*Bibliotheca Sacra*
BZ	*Biblische Zeitschrift*
CBQ	*Catholic Biblical Quarterly*
CBQMS	CBQ Monograph Series
CJT	*Canadian Journal of Theology*
CRINT	Compendia rerum iudaicarum ad Novum Testamentum
CTM	*Concordia Theological Monthly*
DSS	Dead Sea Scrolls
EBib	Etudes bibliques
ETL	*Ephemerides theologicae lovanienses*
EvQ	*Evangelical Quarterly*
EvT	*Evangelische Theologie*
ExpTim	*Expository Times*
FRLANT	Forschungen zur Religion und Literatur des Alten und Neuen Testaments
GTA	Göttinger theologische Arbeiten
Heb.	(Epistle to the/Book of) Hebrews
HNT	Handbuch zum Neuen Testament
HTR	*Harvard Theological Review*
HUCA	*Hebrew Union College Annual*
IBS	*Irish Biblical Studies*
ICC	International Critical Commentary
IDBSup	Supplementary Volume to *Interpreter's Dictionary of the Bible*
Int	*Interpretation*

JBL	*Journal of Biblical Literature*
JES	*Journal of Ecumenical Studies*
JETS	*Journal of the Evangelical Theological Society*
JPS	Jewish Publication Society
JSJ	*Journal for the Study of Judaism in the Persian, Hellenistic and Roman Periods*
JSOTSup	Journal for the Study of the Old Testament—Supplement Series
JTS	*Journal of Theological Studies*
KD	*Kerygma und Dogma*
L.S.	Last Supper
MeyerK	H.A.W. Meyer, Kritisch-exegetischer Kommentar über das Neue Testament
MTZ	*Münchener Theologische Zeitschrift*
NC	New Covenant
Neot	*Neotestamentica*
NICNT	New International Commentary on the New Testament
NJBC	*New Jerome Biblical Commentary* (ed. R.E. Brown et al.)
NovT	*Novum Testamentum*
NRT	*La nouvelle revue théologique*
NT	New Testament
NTD	Das Neue Testament Deutsch
NTS	*New Testament Studies*
OT	Old Testament
OTP	*Old Testament Pseudepigrapha* (ed. J.H. Charlesworth)
PTR	*Princeton Theological Review*
RB	*Revue biblique*
RevExp	*Review and Expositor*
RevQ	*Revue de Qumran*
RNT	Regensburger Neues Testament
RSR	*Recherches de science religieuse*
RSV	Revised Standard Version
RTP	*Revue de Théologie et de Philosophie*
SBLDS	Society of Biblical Literature Dissertation Series
SBT	Studies in Biblical Theology
Sem	*Semitica*
SR	*Studies in Religion*
ST	*Studia theologica*

StudNeot	Studia neotestamentica
TDNT	*Theological Dictionary of the New Testament* (ed. G. Kittel and G. Friedrich)
TGl	*Theologie und Glaube*
TLZ	*Theologische Literaturzeitung*
TRu	*Theologische Rundschau*
VT	*Vetus Testamentum*
VTSup	Vetus Testamentum, Supplements
WMANT	Wissenschaftliche Monographien zum Alten und Neuen Testament
WTJ	*Westminster Theological Journal*
WUNT	Wissenschaftliche Untersuchungen zum Neuen Testament
ZAW	*Zeitschrift für die alttestamentliche Wissenshaft*
ZNW	*Zeitschrift für die neutestamentliche Wissenschaft*
ZTK	*Zeitschrift für Theologie und Kirche*

Chapter 1

INTRODUCTION

No commentator on Hebrews (henceforth Heb.) can afford to overlook the notion of the New Covenant (NC), since it gives rise to the author's insertion of the longest single quotation from the Hebrew Scriptures in the NT. Nonetheless this concept appears to warrant a fuller-scale treatment than it has hitherto received.[1]

Our familiarity with the idea of a 'New Testament', which is after all derived from the concept here in view, somewhat complicates this investigation, because it may tempt us to take references to a NC for granted without further questioning. Alternatively, we might also read more into a first century document from our later experience with the usage of this term. An example of the latter pitfall would be to attribute to the author of Heb. the view that the Hebrew Scriptures are coterminous with the old covenant. Not only would this constitute a patent anachronism,[2] but it would also overlook the document's insistence on the *continuity* of God's speaking in history.

This study will investigate the role of the NC idea in Heb. from the standpoint of the author and of his first readers.[3] It is my suspicion that these standpoints may very well turn out to be distinct, and that the NC concept has been chosen by the writer—perhaps building upon community tradition—in an attempt to respond to the problems of his addressess. I am departing from the assumption that the NC theme is a major one in Heb., a linchpin in fact, without which the structure of the author's thinking would fall apart and lose its coherence. We will seek to verify Wrede's sweeping claim that Heb. is a study 'concerning the relationship of the old and new covenants'.[4]

In so doing one must go beyond actual occurrences of the term 'covenant' in the text, because in accordance with biblical usage the author of Heb. associates a whole symbolic universe with the idea, a particular relationship of God with his people. Therefore the whole document will have to be taken into account, not merely the central section (4.14-10.18) within which all but three (10.29; 12.24; 13.20) of the 17 occurrences of διαθήκη fall. Even the semantic evidence is not clear-cut, for there are six other instances in which διαθήκη may be supplied as the understood noun (8.7 (twice); 8.13 (twice); 9.1, 18). In 9.18 (and perhaps in 9.1) the author may have deliberately left ambiguous the referent of ἡ πρώτη (Tent/covenant).

Over and above these 23 references to διαθήκη, then, the proem (1.1-4), with its picture of two eras of divine revelation, falls within the purview of this study. The juxtaposition of the touchable revelation through the earthly voice, and the unshakable revelation through the heavenly voice (12.18-28), must be regarded of equal importance. Finally there are scattered echoes of covenantal language and thought patterns that are also worthy of consideration, e.g. the invocation of blessing and curse in the simile of 6.7-8.

Since most commentators would agree that a major concern of Heb. is God's speaking and his people's hearing of his Word at various times in history, it is but a small step to the problem of God's covenantal relationship with his people. Would it not be true to say that the notion of covenant stands in the background even of the introductory chapters (1.1-4.13), of which it is often stated that they deal supremely with the Word?[6]

While we do not wish to exclude the possibility that Heb. presents Jesus as a hypostasized Logos in 4.13,[7] our main concern for the purposes of this study lies in the writer's skillful use of the category of 'Word' as revelation and its interplay with the category of 'covenant'. λόγος (or ῥῆμα) can refer to revelation in general (4.12-13), both old (2.2; 4.2; 12.19) and new (6.1, 5; 7.28). The latter is often presented as mediated by the author himself and by other Christian leaders (5.11, 13; 13.7, 17, 22).

The choice of a particular rubric to guide one's exegesis influences one's conclusions about the text. By analyzing the hermeneutics of Heb. under the heading of the 'Word', G. Hughes is bound to stress continuity, in speaking of the 'same Word making the same kinds of demand upon those who are its recipients'.[8] But this accounts for only one side of Heb. At first glance, the rubric of 'covenant' seems to point instead to a picture of sharp contrasts, because of its qualifying adjectives: 'first/second, old/new and better' (chs. 8-10).

Here we have arrived at the crux of the problem of continuity and discontinuity in God's modes of revelation that will continue to haunt us during this inquiry. Granted that 'L'Epître aux Hébreux est de loin l'écrit du Nouveau Testament qui a le plus insisté sur la notion d'alliance',[9] why does our author choose to qualify the new order of Christ by the term διαθήκη? Is it to underline its *continuity* with the old order of Israel? Or is Grässer right in insisting that the issue is 'nicht nur... typologische Entsprechung zur alttestamentlichen *berît*, sondern *Andersartigkeit*,... *Gegensatz*'?[10] Did the author view the relationship between the covenants in a dialectical fashion? Since dialectical thought patterns can be found in most NT writings, we will try to discern what is distinctive about the mode of argumentation in Heb. and where the accent falls. The author's comparative framework has been analyzed by many exegetes from the standpoint of the hermeneutical scheme. 'correspondence, contrast and superiority'.[11] We propose to apply this scheme to the NC concept in Heb. and to test its validity in the process.

To put it another way: how new is the NC? Is its newness of such a drastic quality as to turn it into something wholly other? Is it in fact no longer a 'covenant' at all? Grässer seems to take this radical stand, when he says that the absence of a covenantal theology in the traditions descended from Jesus himself is not an accident.[12]

Briefly, his argument is as follows. The endless debate about the various covenants in the OT and about the relative importance of the category in the OT as a whole[13] resulted in a consensus, that what we find in the OT are various forms of covenantal theology (or even theologies) and later transformations, building on earlier traditions. Common to them all, however, in Grässer's view, is the consciousness on the part of Israel of being an elect people with a national God who intervenes in its history. The category of *berît* presupposes membership in Israel. When this historical continuity is broken in exile, apocalyptic traditions arise that see no possible bridge spanning from history to salvation. The latter can only happen in the creation of something wholly new.

Now, the theory goes, Jesus is an heir to such apocalyptic thinking and calls together various and sundry folk who can no longer claim historical continuity with Israel, nor expect salvation to arise from such historical links. His βασιλεία is an eschatological new creation, no longer rooted in any kind of covenantal theology, but instead taking shape wherever people respond to the call to discipleship. 'Covenant' has ceased to be a useful category for it is too closely

linked to the Law and to descent from Abraham to describe the new reality in Christ.[14]
We have an illustration of what happens when this theory is mechanically applied in Bultmann's question as to whether Jeremiah and Ezekiel might not have been *inconsistent* (emphasis mine) in calling the eschatological covenant a covenant with a future empirical Israel.[15] The point is that they, like Heb., did in fact employ that category, so it must have seemed capable of bearing the new meaning which these authors intended it to convey.

Several other things appear to be problematic with this theory, if it is meant to apply to the NT and does not constitute, as Grässer may have intended in his summary chapter, a possible modern interpretation, formulated with hindsight. The status of the Law and the determination of membership in the 'true Israel', i.e. legitimate inheritance from Abraham, are key topics not only in the struggle of early Christianity over its identity but already in the battles among the Jewish sects.

Israel has long since ceased to be the kind of empirical national body that Bultmann's query above seems to presuppose, even though Jewish communities enjoy some degree of political autonomy in the cities where there are *politeumata* or *collegia*. Religiously speaking, however, the boundaries are rather permeable and there is evidence of eager proselytizing activity in the first centuries BCE and CE.[16] The concept of spiritual descent from Abraham allows for *incorporation* of non-Jews, provided they are willing to live according to the Law, into the body of Israel. The sectarian consciousness of possessing the (only) correct interpretation of the Law and the key to the secret intentions of the prophets leads to *de facto* (if not *de jure*)[17] *exclusion* of parts of Israel from the 'true Israel', most clearly seen in the physical withdrawal of those that were to form the Qumran community in the desert.

These facts form an important matrix for trying to understand the early attempts of Christians to define themselves sociologically and theologically vis-à-vis Israel at large. The aspect of individual response, which is heavily stressed by Grässer, is certainly important in early Christianity, but the corporate conception of the λαὸς τοῦ θεοῦ (Heb. 4.9, 11.25; cf. 13.12) remains vital and its 'borders' are the subject of much debate in the NT.

That the issue of 'Jewish' versus 'Gentile' Christianity is absent in Heb. has often led commentators to conclude that it must be a late document, composed when the rupture between Judaism and Christianity was completed, and addressed to a Gentile church. The fact that this issue plagued some Pauline churches in the fifties and is still reflected in Matthew in the eighties should perhaps warn us against such facile conclusions. The congregation addressed by Heb. was uncertain about what its relationship to the Jewish roots of its new faith ought to be, *regardless* of the cultural-ethnic origin of its members.

We will try to show that the author of Heb. addresses this very uncertainty in his covenantal theology and formulates an independent and highly original conception of Christian identity in the process. Granted that Jesus himself, as he is presented to us in the Gospels, does not seem to have put his message in covenantal terms,[18] one of his followers is nevertheless capable of depicting the Christ event in light of what he remembers about the NC foretold in the Scriptures. In the process he enlarges the meaning of the NC idea, but the link to the old historical traditions, which had attached themselves over time to the OT idea of covenant, is never quite severed. In speaking about the *definitive* NC in Christ, the writer of Heb. may have provided one among several reasons that made that term less useful and attractive for Rabbinic Judaism.[19]

A peculiarity of the covenantal theology of Heb, which seems to alienate some modern interpreters is its cultic thrust. 'L'originalité de l'Epître aux Hébreux dans la théologie de l'alliance est d'avoir rattaché la διαθήκη au sacerdoce et au sacrifice'.[20] This fusion of cult and covenant already began in the OT priestly traditions,[21] and Heb. develops it further. Jeremiah's oracle on the NC (31.31-34), the original locus of the idea in the OT and the acknowledged proof text (among others) for our author's argument, is noteworthy for its lack of any cultic reference. The forgiveness of sins that it envisages happens by divine fiat, not by mediation of priestly sacrifice. It is significant that the author of Heb. never subjects this text to detailed exegesis, but turns instead to Ps. 110 and images of Yom Kippur to undergird his convictions about Christ's priesthood of the NC.

When asking ourselves what might have motivated this cultic perspective, we will look for clues in the pastoral intent of the work. In trying to ascertain the needs of the readers and the problems with which they are faced, we will have to take seriously the author's penchant for basing his argument upon the Law and the cultic institutions of the old Levitical order. Even if he were using these as a foil for displaying the infinite superiority of the new order by comparison, he must know why this particular foil would work better than others. The answer must lie somewhere in the addresses' background, in their tradition and in their presuppositions. These, along with his own preferred patterns of thought and value judgments,[22] as they can be ascertained by reading between the lines, provide the key to this preoccupation with cultic matters.

Whatever the readers' origin might have been by birth, in becoming Christians they inherited and appropriated certain Jewish presuppositions. On the one hand, this Jewish heritage can be taken for granted by the author as the common ground between him and his addressees, and to it he keeps returning to quarry further images in the hope of cementing his case. On the other hand, the writer's perception of the significance of this Jewish past differs markedly from that of his readers.

For conceptual purposes we shall adopt the scheme proposed by Brown and categorize the author of Heb. as a member of 'Group Four' and the recipients as members of 'Group Two' on the spectrum of groups of Jewish Christians and their Gentile converts.[23] We must be aware, however, that the particular species of early Christianity represented by the addressees is hard to characterize, because we have no evidence of their observance of *kashrut*, aside from a few tantalizing references to 'foods' (9.10; 12.16; 13.9).[24] Circumcision and festivals, the two principal elements representing diaspora Judaism in the eyes of outsiders, are also not mentioned in Heb.

Judging from the author's manner of argumentation and exhortation, we can detect on the part of the readers a kind of longing for some form of Jewish cultic observance that they seem to be missing in their new faith-community (see e.g. 7.11; 9.8-10, 13-14; 10.1-2; 13.9-13). Possibly they are attempting to maintain a dual allegiance, as it were, by continuing their association with a local Synagogue of (non-Christian) Jews and simultaneously believing in Jesus.

Even though the passages referring to harassment and persecution speak primarily about events in the past (see 10.32-39; 12.1-13), the tone is sufficiently urgent and severe to suggest that further persecution may be imminent and the readers are ill-equipped to stand up to it.

This study takes the position that the writer of Heb. faces several kinds of problems in the congregation which he addresses. Along with the concrete predicament of abuse and suffering, and a nostalgia for their Jewish heritage (a diagnosis prevalent in the English-speaking world of scholarship), the recipients display a lack of enthusiasm in their faith and hope (the preferred German diagnosis).[25] We believe that these dangers—far from being mutually exclusive as is sometimes thought—may coexist and threaten at least some community members. Clearly the author believes that in correcting and solidifying the readers' grasp of Christ's person and work he will help them combat these external and internal threats.

His portrayal of Jesus as high priest of a new covenantal order is a deliberate reformulation of the Christian story in response to specific needs of his audience. The frequent interruptions of his exposition by paraenetic warnings and urgent appeals to focus on Jesus (see e.g. 3.1; 12.2-3) and to follow him (6.18-20; 10.19-24; 13.13) demonstrate that the writer's purpose is ultimately pastoral. For the people of the NC the 'imperative' of cultic service in the new order is grounded in the (prior) 'indicative' of their salvation in Christ.

Chapters 2-4 of this work will lay the groundwork for our detailed discussion of the NC concept in Heb. In Chapter 2 we will examine which of the various OT covenantal traditions can be traced in Heb. and how they have been made to function in our text. We will touch upon all the major lines of tradition—the Patriarchal covenant, Sinai, the royal Davidic covenant and Jeremiah's NC. Although of unequal importance to the author, they can all be detected.

Chapter 3 will deal with the NC idea in Judaism, as a way of establishing a context for the use of the concept in Heb. With the notable exception of Qumran, there is a singular lack of enthusiasm for the idea, both in the Second Temple period and in later Rabbinic literature. There can be no question of any literary dependence or even any proof of allusions to these writings in Heb. Nevertheless it seems important to try to follow the fate of Jeremiah's prophecy chronologically. In the DSS and in Heb. the prevalence of covenantal thought patterns in general, and the references to the NC in particular, are all the more notable because of the virtual silence before and after this period. Even without positing any literary connections between these near contemporaries, a typological comparison between the DSS and Heb. from the point of view of their covenantal theologies may prove instructive, if only to highlight the distinctive features of Heb.

In Chapter 4 the appropriation of the NC concept by other early Christians besides the author of Heb. will be examined. Most attention will be given to the treatment of the idea in Paul and in the Last Supper accounts. Sadly enough, when we attempt a comparison between these texts and Heb., we are in a similar position as we are with regard to the DSS. Proof of explicit literary interconnections is lacking here too. Yet for establishing a matrix for the genesis of ideas in Heb. these other authors are important witnesses to the way in which the new faith could be formulated under the rubric of the NC, and oral tradition among Christians may have come into play here. To continue the trajectory, the chapter will end with a brief section on the resurgence of the NC concept in the early Fathers.

In Chapter 5 we will draw together the various elements characteristic of the NC concept in Heb., as they will have emerged in the comparisons of this work with others in Chapters 3–4. It will be seen that the NC motif has been deliberately reinterpreted from a cultic perspective, and shapes the author's theological exposition of revelation and priesthood. Then we hope to demonstrate that even the paraenetic sections cannot be understood apart from the idea of the NC people, who face certain consequences—both negative and positive—as a result of their standing in the NC. The nature of the Christian cult envisaged by Heb. is often thought to be rather elusive, so we will briefly examine possible allusions to those rites that would later become central to any Christian cult: baptism and the Eucharist.

Chapter 6 will summarize our findings and show how this study contributes to a better understanding of the author of Heb. as a theologian and as a *Seelsorger*.

Chapter 2

OLD TESTAMENT COVENANTAL TRADITIONS IN HEBREWS

The aim of this chapter will be to investigate which covenantal traditions from the Hebrew Scriptures the author of Heb. chooses to employ and how they have been made to function in his scheme. His lively interest in the OT and his skillful use of various exegetical techniques that were current in his day have been amply documented elsewhere.[1]

At present we will focus on those traditions dealing with the concept of covenant in the narrower (semantic) and in the wider (conceptual) sense, bearing in mind that we will thus account for only a portion of the OT citations and allusions in Heb.

A. *Patriarchal Covenant(s)*

It is difficult to concur with Grässer's judgment, that God's 'promissory covenant' (*Verheissungsbund*) with the fathers plays virtually no role in Heb.[2] Even though the author never refers to it as διαθήκη he uses ἐπαγγελία to describe those same promises that are part and parcel of the Patriarchal covenants in the OT: the land (11.9) and progeny (6.13; 11.11-12). Most often, however, the content of the promise is not explicitly mentioned, as though the author and his readers shared a common understanding of what the category of promise denotes.

Heb. as a whole shows the hand of a careful theologian, and the terminological distinction between διαθήκη and ἐπαγγελία may be deliberate. The former is reserved for the old covenant at Sinai and for the new covenant foretold by Jeremiah and inaugurated by Jesus. Without entering into the long-standing debate about the applicability of the term 'covenant' (in its various translations) to unilateral and/ or bilateral agreements[3] one might say that Heb. avoids any possible ambiguity by referring to the Patriarchal covenant as ἐπαγγελία.

Unfortunately, however, things are more complicated than would seem at first sight. The verb ἐπαγγέλλομαι appears exclusively with God as its subject. It functions to reiterate what could almost be termed an OT cliché about the faithful character of God, as the one who promises (10.23; 11.11). But it also shows that God's promise spans the ages, from Abraham (6.13) to that time when the very heavens will be shaken (12.26). The noun ἐπαγγελία shares this all-embracing character, for it can refer to past promises obtained in the OT era itself, to other promises having found their fulfilment in Christ and to further ones still outstanding.

Whoever tries to derive theological significance from the use of the singular or the plural of ἐπαγγελία in Heb. will be puzzled, for here the author permits himself what modern readers might regard as inconsistencies. A study of the thirteen occurrences of the term in their context reveals that the singular can qualify the heirs (6.17) and the land (11.9) of promise in a rather traditional manner. Furthermore the singular denotes the outstanding promise of entering the land (4.1), the reception of the promised eternal inheritance upon the death of Jesus by those called (9.15), the unambiguous denial of the ancestors' having received any promise apart from 'us' (11.39-40), and the outstanding promise of reward to those who have confidence and endurance (10.35-36).

The *plural* of ἐπαγγελία, on the other hand, usually refers to past promises obtained within the old covenant (6.12, 15; 11.33) or to Abraham's status as a recipient of promises (6.15; 11.17). But there are two important exceptions. In 11.13 we learn from one of the author's editorial comments interrupting his catalogue of heroes that 'all those died in faith not having received the promises'. And in 8.6 the reader is informed that the better (new) covenant, of which Jesus is the mediator, is 'based on better promises'.

So the 'rule' that singularity denotes the new dispensation and plurality the old, which we find operating elsewhere in the document,[5] cannot be applied in this instance. These seemingly inconsistent variations between the singular and the plural of ἐπαγγελία do not trouble the writer,[6] for in his eyes God's promise, like God himself, has an unchangeable character (6.17). It spans the ages and belongs both to the old and the new covenants.

Abraham plays an important role as a *positive* representative of the old people of God, next to Moses and the enigmatic figure of Melchizedek. The author reminds his readers that they are Abraham's seed. As such they are the object of special concern for their high priest Jesus, in contradistinction to angels (2.16-17). The concept of spiritual descent from Abraham is developed further when the new people of God are enjoined to become μιμηταί of those who by faith and patience inherited the promises (6.12)—for Abraham is the classic example of this stance (6.15).

He is also the recipient of God's oath, when he is assured of blessing and progeny (6.14). Along with this reference to Genesis 22, the author's exegesis of Psalms 95 and 110 shows that the divine oath is highly significant. It can function both in a negative way, as the testimony to old Israel's disobedience (3.11, 18; 4.3), and in a positive way as a description for the Word which ushered in the new order (7.20-21, 28).

Abraham's reappearance in ch. 11 confirms that his main function in Heb. is paraenetic. As a sojourner in a foreign land he exemplifies the position of the pilgrim on his way to the heavenly city (11.l8-10), who obeys the call even when, humanly speaking, he does not know where it will lead him. The circumstances of the birth of Isaac are reinterpreted, contrary to the testimony of Genesis, as Sarah's unwavering faith in the face of her barrenness and Abraham's proximity to death (11.11-12). When Abraham is summoned to bind his only son, he can again display the kind of faith that transcends death and hence receives Isaac back ἐν παραβολῇ (11.17-19). These elements from the life of the patriarch are purposefully selected to show how God rewards a life of faith in the unseen, a faith that is undaunted by the human boundary of death. For the author this ought to be the stance of a 'sharer of Christ' (3.13), and so he offers the example of Abraham to his readers.

Solely in the curious story about Melchizedek and Abraham could one say that the latter's place is squarely within the old dispensation. For here Abraham is aligned with his descendants, the Levites, and the inferiority of their priestly order is foreshadowed, as it were, in Abraham's inferior status vis-à-vis Melchizedek: he is the one who gives tithes and he is the recipient of Melchizedek's blessing (7.4-10). This is said after Abraham has just been characterized with the honorific title ὁ πατριάρχης (v. 4) and has been described as 'the one having the promises' (v. 6). So it would be false to conclude that Abraham's role in this story is a negative one. Two positive qualifications of Abraham are outweighed by two interactions with Melchizedek displaying Abraham's inferiority. Thus Abraham's titles of honour have the function of highlighting the far superior honour of Melchizedek, which in the final analysis turns out to be the honor of Christ.

The author's reshaping of this Genesis tradition and its function within his comparison of priestly dispensations in ch. 7 is a good example of his nuanced approach to the old order. We see the hermeneutical scheme of 'correspondence, contrast and superiority' at work. The note of contrast is much more pronounced when Heb. deals with the Law as a further element within the Levitical order. When we return to chap. 7 to examine the author's treatment of νόμος, we will find that the Law ultimately becomes synonymous with the old covenant for Heb. Even though it supplies certain cultic rubrics for understanding the new order it has no place in the NC.[7]

B. *Mosaic Traditions, Sinai and the Law*

There can be no doubt that Moses plays a key role in Heb. P.R. Jones claims that 'Moses and Jesus are yoked throughout the entirety of the Epistle. . . The Mosaic era or covenant is contrasted extensively with the Jesus era or covenant'.[8] For our study of covenantal traditions in Heb. it will be of paramount importance to examine the place of Moses in our text and to determine his relationship to the mediator of the NC. We note that while the author accords Moses the traditional function of a covenant mediator, he never calls him a μεσίτης and reserves this distinction for Jesus.

We must content ourselves with a brief overview of the explicit references to Moses in Heb. His first appearance[9] is in an important passage which has attracted much scholarly attention: 3.1-6.[10] Moses and Jesus are being compared in relation to their position vis-à-vis God's house and in relation to their respective glory attendant upon that position. Moses is the servant in the house, witnessing to the things that would be spoken (3.5) *in the NC*,[11] Jesus is the Son over the house, who turns out to be equal to its builder.[12] Grässer rightly calls this passage a classic example for the hermeneutical procedure of Heb.[13] As usual, the author's goal is to show Jesus' definitive superiority. Although starting from the *likeness* between Jesus and Moses, this comparison is rooted in the dualistic thought patterns characteristic of Heb., whereby the heavenly is *a priori* superior to the earthly.[14] When Jesus' faithfulness is compared to Moses' faithfulness, which is beyond question as attested in Num. 12.7, the greater glory of Jesus has eclipsed the glory of Moses. Here we encounter Moses in his function as trustworthy mediator of revelation and leader of the desert generation (3.16). His function as *lawgiver* becomes important to the author when he deals specifically with priesthood (7.14)[15] and with the realm of covenant (9.19; 10.28; 12.21). It is striking that the context of the latter three passages is in each case a thoroughly cultic one wherein the motif of the *blood of the covenant* plays important role. With the exception of the final blessing, with its echoes of the priestly ברית עלם[16] in the expression ἐν αἵματι διαθήκης αἰωνίου (13.20), Moses is linked to every reference to the blood of the covenant in our text. This is surely significant and we propose to deal with each of these three references in turn.

According to the analysis of D'Angelo,[17] the writer reduces the Law to its cultic prescriptions, its δικαιώματα λατρείας (9.1), which Moses received on the mount and executed in the covenant ceremony. When we compare this ceremon, as it is described in 9.18-22, with its original in Exodus 24, we note major revisions. It takes place on the altar and the blood of the covenant is no longer divided nor dashed against the altar. Instead there is a sprinkling of the people, the book and the tent—an action which bears more resemblance to an expiatory cleansing rite than to a covenant sacrifice. These actions of Moses, together with the two uses of the cultic term ἐνκαινίζω in Heb., give a clue to the author's interpretation of the ceremony. 'The "consecration" of the new way (10.20) is contrasted with the "consecration" of the old covenant (9.18)'.[18] In this presentation the inauguration of the covenant has been merged with the initiation/sprinkling of the Tent and of its worship (Num. 7.1).

The axiomatic rule of 9.22 lies at the basis of all other occurrences of the motif of covenant-blood in Heb. After having established that the death of Jesus brought lasting forgiveness once and for all (4.14-10.18), the author issues serious warnings to anyone who would fail to recognize the definitive nature of Christ's sacrifice. In a *qal-waḥomer* argument he appeals to the procedure of punishment under the Law of Moses in order to highlight the far superior penalty that is deserved by one who would 'trample upon the Son of God, regard as profane the blood of the covenant, by which he was sanctified, and insult the spirit of grace' (10.28-29).[19]

The tone is hardly less severe in the final encounter with Moses as lawgiver in Heb. In the dramatic scene of 12.18-29, comparing the revelations of the old covenant at Sinai and the ingathering of the ἐκκλησία of the new covenant at the heavenly Zion, the motif of 'better blood' reappears. Its listing here, among the phenomena characteristic of the new cultic community, might not appear that significant, if we had not encountered it as a *leitmotif* in chs. 9-10.[20] The writer knows of a tradition of the 'speaking of Abel's blood' (12.24; cf. 11.4), which must have regarded the lasting value of Abel's sacrifice very highly. In his usual manner of argumentation he can underline the superior nature of Jesus' blood by comparing it to this precious antecedent.

Moses' role in this passage is not explicitly cultic, although the terror, which he is made to express, is the result of a divine injunction about sanctifying the mountain and hence keeping one's distance before the Holy One (12.20-21). Stressing that even the great Moses was afraid has the effect of making the scene, replete with all its tangible, audible (in the author's underlying metaphysic read: 'earthly')[21] phenomena, appear that much more terrifying.

Once again we note how the author avoids calling Moses a covenant mediator. In a peculiar circumlocution he speaks of the failure of the first covenant as a refusal of the one warning ἐπὶ γῆς. He contrasts this via yet another *qal-waḥomer* with the rejection of the one warning ἀπ᾽ οὐρανῶν. Like the earlier circumlocution about the 'word spoken by angels' (2.2), which occurs in a similar *qal-waḥomer* construction warning about the neglect of the new revelation, this reference to the revelation at Sinai all but succeeds in leaving God out of the picture altogether. The resulting tension between this manner of viewing the old dispensation and the simultaneous stress on the continuity of God's speaking in the history of his people[22] is never fully resolved in Heb.

We have so far omitted two further references to Moses in Heb. Both 11.23-28 and 8.5 have been discussed at length by D'Angelo and we will content ourselves with summarizing those of her findings pertinent to our study. When Moses appears in ch. 11 among the 'witnesses', it is interesting that the focus is on his early life in Egypt, with a brief mention of his keeping of Passover. The people themselves are the active subject of the Red Sea crossing, without reference to their leader Moses (11.29; but see 3.16). A person reading only ch. 11 would remain ignorant of the Sinai covenant.[23]

As D'Angelo points out, the thrust of Moses' actions and his stance in 11.23-27 is his renunciation of Egypt. In light of the author's paraenetic purpose, 'Moses' early life is explained as a process of endurance... of and separation from Egypt, the world of pleasure, persecution and sin. Moses is made a model for those who must resist and yet survive'.[24] But the remarkable thing is the extent to which the picture of Moses has been 'accommodated paraenetically to the needs of the hearers'.[25] Moses renounces in order to bear the shame of *Christ* (11.26), which is precisely what the addressees are exhorted to do (13.13) and have already done in the past (10.33). Thus Moses here functions as a model for Christian faith and endurance, as a pilgrim who never loses sight of his goal despite all odds.

This leaves us with 8.5, another verse which has puzzled many interpreters.[26] On the surface we are dealing with a quotation from Exod. 25.40, where Moses is instructed to make/perform (everything) according to the τύπος shown to him on the mountain.[27] But, in characteristic fashion, the author probably intends this verse to include allusions to other similar verses from Exodus, all of which deal with patterns that Moses saw and was commanded to carry out.[28]

In the metaphysical scheme of Heb. τύπος is a synonym of εἰκών (10.1). Both of these stand for the heavenly reality which is over against the earthly ἀντίτυπος (9.24)/ὑπόδειγμα (8.5; 9.23)/σκιά (8.5; 10.1)/παραβολή.[29] Taking his point of departure from the τύπος of Christ, the author scans the OT for antitypical features in the history of Israel. Chapters 8-10 discuss the ἀντίτυπος and its fulfilment in Christ. Hence 'Moses' vision of the τύπος is invoked at the beginning of this passage to explain the relation between the first covenant and its fulfilment'.[30] In writing the Law Moses gives his witness to what he saw on the mountain.

But what exactly did Moses see? D'Angelo can show convincingly that Heb. displays a 'high' view of Moses as prophet-mystic.[31] Because of the need both to safeguard God's proximity and his inaccessibility to humans Scripture presents ambiguous and conflicting accounts of what Moses was granted to see.[32] Later traditions continue the debate and emphasize different textual witnesses. Heb., like most Rabbinic sources, en compasses a 'high' view of Moses' glory.

But while the Rabbis discuss Moses' vision of God, the Moses of Heb. has a vision of Christ—of his passage from death to exalted glory, a vision of Christ's τελείωσις. The imperfect, shadowy order of the Levitical cult that Moses instituted is the antitypical reflection of the *typos* of the one and only true τελείωσις which Moses was permitted to see.[33]

Thus Moses enjoys a unique position in Heb. Beyond his *antitypical* role vis-à-vis the Son, which is reflected in the presentation of details from his early life (11.23-28), Moses plays a *predictive* role, when he acts as faithful witness to his vision (3.5; 8.5). D'Angelo would even accord a limited *soteriological* function to Moses, as receiver and deliverer of God's Law.[34] In our view this is going too far, since the ultimate impression one gets after examining the various (and perhaps not altogether consistent) statements about the Law in Heb. is a negative one. As we shall see below, it has no place in the new covenantal order.

In trying to get a clearer picture of the author's view of the Law we will turn to ch. 7, which we have so far left out of the discussion about Moses. All explicit references to νόμος in Heb. are concentrated in chs. 7–10. Since these are the central chapters dealing primarily with cultic material, it becomes obvious that the author subsumes the Law under the rubric of cult. From reading only Heb. someone might think that the Law was exclusively about cultic matters.

Hebrews 7 contrasts the old Levitical order with the ancient but everlasting order of Melchizedek, who is conformed to the Son of God and his new priestly order (7.3).[35] We find some rather disparaging remarks about the Law: it is made up of 'fleshly commands' (7.16), it 'made nothing perfect' (7.19), it 'appointed weak men as high priests' (7.28). It is the ally and the *raison d'être* of the Levitical priesthood (7.11). The Son, on the other hand, enjoys the power of indestructible life (7.16) and is appointed to his priesthood by an oath (7.21), having been made perfect for ever (7.28).

If priesthood and Law are so intimately connected, as posited in 7.11-12, could it then be that Heb. envisages a new Law in the order of the Son? Curiously enough, the verb νομοθετέω—one of the author's *hapax legomena* in the NT—reoccurs when the NC is invoked in 8.6. The NC is said to be 'legally enacted upon better promises'. The way in which the author bases his argument on the Law implies that his *readers* must have accepted it in principle or at least accorded it a certain status. Verses like 2.2, 9.22 or 10.28 would otherwise have fallen on deaf ears. The same applies to the use of parenthetical inserts on the Law in 7.11b and 10.8b which are designed to drive home the author's point in each case and show his skill at working with his readers' presuppositions, while attempting to correct and transcend them in the process.

All these statements function within the author's comparative scheme and ultimately show that the Law belongs squarely within the old order. Since it is conceived as cultic Law, it supplies certain categories of continued validity to the new order, such as covenant, priesthood, and bloody sacrifice. Based on the metaphysical framework provided by the author in 10.1, we conclude that each of these categories is seen as imperfectly foreshadowed in the Levitical system. It is due to the author's genius that he succeeds in still employing these categories to describe the new reality brought about by Christ, even though the new wine seems to bring the old wineskins close to their bursting point. The category of νόμος itself is left behind in the process.

Thus the role of the Law in Heb. is a subtle one. The author obviously could not discuss his vision of the highpriesthood of Christ and the new covenant which he inaugurated without mentioning the Law. What is true of the NT in general is even more true of Heb.: the new order cannot be described and understood without referring to the old order that prepared it. In this sense the Law has a severely limited dispensational function in Heb. Even though its ritual cleanses only the flesh, it does effect cleansing; even though access to the Holy of Holies is limited to the high priest once a year, there is momentary access. By furnishing the (cultic) rubrics for the new covenant, the Law points the way to something better: 'a better hope' (7.19), 'a better covenant' (7.22), 'based on better promises' (8.6); there is a heavenly Tent, which is purified with 'better sacrifices' (9.23) and has been made accessible to all believers by 'better blood' (speaking more graciously than that of Abel 12.24; see 11.4 and also 9.12-14). But nowhere do we hear of a 'new' or 'better' Law.

C. *Royal-Priestly (Davidic) Traditions)*

In trying to trace royal covenantal traditions in Heb. it will be most apparent how artificial are the divisions which we have chosen to adopt for conceptual purposes. In the author's mind they certainly did not exist, for he selected his testimonies and traditions in accordance with his already formed beliefs about the Christ event, and Scripture in turn helped him in the articulation of those beliefs.

As a scholarly construct the 'Davidic covenant' is described as an unconditional, royal grant, which involves God's oath to the king. God promises his eternal favor to David and David's 'house', and God chooses Zion as his eternal abode. This construct as such appears nowhere in Heb., yet elements that have gone into its making do occur.

Chapter 1 is usually thought to contain various traditional elements predating Heb. The string of OT quotations following the proem is modelled after a royal enthronement liturgy and the first two testimonies in the entire work are the adoption formula of Ps. 2.7 and Nathan's oracle (2 Sam. 7.14). Next, the Son is addressed via Ps. 45, an ode for a royal wedding that is used as a testimony to the eternity of the Son's throne. Then his kingship over creation and his eternity are affirmed via Ps. 102. The whole passage celebrates the exaltation of the first-born (Heb. 1.6)—a Davidic title (see the ἐκκλησία πρωτοτόκων in the heavenly Zion, Heb. 12.23)—and is framed by references to his session at God's right hand drawn from Ps. 110.1 (Heb. 1.3, 13).

Already in Hebrews 1, however, there is an important announcement about the Son's *priestly* office, when it is affirmed that he made purification for sins (1.3). The joining together of sonship and high priesthood becomes clear in 5.5-6, where the adoption formula reoccurs in conjunction with Ps. 110.4. Hay stresses the general similarity of 5.5-10 and 1.1-13.[36]

But the ἀρχιερεύς *title* first occurs in 2.17, where it is postulated that Jesus had to become like his brethren in every respect in order to exercise his priesthood with the qualities of the ancient covenant Lord: ἐλεήμων/πιστός (i.e. חסד/אמת).[37] For it is precisely in his lowliness, in his solidarity with his brethren through suffering and death (2.6-15), that Jesus qualifies for the high priesthood and becomes the pioneer of their salvation.[38]

The catchword πιστός is picked up and elucidated in the following section 3.1-6. In addition to the Mosaic traditions that we examined earlier,[39] the passage contains royal-priestly traditions. The play on the word 'house', which already starts in 2 Sam. 7, continues in the tradition surrounding Nathan's oracle, and by the time of Heb. multiple meanings for οἶκος are possible: 1. the household of God/ his heavenly *familia* (hence the references to angels in chs. 1-2); 2.

the Tabernacle/Temple as God's dwelling place; 3. the community of Israel (3.6).[40]

Having established the Son's faithfulness, the author reiterates his ability to sympathize and undergo testing and suffering like his people (4.15-5.8). Thus perfected, the Son qualified for the high priesthood (5.6, 10) and became the 'source of eternal salvation' to all who would walk down the same road of obedience (5.9).

The nature of his high priesthood is explicated in ch. 7, which (apart from its early verses derived from Gen. 14.17-20) is structured around Ps. 110.4.[41] Every element in this verse is stressed at different points in the text: the Lord's *oath* (7.20-21, 28), the fact that Christ is a *priest*[42] (5.6, 10; 7.28), the *permanence* of his priesthood (7.24, 28; see 7.3, 16) and the *order of Melchizedek* (7.11, 17).[43] As stated in note 35, the focus is not on Melchizedek as a person, but he is 'mentioned (only) to demonstrate the reality and superiority of Jesus' priestly office'.[44] Taken together these elements of Ps. 110.4 are presented as conclusive proof that Jesus belongs to an *authentic* priesthood, which definitively superseded the Levitical priesthood and which lasts for ever. The references to Ps. 110.1, on the other hand, testify to the *adequacy* of that priesthood, because Christ is in heaven and his perfect sacrifice has already been consummated once-and-for-all.[45]

Our section on royal-priestly traditions in Heb. would not be complete without mentioning the Tabernacle. We will do so very briefly, because the author's use of Tabernacle traditions—some of which are extra-biblical and go beyond the description of the Tabernacle in Exodus, Leviticus and Numbers—has been thoroughly investigated elsewhere.[46]

In our section on Moses we noted that 8.5 is a key verse. Moses was shown the τύπος, the heavenly prototype (תבנית), according to which *all* covenantal arrangements were given. Heb. is an heir to the tension, already present in the so-called 'P' source, between the horizontal axis (spanning from creation to the final consummation) and the vertical axis (indicated by the transcendent cultic order).[47] A *temporal* dualism, expressed in the sequence of two ages, intersects with a *spatial* dualism of heavenly/abiding and earthly/temporary realities.[73]

This intersection can be studied most clearly in the picture of the divided Tent, that property of the Tabernacle in which Heb. shows the most interest.[49] Later[50] we shall see that Heb. speaks of two Tents and uses the metaphor to illustrate the two covenantal orders/cults or two ages. These cults are differentiated by their varying degrees of cleansing; both affect the flesh, but only the new order reaches the human conscience.

D. *Jeremiah's New Covenant*

In this section we will confine ourselves to an examination of those features within Jeremiah's oracle in which Heb. takes an interest, for a large part of the author's development and exposition of the NC concept takes place independently of this prophecy. As we remarked at the very beginning of this study, Heb. quotes quotes Jeremiah's prophecy on the NC (MT: Jer. 31.31-34; LXX: Jer. 38.31-34) in full and thereby furnishes the longest single quotation from the Hebrew Scriptures in the NT (8.8-12). This extensive quotation is inserted shortly after the first explicit mention of the word διαθήκη (7.22), at the point when the author himself acknowledges that he has reached the κεφάλαιον of his argument (8.1). At the conclusion of the central section on the new cultic order a shortened version of the same oracle is used to clinch the argument (10.16-17).

The author does not subject this text to a detailed exposition, *lemma* by *lemma*, in the way he does with parts of Pss. 8, 95 and 40. Some statements in the prophecy never seem to occupy the author's attention. He deals with the transgression of the ancestors in chs. 3-4. The theme of the inner disposition of the heart appears in 10.22 and 13.9 (where it is intimately related to grace) and finds its negative counterpart in the exegesis of Ps. 95. The 'covenant formula' is developed in the λαός motif[51] and is echoed in the twice quoted adoption formula regarding the Son (1.5; 5.5). Spontaneous knowledge without instruction does not seem foremost in the author's mind, for his whole epistle is extended *paideia* and the recipients are called to be teachers (5.12).

Most of the textual variations from the LXX are minor and insignificant.[52] In the second quotation there are several notable changes which place the accent on the remission of sins. It is introduced as a testimony by the Holy Spirit in 10.15 (in contrast to the earlier 'he says' 8.8) and picks up at Jer. 31.33, omitting the early verses about the failure of the first covenant. The reference to the 'house of Israel' is dropped in favour of the more general third person plural pronoun.

Most importantly, after the reference to the inwardly inscribed Torah, the author skips to the conclusion of the prophecy, the assurance of divine forgiveness. The transition is usually made smooth by renderings such as, 'then he adds...' The form of the verb expressing God's deliberate erasing of human sinfulness from his memory is changed from μνησθῶ (aorist passive subjunctive) to μνησθήσομαι (future passive), and in addition to ἁμαρτιῶν a new category of transgression appears: ἀνομιῶν (in lieu of ἀδικίαις).

Finally, the author's concluding statement reinforces the promise of complete definitive forgiveness. It reads like a rule: 'Where there is forgiveness of these, there is no longer any offering for sin' (RSV). This quasi-dogmatic utterance harks back to the earlier definition of purgation/forgiveness in the 'blood rule' (9.22) and will be restated in the warning of 10.26.

Going back to the first full quotation in ch. 8, one notices that its function is primarily a negative one. It is framed by indictments of the Sinai covenant on two counts. On the one hand, that *first* covenant—quite apart from the ancestors' breaking of it (8.9)—was not blameless to begin with, otherwise there would not have been any grounds for a *second* one (8.7). On the other hand, God's very promise of a *new* covenant amounted to an automatic declaration of obsolescence vis-à-vis the first, which was *becoming old* and was near disappearance (8.13). On the basis of this exegesis by our author, and similar ways of handling Pss. 8, 95 and 110, Caird argues that Heb. regards the OT as an 'avowedly incomplete book, which taught and teaches men to live by faith in the good things that were to come'.[53]

There can be no doubt that the writer puts Jeremiah's oracle to a use rather foreign to the intentions of the prophet. When there is talk about the self-confessed inadequacy and obsolescence of the very nature of the old order, when μετάθεσις of priesthood/Law (7.12) and ἀθέτησις of the former commandment (7.18) occur, and when there is an abolishment of the First in favour of an establishment of the Second (10.9), we have definitively left the realm of the OT.

Summary

In our attempt to account for the OT covenantal traditions in Heb. we have gone very far afield. The way in which one topic seemed to lead to another illustrates the difficulty involved in our enterprise.

The topic of covenant is related to so many subjects and can hardly be contained, since it reflects the central experience of Israel's encounter with God.

We found that Heb. allots a positive exemplary function to Abraham and views Christians as the recipients of the patriarchal promises. In Moses we discovered a figure of pivotal importance in the exposition of the author, both in his role as witness to the NC, of which he had a vision, and in his prophetic role as recorder of an imperfect cultic Law which inchoately foreshadowed the new cultic order.

We noted our text's interest in royal-priestly traditions and saw how Ps. 110.1, 4 in particular provide a vehicle for the articulation of the author's convictions about the new covenantal order of the high priest Jesus. Finally, we reviewed briefly the writer's exegesis of Jeremiah's oracle on the NC.

Excursus I
The Original Meaning of Jeremiah 31.31-34

Translation:[54]

(prose section:)

31	The days are surely coming,	a
	oracle of Yahweh,	
	when I shall make with the house of Israel	
	and the house of Judah a New Covenant,	
32	not like the covenant which I made with their fathers	b
	on the day I took them by the hand	c
	to bring them out of the land of Egypt:	
	it was they who broke that covenant of mine,	b′
	while I was master over them,	
	oracle of Yahweh;	
33	but this is the covenant which I shall make	a′
	with the house of Israel after those days,	
	oracle of Yahweh:	

(poetry:)

1. *Toraverheissung*
   Then I shall put my law within them,   a -b
   and on their hearts I shall write it,   b′-a′
2. *Bundesformel*
   and I shall be to them God,
      and they shall be to me a people

3. *Erkenntnisverheissung*
34 and no longer shall they teach one another
   or each other, saying,
   "Know Yahweh!"
   for they shall all know me,
     from the least of them to the greatest,
                                   oracle of Yahweh,
4. *Vergebungsverheissung*
   for I will forgive their inquity,   a -b
   and their sin remember no more.   b'-a'

We accept the authenticity of this oracle of Jeremiah and believe
that it can be treated essentially as a unit (with the exception of the
phrase 'house of Judah' which probably constitutes a later element,
testifying to a Southern recension of materials originally addressed to
the North).

Holladay has developed an interesting theory about the possible
setting of the prophecy, a theory which seems quite plausible as an
explanation for Jeremiah's word of hope in the context of doom.
Assuming that there were periodic septennial readings of Deuteronomy
ever since Josiah's reform, Holladay suggests that some of the
sermons in the book of Jeremiah can be construed as counter-
proclamations to those occasions. He is most confident about the
sermon in ch. 11 having been delivered at Tabernacles in 594 BCE,
but thinks one can also be reasonably confident that the best setting
for Jer. 31.31-34 would be that same feast in 587 BCE, when he posits
a public reading in the Temple ruins.[55]

This would explain the deuteronomistic language echoes in these
passages. The scribes with their 'vain pen' and those who continue to
rely upon the efficacy of the deuteronomic reform in the face of
overwhelming catastrophe would thus be countered by Jeremiah's
oracle. From the perspective of the scribes and priests, the manner of
Toraverheissung, the *Erkenntnisverheissung* doing away with catechesis,
and the non-cultic *Vergebungsverheissung* can be taken as polemical
references against these groups.

Even a rapid reading of Jeremiah reveals his profound disenchantment
with the possibilities of human faithfulness and obedience. In 11.10
he announces his conviction that the covenant has been broken from
the human side. But in 14.21 he even goes so far as to record the
people's worry that Yahweh for his part might break the covenant!
The problems of a change of heart in Yahweh and the hint of the

inherently imperfect nature of the Sinai covenant due to human nature's inability to fulfil it are never resolved in Jeremiah. His 'confessions' reveal that he can never 'win' an argument against Yahweh and frequently has to learn to view things anew from the deity's standpoint.

Hence he is prompted to proclaim a NC in Yahweh's name, once the Lord's judgment has been carried out to the full by the Babylonians and the only way forward is to begin in a completely different way. Polemics against Yahweh are clearly impossible, but announcing a NC on the Lord's behalf implies opposition to those who are seeking to rebuild within the old norms.

As has often been pointed out, Jeremiah does not envisage a new Torah and is probably not opposed to the written Torah per se.[56] His prophecy contains the traditional links of Torah and covenant, the traditional covenant formula (2) and the often encountered promise of God's complete forgiveness (4). The radical, new elements in the oracle are elements 1 and 3, the manner of God's imparting Torah and the absence of further need for instruction of it. Unlike the deuteronomistic editor in ch. 32 of the book of Jeremiah, Jeremiah himself does not use the phrase ברית עלם which later became characteristic of the priestly promissory covenants. But the double use of לא עד shows that the NC—as a new divine initiative—will effect the conditions for its own permanence.[57]

It seems unwarranted, however, to attribute to Jeremiah the idea that the NC would be inherently unbreakable and that human beings would be turned into marionettes.[58] The text, in our view, does not engage in such speculations. The implications of complete internal appropriation of Torah and perfect knowledge of God are never spelled out as modern psychology might require them to be. The prophet is speaking about future eschatological times when undivided allegiance to Yahweh would become possible. It is only when this prophecy is appropriated by Christians (and probably by the members of the Qumran community) for their own times that the problematic nature of these predictions becomes apparent because of their failure to be realized.

Chapter 3

THE NEW COVENANT IN JUDAISM

A. *The Absence of the Idea in the Second Temple Period*

The literature of this period is abundant and features the most varied genres—apocalypses, narrative fiction, testaments, expansions and paraphrases to biblical books, historiography, wisdom literature, hymnic material and the works of Josephus, Philo and the Qumran sectaries.[1] It is curious, therefore, that in all of these writings—with the exception of the Dead Sea Scrolls, which will occupy us in the next section—there seems to be a studious avoidance of Jeremiah's phrase ברית חדשה or its Greek equivalent καινὴ διαθήκη. In fact, even the word 'covenant' seems to appear less frequently than in the Hebrew Scriptures.[2]

As is well known, however, word studies can be deceptive. E.P. Sanders' critique[3] of the widespread bias in Christian scholarship regarding the posited degeneration of post-biblical Judaism—while principally pertaining to Rabbinic literature—is nonetheless applicable here. According to this old view, the notion of God's precious gift of the covenant was all but swallowed up by the growing importance of the Law and its tyranny over post-biblical Jewry.[4] Even a cursory reading of the fine study by A. Jaubert,[5] which traces the covenant idea in the Second Temple period, will show that the idea remained alive and functioned as a significant concept in Israel's self-definition, both in Palestine and in the diaspora. It is therefore important to pay attention to the *relationship* between the covenant and the Law as it emerges from the literature of this time.

But for our purposes we must concentrate on the *new* covenant. Was Jeremiah's prophecy simply forgotten or was there something too ambiguous or disturbing in its content to allow for an appropriation by Jewish groups before the first century CE?

Let us first dispense with what seems to be an ill-guided approach to the problem. Levin subjects Jeremiah's oracle to a complicated dissection and concludes that v. 33a, about God's new manner of giving Torah/his inscription of it on human hearts, is a late addition (possibly as late as the second century BCE).[6] Levin reasons that this addition was prompted by the tension between the announcement of a NC and the lack of new content in the original prophecy. He then sees this same tension as the reason for the avoidance of the expression 'New Covenant' in subsequent writings, presumably because it would have seemed inappropriate without clear indications of what kind of *newness* was to be expected. Levin admits that v. 33a occupies the central place in the pericope, but to him its 'excessively long' prose introduction, followed by the abrupt transition to poetic style, confirms his case for the lateness of this phrase.[7]

We prefer to follow Holladay's analysis, which uses some of the same stylistic features that Levin isolated, to argue for the literary unity of the passage. Holladay points to several chiasms that tie the oracle together, and regards 'the contrast between prose and poetry (as) part of the intentional effect of the passage, manifesting in the mode of presentation the contrast between the old covenant and the new.[8]

If we then assume that biblical and post-biblical tradition following Jeremiah possessed his oracle on the NC essentially in the form in which we know it, why did so many centuries have to elapse until communities arose who dared to apply the prophecy to themselves? Are we perhaps overlooking echoes of this tradition in the literature under consideration which may have been formulated differently while alluding to the same idea? And where we come across the NC phrase, are we justified in positing a relationship to Jeremiah's oracle or could we be dealing with independent traditions, formulated as a conscious antithesis to the old Sinai covenant?[9]

We will analyze in turn each of these three possibilities: (1) echoes of Jeremiah without the NC phrase, (2) occurrence of the NC phrase and its possible allusions to Jeremiah, (3) actual quotations of the prophecy of the NC—. Case 3 will occupy our attention in Chapter 5, case 2 will be treated in section B of this Chapter and in Chapter 4. First, however, we will turn to case 1.

Schreiber[10] is the only author we could find who believes that there are three specific texts of the Second Temple period, namely Bar. 2.30-35, *Jub.* 1.16-25 and *4 Ezra* 6.26b-28, that betray a knowledge of Jeremiah's prophecy on the NC and contain echoes of its content. We will therefore use Schreiber's treatment as a basis for our discussion and, in debating his contentions, we hope to raise some important questions about the tradition history of the NC concept. Let us now examine each of the three passages in turn.

(1) *Bar. 2.30-35* belongs to a long prose section (1.15–3.8) devoted to the confession of Israel's guilt. The book, redacted sometime in the second or first century BCE, has the time of the first Babylonian exile as its fictional setting. The author fully acknowledges Israel's guilt, from the very beginning of its relationship with the Lord at the Exodus (1.19) to his own time, and finds the Lord's punishment completely justified and in accordance with his curses announced through Moses (1.20) and through the prophets (1.21; 2.24-25). As a constant refrain we hear of the Lord's righteousness in carrying out his words of doom and of his people's wickedness in not heeding any of those words.

The passage with which we are concerned follows an appeal to the Lord for mercy (starting at 2.11) based on his past covenantal actions on behalf of Israel at the Exodus (2.11) and in giving the Law (2.28). The writer remembers that God has predicted a change of heart on the part of his people in the misery of their exile (2.30-33). They will acknowledge his Lordship over them and will be rewarded with a 'heart that obeys and ears that hear' (2.31, RSV). They will praise God and give up their sinful ways (2.32-33). The traditional promises of restoration of the land and abundant progeny follow (2.34). Finally a ברית עלם is announced, coupled with the 'covenant formula' and the promise never to remove Israel from the land (2.35).

Does this passage bear any relationship to Jeremiah's oracle on the NC? As Schreiber himself admits, 'Was den Ausdruck ברית עלם anbelangt, so zeigt schon ein Blick auf die Konkordanz, dass es sich hier... um einen stehenden Ausdruck handelt und in diesem Rahmen kann keinesfalls der Neue Bund gemeint sein'.[11] While he is certain that the 'everlasting covenant' in Isa. 24.5 must refer to the *old* covenant, Schreiber thinks that the same expression in the deutero-Jeremianic prophecies of Jer. 32.40 and 50.5, and especially in Bar. 2.34, reflects a tradition familiar with the NC prophecy. He would have it that the 'NC' terminology is shunned but echoes of its ethical content are present under the more general, less daring rubric of the 'eternal covenant'. In this view, Bar. 2.34-35 mixes traditional OT promises about what Schreiber calls the 'external fate of Israel' with 'ethical' promises of a more 'demanding character' (2.31-33). As a result, the text dissolves the tension between the old and the new covenants which is so marked in Jer. 31.31-34.[12]

It becomes immediately apparent that Schreiber starts from preconceived notions about the old covenant, said to contain *external* promises, and the NC, supposedly pertaining to *internal, ethical* demands. He absolutizes this dichotomy, which is derived from modern notions about the superiority of the spiritual over the material,[13] to such an extent that he believes one can easily compare *the* old covenant with *the* NC as if they were fixed entities. Schreiber fails to appreciate the fact that because these categories were interpreted and appropriated by living communities they were subject to variations. One fears that Schreiber is in fact taking later Christian notions as the basis for his understanding of the 'essence' of the NC.

From our point of view, Bar. 2.30-35 gives no evidence of a real attempt to grapple with Jeremiah's prophecy on the NC. The mere presence of phrases alluding to an internal disposition and change of heart (2.31) is not sufficient to prove that the author had Jeremiah's oracle in mind, and can easily be explained by reference to similar phrases elsewhere in the OT.[14]

The tone of Baruch 2 seems much more akin to that of Deut. 4.25-31 and Deut. 30.1-14 than to Jer. 31.31-34. We do not hear of a covenant rupture as in Jeremiah. In its negative sense the covenant is still operative in the curses that it brings. The people's coming to their senses because of the plight of exile brings about a concomitant return on the Lord's part. Even though all these prophecies share the idea of a divine action to change human hearts, Jeremiah's pessimism about human nature (see Jer. 13.23) allows no more human initiative in the formation of the NC: it is solely God's doing.

The deuteronomistic passages and Baruch 2, on the other hand, allow for a spontaneous human return to the Lord and envisage a restoration of the *prior* covenantal relationship: human obedience and the renewal (everlasting and irrevocable in Bar. 2.35) of the divine gifts of land and progeny. In the deuteronomistic scheme of history: sin—dispersion—return—ingathering, the last element of the reassembling of the exiles has been coupled with the covenant idea in our text. The specific characteristicis of Jer. 31.3-34 are missing, while a kinship to passages like Jer. 32.37-41 and Ezek. 36.17-28 is evident.[15]

(2) *Jub. 1.16-25* belongs to the introduction of the book of *Jubilees* (second century BCE) in which 'God describes to Moses the apostasy and ultimate restoration of his people, which will take place in the future'.[16] The remainder of the book contains a series of revelations given to Moses on Sinai by an angel in which the traditions of Genesis and the early chapters of Exodus are freely reworked according to the author's theological concerns. While *Jubilees* resembles apocalyptic works in certain features (pseudonymity, private revelation to a famous hero of the past by an angel, periodization of history according to a special calendar, with the goal of instruction to the author's contemporaries), it is also distinct from such works in its lack of bizarre imagery and its limited interest in eschatology[17] (no discussions about the future Messiah or his age or the nature of an afterlife).[18]

Most important for our purposes, however, is the growing scholarly consensus about Jubilees' intent to address *all Israel*, not just a limited esoteric group.[19] The book stems from the Maccabean period, during which most of the sects known to us are said to have emerged (which is of course not to deny their roots in earlier traditions), and is notable for its 'proestablishment stance'.[20] Jaubert, in seeking to distinguish *Jubilees* from the DSS, while allowing for the peculiarity of some of the author's convictions about the Law and the calendar, postulates that the book is addressed to a *confrérie* rather than a sect.[21] The fact that Jubilees was used at Qumran shows its appeal for the sectaries and may suggest a parentage in similar circles.[22]

Jub. 1.16-25, Schreiber's second candidate for a text reflecting Jeremiah's oracle, contains strong deuteronomistic echoes. God tells Moses that Israel will return to him in exile 'with all their heart and with all their soul and with all their might' (1.15). In exchange, God himself will gather and transplant them 'with all my heart and with all my soul' (1.16). This mutual return of the covenant partners is reinforced by the 'covenant formula' (1.17) and God's promise not to forsake Israel (1.18). Thereupon we read Moses' prayer of intercession for Israel and his entreaty for God's mercy in spite of Israel's sinfulness (1.19-21).

God's reply contains several promises. He will circumcise the foreskin of their heart and create for them a holy spirit and purify them for eternal obedience (1.23) to the Law (1.24). Finally, the culminating promise predicts that the Israelites will be universally acknowledged as 'sons of the living God' and God will love them as their father (1.24-25).

Schreiber's analysis of his passage is not very satisfactory and at points even contradictory. In his wish to detect reminiscences of Jeremiah's NC, he regards the mere predictions of complete obedience to the commandments and of a filial relationship with God (1.24) as sufficient evidence to suspect such reminiscences. He sees this reinforced by *Jub*. 1.14 where he detects the prior rupture of the covenant (à la Jer. 31.32) in Israel's total neglect of the Law.[23]

Immediately thereafter, however, the 'new moons, sabbaths, festivals, jubilees, and ordinances' (1.14) are qualified as 'äussere Ordnungen', i.e. phenomena within the realm of the *old* covenant and hence far from Jeremiah's purview. Since *Jub*. envisages a restitution of these external realities, along with what Schreiber recognizes as typically deuteronomic concerns, it is essentially characterized by the spirit of the *old* covenant. Schreiber is entirely correct when he finds in *Jubilees* a fusion of 'P''s ברית עלם with the Mosaic covenant. But it is highly questionable whether the vision of the covenant in *Jubilees* also bears traits of the Jeremianic NC.[24]

How difficult it is for Schreiber to uphold this contention becomes apparent when he is at pains to compare the tension between the old and the new covenants in Jeremiah with the apocalyptic tension which he finds in *Jubilees*. In the latter book the presentation of God's predestined plan for Israel clashes, in Schreiber's view, with the political and social realities of oppression experienced by the author and his contemporaries. The remission of sins and the new creation (1.29) necessitated by this state of affairs is premised on Israel's faithfulness to the *old* external order. The covenantal conception, even in its eschatological form, is yoked to the demand for this uncompromising faithfulness to the cultic and religious order of which Jeremiah's NC says nothing.[25]

We concur with Sanders' judgment that 'There is no discussion of a NC (in *Jubilees*), but the expectation. . . of the fulfilment of the old by the elimination of transgression'.[26] Apparently the author expects a general return to the proper covenantal relationship between God and his people within his own lifetime[27] and presents his peculiar legal prescriptions as the norm for all Israel to follow.[28]

(3) *4 Ezra 6.26b* can be dealt with more briefly than Schreiber's other two passages, for if anything this is an even weaker candidate

for an echo of Jeremiah's NC.[29] *4 Ezra* 3-14 is a Jewish[30] apocalyptic work, of the late first century CE, commonly thought to reflect the events of the fall of Jerusalem in 70 CE.[31] In the fictional setting of Babylon after the first destruction of the Temple, the priestly seer Ezra engages God in a series of dialogues, which are answered both by an angel and by seven visions granted to Ezra.

We cannot be detained by the complicated problems of authorship of this apocalypse and the debates about the disparate viewpoints represented in it.[32] For Sanders it 'appears best to consider the *view of the main author* of the book *to be that of the angel* in the dialogues' and thus to treat the final vision and ch. 14 as '"saving" appendix to make IV Ezra more palatable in Jewish circles'.[33]

Sanders labels this view 'legalistic perfectionism'.[34] The book evinces a profound pessimism about the plight of Israel vis-à-vis 'God Most High'. The power of sin is virtually inescapable, only a few perfectly righteous individuals will be saved after many tribulations, and the majority of Israel will be judged without mercy according to their transgressions and will consequently suffer eternal damnation. God's election of Israel and membership in the covenant no longer protect Israelites from destruction; 'covenantal nomism', the pattern commonly observed by Sanders in the rest of Palestinian Judaism, has collapsed in this case.[35]

4 Ezra 6.26b forms part of the conclusion of the second vision wherein the signs of the end times are enumerated (6.11-28). We learn that 'the heart of the (earth's) inhabitants shall be changed and converted to a different spirit'.[36] One wonders why Schreiber is again reminded by this verse of Jeremiah's oracle,[37] since that oracle predicts nothing about the Spirit, and such passages as Ezek. 11.19-20; 36.26-27, or even the eschatological outpouring of the Spirit in Joel 2.28-29 come to mind much more readily.

As Schreiber correctly notes, the context of the second vision raises the question of the election and the fate of the covenant people (5.23-30).[38] Ezra complains that 'those who opposed your promises have trodden down on those who believed your covenants'[39] (5.29). God's reply is shrouded in the mystery of his inscrutable judgment and his eternally preordained plan about the sequence of events in creation and time. The fact that the book continues with five more dialogues and visions shows that Ezra is in no way reassured by this answer.

It is puzzling why Schreiber insists that the eschatological facts listed in 6.11-28, while attached to the *old* Patriarchal covenant (see 6.8), nonetheless bear traits of the NC.[40] There is nothing here about a *new* divine action on behalf of Israel, as we would expect if there were a relationship to Jeremiah's prophecy. The Torah is eternal (9.37), but its main function in *4 Ezra* seems to be to condemn. This could not be further from Jer. 31.33a, where the Law will become readily accessible and understandable to the human heart on which it will be inscribed. As Schreiber himself admits, there is no tension between the old and the new covenants in *4 Ezra*. Creation has become old (5.55b) and needs to be renewed, but the covenant remains the same.[41]

To sum up, our brief search for traces of Jeremiah's prophecy of the NC in the Second Temple Period confirmed the negative hypothesis with which we started out. Jaubert's verdict reads: 'Dans l'ensemble du judaïsme, l'expression "nouvelle alliance", qui était celle de Jérémie, n'est attestée qu'à Qumrân...'[42] More recently Levin writes, 'Die Einmaligkeit des Stichworts "*neuer* Bund" in Jer. 31, 31 und sein Fehlen in der zwischentestamentlichen Überlieferung machen die traditionsgeschichtliche Untersuchung zu einer einfachen Sache...'[43] Given this absence of the NC phrase, we found Schreiber's readiness to detect echoes of the NC oracle in three texts of this period unwarranted. Without the *NC terminology* and without clear allusions to the *specific content* of Jeremiah's prophecy one is not justified in speaking about a relationship to Jer. 31.31-34.

In debating Schreiber's contentions we were brought face to face with some important questions about the nature of the NC that have bearing on our own enterprise. We simply list them here and will have occasion to raise them again at appropriate points in this study. Does the idea of a NC automatically imply a clear break with the old covenant, or can there be elements of continuity? Assuming one has decided what *Jeremiah's* understanding of the NC idea might have been,[44] would that understanding still apply to a later age? Is the very idea of a *new* covenant disturbing to the Jewish understanding of a God who has an ongoing covenantal relationship with his people? Was Jeremiah therefore a lone radical in proclaiming this prophecy? Did the NC concept already bear the seeds of polemical sectarianism within it? Can one distill the *essence* of the NC? Which features allow us to distinguish a NC from a renewed covenant?

B. *The New Covenant in the DSS—Compared to the Idea in Hebrews*

One has to approach the NC idea in the DSS within the larger context of the many covenantal expressions used at Qumran.[45] The phrase ברית חדשה occurs relatively rarely. It is found exclusively in the *Damascus Document* (MS A 1: CD 6.19; 8.21; B: 19.33-34; 20.12),[46] and once in the *pesher on Habakkuk* (1QpHab 2.3), where ברית has to be supplied to fill in a lacuna before חדשה.[47]

Most commentators hold that the notion of the NC in CD comes from Jeremiah's prophecy, even though Jer. 31.31-34 is unfortunately never quoted there, nor in the rest of the extant sectarian literature of Qumran.[48] Since CD formed part of the sectaries' library we have to relate the 'NC' phrase in CD to favourite covenantal expressions in the other DSS, such as 'covenant of the fathers', 'covenant of God/ His covenant/Thy covenant', 'this covenant', 'covenant of the (everlasting) community', 'covenant with (all) Israel', 'eternal priestly covenant',[49] and consequently it cannot be maintained that the presence of the adjective 'new' signals a different kind of covenant. The Qumran sectaries demonstrate a consistent self-understanding vis-à-vis the outside world and הברית החדשה, even if it may have been appropriated from elsewhere, has become one of the phrases employed to express that understanding.

A few general remarks about the community's sectarian self-perception are in order before turning to a closer examination of the passages in which the NC idea occurs.

The sectaries live in the conviction that the final age is dawning and that they have been especially predestined and chosen by God—as individuals—to form the community of his covenant and to lead a life based on special secret revelations granted to their community alone. The very formation of the sect is intimately bound up with the need to prepare for the end-time by an exemplary life-style. Having separated from the rest of Israelite society and its wicked ways and voluntarily joined a group of like-minded people, the sectaries establish themselves in the desert and apparently model their lives after the wilderness generation, living in camps, and readying themselves for the renewed conquest. This final eschatological battle is expected to occur under the auspices of the Princes of Darkness and Light who are thought to govern the interim time and to hold sway over human beings. The latter then act accordingly as Sons of Darkness or of Light. The Qumranites are convinced that, at the end of the battle between these forces, their lot will prevail and settle in a purified land with a purified Temple at its center.

The community's hermeneutical axioms follow directly from its self-understanding. The sectaries interpret the prophets with reference to the eschaton and under the conviction that theirs is indeed the age of the dawning eschaton. Under the leadership of the Teacher of Righteousness and of his followers, who are believed to be recipients of a special key for unlocking the hidden meanings in Scripture, they go about the exegetical task of deciphering the mysteries of the prophets and apply them to their circumstances. Likewise, their interpretation of Torah is derived from their sectarian consciousness of possessing the only true understanding of the Law of Moses, in contradistinction to the ways in which the Law is practised in the rest of Israel. In typically sectarian fashion, Qumran exegesis employs the ancient traditions in a way favorable to the sect's self-perception and to its legal rulings. Thus all the blessings foretold are imputed to the in-group and all the curses are reserved for Qumran's numerous enemies.

This seemingly self-righteous attitude vis-à-vis *outsiders* and the firm assurance of the sect's chosen status vis-à-vis *Israel at large* is coupled with a profound recognition of personal and collective sinfulness vis-à-vis *God*, as we can glean from their *Thanksgiving Hymns* and from their public rituals of confession.[50] The community even goes so far as to attribute a measure of expiatory atoning power for the sins of outsiders to its way of life in preparation for the final conflagration.

This brief sketch of the comunity's self-perception must suffice to put the notion of the NC in its context. Even though they do not spell this out as clearly as we might lke, the people who composed CD— whether they were Qumranites or not—were probably thinking of themselves as actualizing Jeremiah's oracle, which the prophet prounounced for the end-time. 'After those days' is applied to their contemporary situation. ברית חדשה not only serves as a convenient self-designation, but is simultaneously used in a polemical fashion. In sectarian contexts these uses are often only two sides of the same coin.

(1) *1 QpHab 1.16–2.10a*

In 1QpHab 1.16–2.10a Hab. 1.5 is being interpreted. The גוים have become בגדים in the *pesher* which proceeds to describe three types of such traitors: 1. those who are associated with the Man of Lies and who would not listen to the words of the Teacher of Righteousness; 2. those who had already entered the NC, but were not faithful to the covenant of God (=NC) and profaned his holy name; 3. all those traitors of the end-time who would mock the predictions of the Priest concerning the last generation, even though he had been given God's special revelation about how to interpret the prophetic message.[51] It is noteworthy how harshly the Qumran covenanters condemn people who have joined their covenant and subsequently abandoned it.

(2) *CD 6.18-19*
In CD 6.18-19 the text is concerned with the sectarian observance of sabbaths, feasts and fasting 'according to the findings of those who entered the NC in the land of Damascus'. The passage continues with an elaboration upon principles of ethical conduct required of the sectaries vis-à-vis the oppressed, the stranger and fellows within the group. The immediate context does not seem particularly polemical, but we should view it in light of the fact that Qumran's calendar differs from the official one in use by the Jerusalem priesthood. Thus the sectaries condemn any calendric or legal rulings that do not stem from the interpretation of the Sons of Zadok.

(3) *CD 8.20-21*
Unfortunately the A 1 manuscript of CD breaks off after 8.20-21,[52] so one cannot determine what function the phrase 'all of the men who entered into the NC in the land of Damascus' is meant to have in relation to what Jeremiah told Baruch, and what Elisha told Gehazi. One can note, however, that the immediate context preceding these scriptural allusions mentions 'those converts of Israel who depart from the way of the people'. Then the 'covenant with the first ones' is invoked, which shows that the sectaries see themselves as following in the footsteps of the patriarchs and enjoying God's special favor as their heirs. Belonging to the ברית האבת entails hatred of the Builders of the Wall, a frequent epithet for Qumran's enemies, based on Ezekiel's word about the wall that was whitewashed to hide its cracks (Ezek. 13.10).

(4) *CD 19.34*
The situations envisaged by CD 8.21 and 19.34 are similar, for there

are repeated references to the 'stubbornness of hearts' (a very frequent cliché for sinful behaviour in the DSS) and to abandoning the Law. Vermes therefore joined the texts of manuscripts A 1 (8.21) and B (19.34) in his English translation.[53] Once again we find in 19.33-34 an indictment of 'all those who entered the NC in the land of Damascus and turned, deceived and forsook the well of living waters' (i.e. the Law, cf. CD 6.4). The names of these people are to be erased from the Book and they are to be expelled from the congregation 'according to the interpretation of the Law in which the men of perfect holiness walk'.[54]

(5) CD 20.11-13

The last use of the NC phrase occurs only a few verses later, within the same eschatological judgment context. CD 20.11-13 speaks of 'those who rejected the covenant and the pact, which was established in the land of Damascus—that is the NC—and neither they nor their families shall have a portion in the house of the Law'.

To summarize briefly, it appears that ברית חדשה is used *both* as a self-designation *and* in a polemical fashion vis-à-vis several groups of traitors by the Qumran covenanters. On the one hand, the concept of the NC is linked closely to the group's particular understanding and practice of the Law and its self-consciousness as collective recipient of God's special revelation. On the other hand, the NC is evoked when various groups of apostates are being condemned. Not only people who initially refused to join the Teacher and his group, but especially backsliders who later opted against their special way of life and understanding of Torah, as well as people still attached to the sect, but secretly disobedient, are treated like apostates and judged accordingly.

Even though Sanders is probably right to insist upon the reserve with which the term 'true Israel' is employed only in *eschatological* contexts at Qumran, in many cases the harsh rhetoric of the sectaries vis-à-vis Jews favouring different legal practice comes close to abolishing the distinction between the rest of Israel and the Gentiles.[55] 'Thus the sect tends to adopt the same attitude to those who rejected the covenant of the sect and to those who have no covenant at all'.[56]

C. *Comparison between the NC in the DSS and in Hebrews*

(1) *Similarities Between Covenantal Traditions in the DSS and in Hebrews*

The conception of two covenants and the eschatological viewpoint from which the old institutions are newly interpreted point to a kindred milieu between the DSS sect and Heb. Flusser detects similarities in the way in which Israel's history is reinterpreted from a sectarian angle. Spiritual descent from Abraham is stressed by both groups. They see themselves as heirs of the promise to the patriarchs (the ברית ראשנים of Lev. 26.45/LXX ἡ διαθήκη ἡ πρότερα). At Qumran we hear of 'those who came into the first covenant/covenant of the first ones' (CD 3.10; cf. 1.4; 6.2) and of God's special favour for the patriarchs (CD 8.16).

Flusser shows that when Heb speaks of ἡ πρώτη (9.1) and οἱ πρότερον εὐαγγελισθέντες (4.6; cf. 4.2) a similar conflation of the patriarchal covenant with the Sinai covenant has occurred. In this reading Sinai is turned into a kind of first Gospel.[57]

Another important point of resemblance, which is not sufficiently stressed by Flusser, can be found in both groups' insistence that the NC does not simply arise through a *negative* process of attrition as it were, i.e. unfaithful Israelites betraying the old covenant and leaving behind a remnant of faithful adherents. Equally important, if not more so, is the *positive* element of God's wholly new action on behalf of his elect. The vocabulary of election is too numerous and multifold in the DSS to document here.[58] In Heb. the μετέχω-word group (3.1, 14; 6.4; cf. 5.13, 12.8) signals the idea of participation in a special heavenly reality and κεκλημένοι (9.15; cf. 3.1) is another characteristic expression of election.

More concretely, the Qumranites regard themselves as recipients of a secret new revelation, not accessible to non-members of their body, which profoundly affects the way in which they interpret the Torah and the prophets and therefore governs their whole life-style as members of the NC.[59] The author of Heb., on the other hand, seeks to imprint on the minds and hearts of his addressees the special unique significance of their *new* high priest, the Christ, whose death and exaltation to the Father's right hand brought about a *new* era of salvation and called into being a *new* ἐκκλησία.

Both communities appropriate and blend various covenantal traditions from the Hebrew Scriptures: the covenant with the Fathers, 'P''s ברית עלם, and the Mosaic covenant. The NC absorbs elements from those earlier covenants in its Qumranite form, and in Heb. Jeremiah's oracle is made to function as an indictment of the Sinai covenant. Not explicitly derived from Jeremiah at Qumran, but referred to by the definite הברית החדשה, the NC has clear eschatological dimensions in both instances. It is thought of as realized in the present and concretely actualized in the life of the sect and of the Christian community repspectively. Royal-priestly traditions, while present in Heb. are exploited much more fully by the sectarians, presumably because of the large number of priestly members of the sect. In their cultic self-conception both groups mimic the cultic ritual associated with the Tabernacle (and/or Temple in the DSS) and transfer its sanctity to themselves, but the unique role of Christ leads to rather different conceptions in Christianity.[60]

(2) Differences between the NC Communities
(a) *Covenantal Dualism.* The precise way in which the various strands of OT covenantal traditions are reworked shows profound differences between the world of Qumran and that of Heb. At Qumran the social aspect of membership in the NC, and indeed the sectarian self-conception that follows from such a life of conscious physical withdrawal from the rest of Israel, are spelled out much more clearly than in Heb. There are institutionalized rites of entry for the individual wishing to join the sect and yearly ceremonies of covenant renewal. During these rites individuals are asked to swear the oath of the covenant (CD 15.1–16.2a) and the history of God's dealings with his people is recited; blessings and curses are invoked (1QS 1.16–2.19). The distribution of blessings and curses reveals the pronounced dualism of the sect and its strong conviction about the elect status of its members.

This kind of division of the world into two camps under the domination of the Prince of Light and Belial is absent in Heb. although the Devil's hold over death appears in a traditional piece (2.14-15). It is significant that in the same passage Jesus, the conqueror of the Devil, is characterized in terms reminiscent of the OT covenant Lord.[61] Further echoes of dualistic OT covenant language can be found in the agricultural simile (6.7-8) which proclaims either εὐλογία or κατάρα upon the readers in accordance with their 'fruits'.[62]

Despite these examples, however, the tone of Heb. differs from that prevalent in the DSS. While it is true that the author issues repeated severe warnings about judgment, which are so absolute and uncompromising as to remind us of the sharp condemnations of back-sliders in CD (e.g. Heb. 3.12-13; 4.11; 6.4-6; 10.27-31; 12.15-17, 29), the milieu of Heb. does not display the characteristic sectarian 'we-they' mentality. The author emphasizes the positive presentation of the Christ event and the NC for his followers more than its negative effects on those who oppose or neglect it.

(b) *The Relationship to the Temple and the Cult.* Flusser already points out the importance of the Temple as a symbol of religious unity with which the Qumran covenanters have to wrestle.[63] Cohen develops this idea and applies it to those other groups in the first century CE that are known to us. He postulates that 'By whatever means the sects explained their origins, their fundamental claim to be the antithesis/supplement/equivalent of the temple meant that the group derived its legitimacy from its status as a temple community'.[64] Thus the Temple's monistic and exclusivistic claims were arrogated by the sects.

The Qumran sectaries regard the Jerusalem Temple, its priesthood and its cult as polluted and refrain from taking part in its rites. Their writings reveal an ambivalent attitude about sacrifice. 'On the one hand the sect hoped to offer sacrifices according to its own rites and by its own priests in a purified future Temple; on the other hand they believed that their non-sacrificial rites (lustrations, prayers, strict observance of the Law) could serve as a full substitute for Temple service. This belief led them to speculation about the equality of the two services, to the use of symbols taken from the Temple ritual when describing Sectarian rites, and, finally, to the view that the sect itself was a kind of spiritual Temple'.[65] There is also a debate among archaeologists about the possibility of animal sacrifice having been carried out on the site of the Qumran settlement.[66]

In contrast to an intensified devotion to the Law and a yearning for a purified Temple with a proper cultic order, under the supervision of a legitimate priesthood,[67] we find in Heb. the abrogation of all these institutions *in their Levitical form* and the transferral of their symbolism and sanctity to Jesus. The monism of one Temple becomes the monism of only *one* high priest and *one* (ἐφάπαξ) ever efficacious sacrifice. The symbolism of a new, living Temple embodied in the praying community is not exploited in Heb. as it is in Paul and in the *Manual of Discipline*.[68]

The author of Heb. calls the community the οἶκος of the Son (3.6; cf. 10.21), but refrains from elaborating upon this image. Nor is the Temple/Tabernacle symbolism applied to Jesus himself as it is in John.[69] Curiously enough, the Temple as such is never mentioned in Heb.: instead, the image of the divided Tabernacle is used to undergird the author's intricate metaphysical scheme of two realities and two ages.[70]

In a way that appears paradoxical, but which is characteristic of the genius of our author, he uses cultic language throughout to describe the Christ event and its import, while clearly rejecting a continuation of the old Levitical cult. The sectaries' hope in a purified *material* cult of the future is not shared by Heb. Forced by their circumstances, the people at Qumran develop an interim worship style[71] that can be likened to the 'sacrifice of praise' prescribed in Heb. (13.15).[72] For the latter document this non-material form of worship becomes the only legitimate cultic activity during the earthly pilgrimage of the citizens of the 'lasting city that is to come' (13.14).

(c) *What is Meant by 'New'?* In seeking to account for the elements of *newness* in the Qumran covenant one must keep in mind that there can be various degrees of newness (in time and quality) vis-à-vis something old. If most interpreters regard the Essene covenant as a *renewed* one, in contradistinction to a NC,[73] one suspects that this is so because their point of departure may be a simplified understanding of the Christian NC as *always* meaning new in place of old. In fact—if one envisages a spectrum of 'newness'—parts of the NT may be closer to Qumran in their interpretation of 'NC' than to Heb. which we regard as the most radical and clear NT formulation of 'newness' understood as a break with the old cultic order.

Hence careful distinctions are in order, if the Qumran covenant is to be comprehended in its own right. On the one hand, the sectaries' custom of yearly ceremonies of covenant renewal allows one to describe their movement as one of renewal and repristination. Their goal is a return to what were thought to be the true intentions of the early days in the wilderness and at Sinai. Far from rejecting the Law, as the author of Heb. ultimately does,[74] the Qumran sectaries regard themselves as fierce defenders of its only true interpretation, as it has been revealed to them through the Teacher of Righteousness and his successors in the exegesis of Scripture for their own times.

On the other hand, this very element of new revelation is crucial and clearly sets the Essene covenant apart from earlier reform movements in the OT. The fact that the sectaries are convinced that they, and they alone, possess a new key for unlocking the secret oracles in Scripture and for interpreting history accordingly makes it legitimate to speak of their covenant as a *new* one, set apart from the old Mosaic revelation.

The weight given to this new revelation at Qumran makes it illegitimate to emphasize the *human* initiative in renewing the covenant to such a degree that the *divine* initiative is downplayed.[75] While it is true that God's part in making the NC is stressed much more strongly in Jeremiah's oracle than in the DSS, the sectaries' firm belief in election demonstrates their conviction that God played a part in calling them into his 'NC in the land of Damascus'. Two examples in the next paragraph cite God as the agent of covenant renewal.

It is noteworthy that the verb חָרַשׁ and the adjective חָרָשׁ are used relatively rarely in the DSS, and most often in connection with covenantal expressions. The *verb* is employed twice to express the self-renewal of the sectaries (1QS 10.4; 1QH 11.13) and three times in a covenant context (1QSb 3.26—'May He (God!) make new for you the covenant of (everlasting) priesthood'; 1QSb 5.21—'May he (the Prince of the Congregation) make new for him the covenant of the community' and 1Q34 3.2.6—'You (God!) made new for them Your covenant').[76] In each of these instances the verb might also be translated as 'renew', which would emphasize continuity with the past. The *adjective* occurs twice in the context of new creation (1QS 4.25; 1QH 13.12) and in the five passages dealing with the NC that we discussed above.[77]

Another essential element of *newness* in the Essene covenant consists in its eschatological character. As noted above,[78] the sectaries see themselves as already participating in some sense in the eschatological time of the 'last generation' (CD 1.12) and some of their former associates have already broken the eschatological covenant.[79] The presence of the Holy Spirit (CD 5.11; 7.14) and of holy angels in their midst (e.g. 1QS 11.8) testify to the partial inbreaking of the new age in the life of the Qumran community. If we accept the ascription of a theological meaning to 'Damascus' as the place of exile, then this further concretizes the meaning of the NC at Qumran. The decisive step of 'entering' (בוא) the Damascene covenant has been realized[80] by those who have withdrawn to the Qumran desert and are attempting to live proleptically in the new order and to prepare for its full inception.

A few further remarks on the Law are in order before we turn to Heb., because what most distinguishes the two eschatological covenant communities is ultimately their attitude to the Law and their consequent divergent views of 'newness'. J.A. Huntjens[81] analyzes three of the NC passages in CD, which we examined above, and concludes that 'the "New Covenant" is identified almost exclusively with the issue of the interpretation of the Torah and with the question of the Sabbath and the festivals'.[82] He agrees with our contention that the NC references occur in highly polemical contexts, in which the points at stake have to do with the correct interpretation and practice of legal precepts—understood to be the exclusive prerogative of the sect. The observation of this close link between the areas of covenant and Law can be generalized to other documents, since 'by far the largest number of occurrences of the word "covenant" in the Qumran texts can be explained in terms of this very rigid and severely legalistic understanding of the law as an absolute maxim to be followed and obeyed'.[83]

Alongside this legalistic and technical notion of covenant, however, or perhaps we should say intertwined with it, there exists at Qumran 'a highly spiritualized notion of covenant law as faith in the eschatological purpose of God revealed through scripture. . .'[84] It is the merit of Huntjens' article to have shown how these supposedly conflicting attitudes could coexist in the DSS. The role of the Teacher of Righteousness as prophet and mediator of the new revelation—a NC—comes into play here.

In the *Thanksgiving Hymns* the word 'covenant' is applied to the redemptive work of God in the life of the Teacher who seeks to discover God's redemptive eschatological purpose and judgment as it applies to the sect. Here we find a different understanding of Law, in some sense realizing the prediction of Jer. 31.33a. The Teacher dares to say that God has engraved His Law in the Teacher's own heart (1QH 4.10) and has hidden it in him (1QH 5.11).[85] Obedience to the Law is always of utmost importance at Qumran, an issue of blessing or curse, life or death. But the sectaries' faith in God's eschatological mysteries means that 'covenant obedience is (also) the act of worship in which God's purpose is celebrated'.[86]

The exploration of the NC motif and its specific function in Heb.

will be the object of Chapter 5. At this stage we will attempt briefly to show the different perception of the 'newness' of the NC in Heb. compared to the view of the DSS which we just analyzed. Whereas we had to guess that Jeremiah's oracle probably underlies the usage of the term הברית החדשה (with the definite article!) in CD and whereas the majority of texts in the DSS admittedly refrain from calling the Essene covenant a 'NC', the author of Heb. leaves us in no doubt as to his source. He chooses to quote Jeremiah's prophecy twice, but then develops the NC theme largely independently of his proof-text.[87]

As we stated above, both communities contemporize the notion of the eschatological covenant and apply it to their own times. But in Heb. we have left behind the realm of annual covenant renewals, for here the NC is presented as inaugurated, once-and-for-all, by the definitive action of Christ's sacrificial death and exaltation. The NC motif is employed by the author to underline the break in salvation history that happened in Christ. The NC community, which is called into being as a result, is summoned by the author to a radically new existence, demonstrated and inaugurated by Christ for his followers, by virtue of his passage from death to life.

The adjectives καινός (8.8, 13; 9.15) and νέος (12.24) are reserved exclusively for διαθήκη.[88] E.A.C. Pretorius discerns a threefold meaning of newness at work in Heb.: (1) the *temporal* element is present in the 'days' which Jeremiah foretold; (2) the *qualitative* element is revealed by the way in which the NC 'surpasses the old decisively in power, functioning and result'; and (3) the *dynamic* element lies in the very appearance of the new, which demonstrates the aging of the old and puts it out of action.[89] In the author's own language we find this confirmed. (1) ἡ πρώτη/δεύτερα (8.7), (2) κρείττων (7.22; 8.6) and (3) παλαιόω/καινή (8.13) express the three elements.

In Heb. the first, old covenant has a provisional character and the author considers it inherently inefficacious. This is so because the covenant is viewed almost exclusively in cultic terms—a perspective which we find nowhere in CD. Here, if we analyze correctly, the problem with the old covenant is human failure to interpret correctly and to keep the Mosaic Law in all its aspects, cultic and moral. In CD even the NC has already been broken/left by certain groups. In Heb. on the other hand, the covenant notion is centered upon the areas of priesthood and sacrifice; and it is argued that the very appearance of a new high priest of a new order, who is able to deal decisively with the problem of human sin and can provide lasting access to God, demonstrates the imperfect quality of the old covenant and its Levitical system (7.11; 8.7; 10.1-4).

Here *newness signals rupture with the ways of old* and any attempts to revitalize the old legal order or to combine elements from both orders are flatly condemned by the author of Heb. Paradoxically, most of the elements that went into the making of the old cultic order are retained in *form*: bloody sacrifice cleanses sinfulness/inaugurates the covenant and a high priest enters the Tabernacle. But the *content* of these elements is utterly transformed in the new covenantal order as they are invested with new meaning by the Christ event. The Qumran sectaries would no longer have recognized this complex of ideas as a covenant, especially since the Law has been severed from its intimate connection to the covenant and no longer has a place within the NC of Christ.

D. *The Fate of the New Covenant in Early Rabbinic Literature*

We wish to conclude this chapter on the NC in Judaism with a brief section on early Rabbinic literature. In the interest of following the fate of the NC idea chronologically such a section seems necessary, even though we are very aware of the difficult nature of the subject matter. Not only is the material notoriously hard to date, but 'the organizing principles and functions of rabbinic literature are still something of a mystery, even to those who are skilled in reading Mishnah, midrash, and Talmud'.[90]

In his concluding chapter of *Torah in the Messianic Age and/or the Age to Come*, W.D. Davies refers to the peril of systematizing 'what was vague and amorphous'. In the Rabbinic corpus, perhaps even more so than elsewhere, 'the isolation of passages dealing with one theme and their presentation in a concentrated, consecutive manner can too easily create an erroneous impression of their significance: to isolate in this context is to magnify. . .'[91]

Furthermore, Davies notes that the passages which he employs in his study of the Law—and the same will be true in our search for the NC concept—are all haggadic,[92] whereas the emphasis in Tannaitic literature is clearly halakic. Whether or not one likes to use catch-phrases such as 'orthopraxis' in this context, the important point remains that the Tannaim tried to build a new community of Law on the basis of their halakic rulings for Jewry at large.[93] They were much less interested in what Christianity terms 'doctrines' and 'could tolerate the widest varieties and even contradictions of beliefs'.[94] This phenomenon, as it developed at Yavneh, has been characterized as a 'grand coalition',[95] displaying a 'hospitable comprehensiveness'[96] in its 'new desire to define a catholic Israel'.[97] The resulting body of literature is therefore quite *sui generis* and it is particularly inappropriate to try to distill its *essence*.[98] Caution is even in order when it comes to comparison of *individual motifs* in Judaism and Christianity such as we are here undertaking, since the context and significance may be vastly different in each case.[99]

Finally, we ought to mention that even Jaubert's otherwise acclaimed study has been repeatedly criticized for its all-too-brief treatment of Rabbinic Judaism.[100] We are aware that what follows here will be subject to similar strictures. While the time-frame of Jaubert's book ended in 70 CE (and hence in some sense justified her short section on the Rabbis), we are willing to take second (and perhaps third) century materials into consideration for our purposes. We are not, however, dealing with the covenant concept as such but with the specific idea of the *NC*. Nonetheless, as we discovered throughout this chapter on Judaism, whenever explicit references to the NC are rare or completely absent, we have to engage in a more general discussion of covenantal theology. This we will now undertake for Rabbinic literature.

In his study of the nature of Rabbinic religion Sanders has to rely on haggadic materials more often than not in order to locate the different elements that account for the basic similarity of the religious world of the Rabbis to other types of Palestinian Judaism. He concludes that the pattern of 'covenantal nomism' is applicable here too, if one realizes that the basic theological concepts are *assumed* rather than explicitly stated in this literature. God's role in the covenant is seldom discussed, 'but that role is nevertheless the presupposition upon which all the halakic material rests. The only reason for elaborating and defining man's obligations under the covenant is that God's faithfulness and justice in keeping his side are beyond question'.[101] In this scheme atonement functions to restore someone to a pre-existing relationship. In a way similar to Christianity, the elements of corporate election of *all* Israel and of an individual/ personal relationship to God through piety are combined.[102]

To those who miss direct references to the term 'covenant',

Sanders replies that there are several Rabbinic expressions denoting the same idea. Some of the favorite ways of expressing the covenantal relationship are: 'confessing the Exodus/the commandments', referring to God as 'King', and to his reign as the '(Yoke of the) Kingdom of Heaven', which one freely assumes.[103]

Segal's article acknowledges the methodological problems involved in the search for the Rabbinic view of covenant and admits that 'there is not a lot of explicit evidence on which to found' such a view.[104] He suggests that 'One way to resolve this issue would be to emphasize that the term "Torah" has very broad implications in Judaism and that it subsumes "grace" and "covenant"... (which) is true, yet it does not give us a positive doctrine with which to work'.[105] Segal then proceeds to survey the areas of liturgy and ritual in which he believes one can find a wealth of sources to help one formulate a Rabbinic conception of covenant. Most notably the area of circumcision, but also daily and Shabbat services, as well as various aspects of the *Shema*, are worthy of further study in Segal's view. The problem of dating these materials may be even thornier than in the case of the midrashim, and the growing evidence of non-rabbinic assemblies constitutes another stumbling block.[106] Nonetheless Segal at least makes an interesting case for further exploration of the liturgy, in which a communal and/or personal relationship to God is of course expressed very differently than in *Halakah*.

Yet in all this we find no trace of a NC idea. Schreiber's study devotes eight pages to the Rabbis in which he analyzes precisely the passages listed in Strack–Billerbeck under Heb. 8.8-12, with one exception: *Sipra* Lev. 26.9 (111a).[107] Unfortunately this latter passage, which is the only one we could reasonably consider early enough to fall within our purview, also turns out to be the least interesting one, from the point of view of wrestling with the issues of Jer. 31.31-34, since its accent falls on the promise of progeny to Abraham.

Schreiber discusses one passage also found in Davies,[108] namely *Midr. Qoh.* 2.1. This midrash, while appearing in the name of R. Simon b. Zabda (ca. 300), is also too late for serious consideration here. But we wish to note that the issue of what will happen to the *Torah in the future* is the one that most seems to engage the later Rabbis' attention in connection with Jeremiah's oracle. Therefore Davies' book deserves mention here. He believes that the Rabbis understood the Law of Jeremiah's NC to be the *Mosaic Torah*[109] and the overall thrust of the texts he studied is that, apart from minor changes in details and a better apprehension on the human side because of divine instruction, the Torah is *not* expected to change in the Messianic Age/Age to Come.[110]

Thus Schreiber is correct when he detects a shift of emphasis from Jeremiah's problem of two covenants to a tension between the conditions of this old aeon and the new coming aeon. But he incorrectly assumes that the Rabbinic texts speak of two *Gesetzgebungen*.[111]

In seeking the reason for the neglect of Jeremiah's prophecy, both Schreiber[112] and Davies[113] suspect anti-Christian polemics at work. In the course of discussion of the idea of Christ as a new Moses, H.J. Schoeps reaches the following conclusion about the Jewish-Christian contest over the appropriation of the Hebrew Scriptures: 'Es begegnet uns hier dieselbe Erscheinung wie bei der Auslegungsgeschichte von Jes. 53, Ps. 2.7, 110.1; *Jer. 31.31f*; Hosea 2.25 usw. Die jüdische Theologie der ersten Jahrhunderte n. Chr. fand diese Schriftstellen bereits *durch die Christliche Auslegung präokkupiert* und verzichtete daher auf ihre Verwendung innerhalb messianischer Diskussionen oder legte die betont *uneschatologisch* aus'.[114]

The problem with this explanation for the lack of enthusiasm for the NC motiv in early Rabbinic Judaism is that, as we will discover in Chapter 4 below, the NC idea does not appear very frequently in *early Christianity* either. It does not constitute a major theological idea anywhere in the NT except in the Last Supper accounts and in Heb. Of course the NC idea might have been better known than the NT writings indicate, if oral tradition about liturgical use of Jer. 31.31-34 was familiar to the Rabbis. Even so, it is not very plausible that they reacted against an early Christian appropriation of the NC idea.

Given the nature of their literature, it is also hard to tell whether *sectarian Jewish* usage of the idea might have led to a Rabbinic avoidance of it. Wolff suggests that the 'Unbedeutsamkeit dieser Stelle für das Frühjudentum' may have played a role in its rare appearance in Rabbinic literature.[115] While it is probably true that certain passages keep reappearing due to their earlier popularity in the tradition, and others are ignored due to earlier neglect of them, thus explanation merely pushes the problem further back in time and ultimately begs the question.

Reventlow notes 'die Gedanken von Jer. 31, 31ff. (bilden) keine der entscheidend weiterwirkenden Strukturlinien in der Botschaft des Alten Testaments'. He would deny a generalized applicability of the prophecy to later times beyond its particular, highly critical historical hour, on the grounds that the contents of the oracle deprive the covenant relationship of the element of human freedom to rebel.[116] Even though one might push the contents of Jer. 31.31-34 to their extreme limits, and read the text as announcing a lobotomy of the human heart,[117] this seems to be a rather modern preoccupation which probably never occurred to Jeremiah himself, and which we do not find in the ancient sources that deal with his prophecy.

In speculating about possible reasons for a dislike of the NC concept in Second Temple Judaism and in the early Rabbinic period, it seems more plausible that the disturbing implication of a NC affected the *divine* side of the relationship. OT history is replete with accounts of human failure and human breaking of the covenant. But a NC initiated by God—as opposed to periodic renewals of the old covenant—might have implied a questioning of God's prior faithful relationship and thus might have led to doubts about the future reliability of the covenant bond.[118]

Summary

In this chapter we tried to trace the NC idea in Judaism. We discussed three passages from the Second Temple period which seem at first glance to reflect Jeremiah's prophecy of the NC. Our analysis showed that these texts—and indeed the vast corpus of literature from this period—do not really grapple with the problem of the failure of the old covenant along Jeremiah's lines, but rather envisage a return to the *old* relationship with God and a *renewal* of the old covenantal promises by God in response.

The notable exception is of course the Qumran community, whose library contains a literature replete with covenantal expressions, including several uses of the term 'New Covenant'. We found many affinities between the DSS and Heb., even though the sectarian covenantal conception is much less radical in its view of newness and is of course unwilling to reject the Law. The sectaries' ideal consists in a return to the original intentions of the Mosaic Torah as they have come to understand its true import under the guidance of the Teacher of Righteousness. In this sense the Essene covenant can be thought of as a renewal of the old Sinai covenant, but it transcends that covenant in important ways, because it contains an element of new revelation granted exclusively to the sect. It also envisages a partial realization and fulfilment of the eschatological covenant promises in the life of the sect.

Heb., on the other hand, works explicitly with Jeremiah's sharp contrast between the two covenants, and views the old Sinai covenant and its institutions as inherently defective and inefficacious in light of the Christ event. The author develops his conception of the NC on the basis of the new and only high priestly ministry of Christ, the NC mediator, who definitively superseded the old covenant and its cult. Despite the lack of evidence for a literary connection between Heb. and Qumran,[119] we regard the DSS as an important witness that can help us to discover the unique features of the NC idea in Heb.

Finally, we took a brief look at early Rabbinic literature in order to follow the fate of the NC concept into the early centuries of the Common Era. We found no passages early enough to warrant inclusion in this study and had to content ourselves with general remarks about the Rabbinic view of covenant as far as it can be deduced implicitly from similar expressions and *haggadah*.

Excursus II
Translations of the NC Texts in the DSS

Cairo Damascus Document

Manuscript A 1:

6.11	'And all who have been admitted into the covenant
6.12	(are not) to enter the sanctuary...
6.14	... unless they are observant in doing according to the law as detailed for the period of wickedness: to separate
6.15	from the children of the Pit; to refrain from unjust wealth...
6.17	... to separate the unclean from the clean and to make clear the difference between
6.18	the holy and the profane; to keep the Sabbath day according to the details; and the festivals days
6.19	and the Fast Day *according to the finding of the members of the NC in the land of Damascus*
6.20	to offer the holy things according to their details; to love each one his brother

6.21	as himself; to support the poor, etc.'
8.2	'This is the day
8.3	when God shall visit 'the princes of Judah'...
8.4	... All are rebellious, because they did not depart from the way
8.5	of traitors but defiled themselves...
8.8	and chose each one in accordance with the stubbornness of his heart. They did not separate from the people and rebelled with a high hand
8.9	to walk in the way of the wicked...
8.16	And this is the judgment of the 'captivity of Israel' who departed from the way of the people: because of God's love for
8.17	the founders who walked after him, He loves those who come after them, for theirs is
8.18	the 'covenant of the fathers'. But against those who hate the 'builders of the wall' His anger is aroused. And like this
8.19	judgment (it will be) for every one who rejects the commandments of God and forsakes them and turns in the stubbornness of his heart.
8.20	This is the word which Jeremiah spoke to Baruch the son of Neraiah and Elisha
8.21	to Gehazi his servant. All men who entered into the NC in the land of Damascus...' *(A 1 breaks off here).*

Manuscript B:

*	19.33	*'(And) thus all the men who entered the new*
	19.34	*covenant in the land of Damascus* and have turned back and acted treacherously and departed from the well of living water
	19.35	shall not be reckoned in the 'council of the people' and shall not be written in the rec(ords) from the time the Teacher
	20.1	of the community is gathered in until the arrival of the Messiah from Aaron and from Israel. And thus is the judgment (also)
*		
	20.2	for all who have entered the congregation of men of perfect holiness and is (sic) loth to do what is stipulated for upright men.
	20.3	He is the man who is 'melted in the middle of a furnace'. When his deeds become apparent, he shall be dismissed from the congregation
	20.4	as one whose lot has not fallen among those 'taught by God'...

20.6	Once his deeds have become clear in the light of the study of the law by which
20.7	the men of perfect holiness walk, no man may have dealings with him in respect of property or work,
20.8	for all the holy ones of the Most High have cursed him. And the same judgment applies to everyone who rejects the former
20.9	and the latter (ordinances), who have placed idols on their heart and walked in the stubbornness
20.10	of their heart. They have no share in the House of the Law. They shall receive the same judgment as their companions who turned back
20.11	with the 'men of scoffing', for they spoke heresy against the ordinances of righteousness and *rejected*
20.12	*the covenant and bond which they affirmed in the land of Damascus that is, the NC.*
20.13	There i(s) no share for those or for their families in the House of the Law'.[120]

Pesher on Habakkuk

1QpHab 1.16, 17–2.1 = Hab. 1.5

2.1	'(The interpretation of the passage concerns) the traitors together with the Man of
2.2	the Lie, for (they did) not (believe the words of) the Teacher of Righteousness (which were) from the mouth of
2.3	God. And it concerns *the trai(tors to) the new (covenant)*, f(o)r they were not
2.4	faithful to the covenant of God, (but they profaned) his holy name.
2.5	Likewise, the interpretation of the passage (concerns the trai)tors at the end of
2.6	days. They are the ruthless (ones of the coven)ant who will not believe
2.7	when they hear all that is going to co(me upon) the last generation from the mouth of
2.8	the priest into (whose heart) God put (understandi)ng to interpret all
2.9	the words of his servants the prophets by (whose) hand God enumerated
2.10	all that is going to come upon his people and up(on his congregation)'.[121]

Chapter 4

THE NEW COVENANT IN THE NEW TESTAMENT
(APART FROM HEBREWS) AND IN THE EARLY FATHERS

It has often been noted,[1] that apart from Heb. the collection which came to be known as the 'New Testament' contains very few occurrences of the phrase καινὴ διαθήκη, and even has relatively few instances of the simple use of διαθήκη.[2] Leaving Heb. to the next chapter, we will here deal with those covenantal passages that are theologically significant in relation to the *new order* introduced by Christ, even if they lack the explicit phrase 'New Covenant'. We will concentrate on the use of (new) covenant language in Paul and in the four parallel accounts of the Last Supper (1 Cor. 11.23-26; and in the Synoptics: Mk 14.22-25; Mt. 26.26-29; Lk. 22.15-20) and will conclude each section with a comparison to Heb. Traditional references to διαθήκη pertaining to the old covenant(s) of the Hebrew Scriptures (Eph. 2.12; Acts 3.25; 7.8; Lk. 1.72) and the ark of the covenant (Rev. 11.19) will be ignored. At the end of the chapter we will briefly trace the reemergence of the NC concept in the early Fathers.

A. *The New Covenant in Paul*

There are eight usages of διαθήκη in Paul. 1 Cor. 11.23-26 will be considered in section B. on the last Supper. In this section we will first deal with the usages in Galatians and in 2 Corinthians 3, and then with those in Romans. Finally, Paul's thinking on the relationship between the old and the new covenants will be compared to that of Heb.

At first there will be a brief treatment of the problem of how to render διαθήκη in Gal. 3.15, 17 and how to interpret this passage as a consequence. Then our exposition will focus on the two midrashic passages of Gal. 4.21-31 and 2 Corinthians 3, which contain the three main occurrences of interest to us, namely Gal. 4.24, 2 Cor. 3.6 (the only use of καινὴ διαθήκη in Paul apart from 1 Cor. 11.25), and 2 Cor. 3.14 (where we find παλαιὰ διαθήκη).

(1) *Galatians 3.15, 17*

The majority of interpreters believe that in Gal. 3.15 Paul intends διαθήκη to mean 'will' according to the secular Hellenistic usage of the Greek term. We are convinced by J.J. Hughes's thorough investigation[3] of the internal (lexical, syntactical and semantic) and external evidence (Greek, Egyptian and Roman legal custom involving wills) and accept his conclusion that 'covenant' in the biblical sense is the *only* possible translation for διαθήκη in Gal. 3.15 and 3.17.

In 3.15 Paul wishes to give a 'human example' of covenant ratification and its inviolability among human covenant partners, of which the OT reports plenty of cases. The curses listed as part of the agreements are designed to show what the fate of the party violating the covenant will be. Paul compares this general case (3.15) to the specific situation of God's promise to Abraham and to his seed, which constitutes a ratified covenant *prior* to the Mosaic covenant (3.16-18).

The issue at stake for Paul is the relationship between the Abrahamic and Mosaic covenants. Since Paul views the former as a paradigm for the principle that inheritance of God's promises comes by faith rather than by works of the Law, the Mosaic covenant is made subsidiary to the Abrahamic one.[4] Unlike human *wills*, which 'could be changed, added to or modified by the testator'.[5], God's *covenant* with Abraham—into which Christians are subsumed in Christ, the 'seed'—is neither nullified nor added to by the later Sinai covenant.

It would go beyond our present scope to discuss the problematic 'scene at the addition of the Law'[6] in 3.19-20. For our purposes it is sufficient to stress that Paul insists on the clearly limited, temporary function of the Law as a παιδαγωγός (3.25). The Law remained in office only until the coming of the promised seed in whom all became heirs by faith (3.24-29). Christ met the demands of the Mosaic covenant and freed people from bondage to the Law by taking the curse of the Law upon himself and thus making available the reception of the blessing promised to Abraham (3.13-14). 'His death was that of a representative, substitutionary covenant servant who vicariously underwent judgment on behalf of his people. It was not the death of a testator'.[7]

(2) *Galatians 4.21-32*

An examination of the relationship between the δύο διαθῆκαι (4.24) in Galatians 4 must be mindful of the larger context of this highly polemical letter. C.K. Barrett[8] and Alexandra Brown[9] argue convincingly that the allegory of Gal 4.21-31 must be viewed, not as incidental,[10] but as the climactic point in Paul's ongoing argument with the Galatians and their Teachers.[11]

For the sake of brevity and clarity we will reproduce Martyn's schematic presentation of the scene depicting the two covenants. Martyn's analysis follows up Barrett's suggestions that (1) Paul is using Scriptural texts which have been forced upon him by the Teachers' exegesis and (2) that the whole debate about true descent from Abraham has arisen because the Teachers have been questioning the lineage of the Galatians and urging them to legitimize themselves by circumcision and submission to the Law.[12] As reconstructed by Martyn[13] *the Teachers' view* of the family tree is as follows:

Hagar	*Sarah*
—slave	—free
—Gentiles	—Jews
—The Nations	—The church of the circumcised (i.e. the ruling powers of the Jerusalem church and the Law-observant mission sponsored by them).

According to Martyn,[14] *Paul's exegesis* is meant to replace the Teachers' table of opposites/correspondences (to wit the technical term συστοιχέω in 4.25) by another:

Hagar	*(Sarah)*
—slave	—free
—the covenant from Mount Sinai	—the covenant of God's promise to Abraham (3.17)
—the present Jerusalem (i.e. the False Brothers in the Jerusalem church as sponsors of the Law-observant mission to Gentiles)	—the Jerusalem above, our mother (an apocalyptic expression in Rev. 3.12; 21.2)
—children of the slave woman born into slavery	—children of the free woman
—one born in accordance	—one born in accordance with the

with the Flesh
—the slave woman and her
son (i.e. the Teachers
who are to be expelled)

Spirit, i.e. the promise of God
—the son of the free woman
(i.e. the Galatians as those
born of the promised Spirit)

The passage is framed by references to the Galatians' danger of becoming against subject to the Law and to the στοιχεῖα (ὑπὸ νόμον θέλοντες εἶναι—4.21; ζυγῷ δουλείας ἐνέχεσθε—5.1). These references form a clear link with earlier passages of subjection-language: ὑπὸ κατάραν (3.10), ὑπὸ ἁμαρτίαν (3.22), ὑπὸ νόμον (3.23), ὑπὸ παιδαγώγον (3.25), ὑπὸ ἐπιτρόπους καὶ οἰκονόμους (4.2), ὑπὸ τὰ στοιχεῖα (4.3), ὑπὸ νόμον (state of the Son—4.4, state of the children—4.5). All these conditions refer to the left column in Paul's antinomy-scheme above, while the groundwork for the right side has already been laid in Paul's exposition of how Christ enabled the Galatians to become heirs to the promise made to Abraham (3.6-29).

Paul shows himself to be a master in playing off Scripture passages against one another. Just as he has done this in 3.11-12 by quoting Hab. 2.4 against Lev. 18.5, so here in 4.21-31 he juxtaposes the stories from Gen. 16–21 (from which he never quotes) with the *haphtarah* passage from Isa. 54.1. The argument shifts from one pair of mothers (Hagar/Sarah) to another pair (the νῦν Jerusalem/the ἄνω Jerusalem). Against Barrett's contention that this association of texts, which has puzzled several interpreters, had never been made before,[15] Mary Callaway can show that the link could be based on liturgical tradition that Paul may have encountered in the Synagogue.[16]

Furthermore Paul seems to be familiar with midrashic traditions in which 'the image of *Jerusalem* giving birth to sons, whether it signifies the restoration of Jerusalem in history or the beginning of the world to come, is based on *Sarah*, who gave birth when it seemed impossible'.[17] Thus it is likely that Paul is using traditional texts and methods to come to startling new results. For Paul the prophecy of Isa. 54.1 becomes a paradigm for God's action in Christ. Just as God brought forth Isaac from barren parents/as good as dead (see Rom. 4.19), so God raised his Son from death and thereby raised up descendants for Abraham κατὰ ἐπαγγελίας (4.28).[18]

Thus Paul employs Isa. 54.1 to reach the opposite exegetical conclusion from what one might have expected. As Barrett points out,[19] the Sarah story of the barren woman who is granted a child by promise clearly seems to favor the Teachers' claim to being

Abraham's rightful heirs and seems to put the Gentiles[20] outside the pale with the rejected slave-woman. But in Paul's exegesis Sinai and those who desire to be under the Law through circumcision end up in Arabia with the outcast slave and slip over into the left column,[21] while Sarah becomes the mother of the non-circumcised and stands for the covenant of the ἄνω Jerusalem.

Underlying Paul's exegetical endeavor is as always the fundamental axiom of Χριστὸς ἐσταυρωμένος (3.1). His main contention against the Teachers, from which all other arguments follow, is the fact that they have failed to realize the import of the Christ event in its head-on collision with the Law. Thus Paul has to remind them that Christ 'became a curse for us' (3.13) so that those who remain ἐξ ἔργων νόμου are henceforth themselves under a curse (3.10). They cannot enjoy the freedom which Christ brought or possess true 'hearing of faith' (3.2).

Hearing the Scriptures from the standpoint of one in whom Christ is being formed (4.19) and who knows himself to be a son κατὰ πνεῦμα entails the realization that an antinomy has been opened up internal to the Law itself (4.21). ἡ γραφή can now be used *both* to bear witness against itself (4.30) and to speak the Gospel truth about God's new freeing act on behalf of the barren/in bondage (4.26-27), even as it already announced that Gospel in the promise to Abraham long ago (see προευαγγελίζομαι in 3.8). In Paul's reading the texts do not function to portray a continuous salvation history (as they probably did in the missionary preaching of the Teachers), but rather 'they speak of two realms, one of freedom, the other of slavery'.[22]

In Galatians, therefore, the two covenants are portrayed by Paul as polar opposites with no middle ground between them. The children κατὰ σάρκα cannot but persecute those κατὰ πνεῦμα, but the latter expect this since they know that an apocalyptic battle is being waged. Even in the midst of this battle they know themselves to be a 'new creation', the 'Israel of God', whose only boast consists—not in circumcision and works of the Law, nor in uncircumcision—but in the cross of Christ (6.13-16).

The Spirit of Christ has begun to invade the world at the resurrection and has altered the basic structures of the cosmos. The fundamental antinomies that characterized the old world (3.28) have ceased to be meaningful in the new world/new time because a radical realignment of forces has occurred. The Law, which used to be considered an antidote to the fleshy Impulse (and is still so regarded by the Teachers!), has turned into an ally of the Flesh, and consequently functions as an enemy of the Spirit.[23]

At the dawn of the 'new creation' the Law is no longer an effective shield and belongs irrevocably to the old covenant of slavery/the present Jerusalem. Those who would belong to the NC of freedom and who would claim the Jerusalem above as their mother are summoned by Paul to 'hear' the Scriptures with faith (see 3.2-5) and to be seized by the apocalypse of Christ's death, so that they might 'know what time it is, thereby coming once again to live in the real world'.[24]

(3) *2 Corinthians 3*

In 2 Corinthians 3 Paul brings up a similar set of antinomies in his discussion of the two covenants, although his opponents are of a rather different kind[25] and are forcing him to interpret a different Scripture passage.[26] The chapter is part of the long section from 2 Cor. 2.14 to 6.10, in which Paul's apostolic office and its authority constitute the major theme.[27]

The Corinthian community is presented by Paul as his letter of recommendation[28] (vv. 2-3):

| carved | —not in ink | —but by the Spirit of the living God |
| | —not on stone tablets | —but on tablets of human hearts |

In defending his apostolic office, Paul is unwilling at this stage to point to his own accomplishments—something he later does in chs. 11-12, when he speaks as a 'fool'—and refers to the Corinthians instead. Curiously enough, they constitute a letter of recommendation which can be 'known and read by all' (v. 2), even though it is written on Paul's *heart*.[29]

The motifs of *revelation and concealment/veiling*, as well as the related actions of *seeing/understanding/knowing* and their opposites, occupy a large place throughout 2 Corinthians.[30] In 3.2-3 Paul prepares both for the subsequent midrash on Exod. 34.29-35 LXX with its multifold play on the word κάλυμμα (3.13-15) and for ch. 4.

There he will once again command himself to everyone's conscience by the '*open* statement of the truth' (4.2). In a characteristic paradox this is followed by the declaration that 'the gospel is *veiled*, ... (but) only to those who are perishing', while those whose hearts are guided by the light of Christ's glory, know that they possess a 'treasure in earthen vessels' (4.5-7).[31] The rest of ch. 4 continues to develop the antinomies of ch. 3 which we will now explore: darkness-blindness/light-sight, weakness manifesting glory, outer/inner nature, mortality-transience-death/resurrection-eternity-life.

Paul's ministry finds its source of empowerment in God (3.4-5), 'who enabled us to be ministers of a NC' (v. 6).

—not of the letter	—but of the Spirit
—which kills	—which gives life

This introduction of the NC theme may at first glance seem rather abrupt after the preceding theme of recommendation letters.[32] Yet it is not at all implausible that the 'magnet' words,[33] attracting Paul's attention—or even that of his opponents, whose Moses-midrash he is reshaping—to the covenant theme, were the words 'writing' and 'hearts', which had already been connected with the NC by Jer. 31.31-34.[34]

Paul extends the antithetical comparison between tbe two types of covenantal ministries by means of three carefully structured *qal-waḥomers* (vv. 7-11):

1. διακονία[35] of death	διακονία of the Spirit
—carved in letters of stone	
—had glory	πῶς οὐχὶ μᾶλλον... glory
2. διακονία of condemnation	διακονία of righteousness
	—exceeds πολλῷ μᾶλλον in glory
—in glory	
(what was once glory	
—is no longer glory	—because of surpassing glory)
3. what faded	what is permanent
—once possessed glory	—πολλῷ μᾶλλον glory

By this threefold variation on the same typological theme of comparative glory 'Paul met en relief la gloire supérieure et durable de la Nouvelle Alliance'.[36] Clearly a *measure* of glory has to be conceded by Paul to the old dispensation to establish a basis for his comparisons *a minori ad maius*. But this form of argumentation should not blind us to the absolute nature of the antitheses involved.[37] The parenthetical verse 10 leaves no doubt as to the ultimate verdict about the old covenant: even its former relative glory is questioned by Paul. *In light of the surpassing glory of Christ* the old and new covenants are viewed as mutually exclusive opposites.[38]

We find this verdict confirmed by Paul's blatant violation of the

OT sense of Exod. 34.29-35 LXX[39] in his peculiar employment of the κάλυμμα-motif for his own purposes. The veil functions in a three-fold manner. First, it retains the OT sense of a cover upon Moses' face, but instead of preventing fear of the transcendent on the Israelites' part, its purpose is now to hide fading glory (v. 13). Second, the veil obscures the reading of the παλαιὰ διαθήκη by the Israelites to this day and can only be removed in Christ (v. 14). Third, the veil covers their hearts whenever Moses is read to this day and is removed only when someone turns to the Lord (vv. 15-16). The virtually synonymous nature of the second and third functions of the veil shows how 'Moses' is all but equated here by Paul with his ministry as mediator of the 'old covenant'.

Thus the antithesis between Moses and Christ runs parallel to the antithesis between the old and new covenants. While Moses is characterized by the motifs of fading glory and the veil, Christ is equated with unsurpassable, permanent glory and unveiling by the action of his Spirit. Thereby Christ's followers are gradually being changed into his likeness and become partakers of his glory and of his freedom (vv. 17-18).

Despite his labelling of the scriptural book in 3.14 as παλαιὰ διαθήκη (which happens nowhere else in the NT), Paul still distinguishes between the old covenant as Scripture, giving witness to the NC,[40] and the old covenant as dispensational era.[41] In Christ God has opened up a new present, the time of life-giving πνεῦμα (3.3, 17-18 form a frame for the midrash!), which confronts the past as an era of γράμμα.[42] Even though 'covenant' is a salvation-historical category, Paul's focus is on the *present*, as the time of the turn of the ages. As Vielhauer puts it, 'zwar [spielt] der zeitliche *Abstand* [see also Gal. 3.17!], nicht aber der zeitliche *Ablauf* eine Rolle: Die Ausführungen des Paulus sind nicht geschichtstheologisch, sondern soteriologisch orientiert'.[43] The now-time (see νῦν in 2 Cor. 6.2; Gal. 3.25, 29) is the time in which the antinomies between the covenants are revealed and played out in dialectical fashion.

As Martyn points out,[44] the underlying debate between Paul and the super-apostles is one over correct ways of knowing. The frequency of references to the suffering and burden entailed by Paul's apostolic office in 2 Corinthians is overwhelming. Yet these statements are always couched in dialectical terms, mirroring Paul's self-understanding as one living at the turn of the ages.[45] On the one hand, he knows himself to be a 'new creation' in Christ (5.17), on the other hand he is continually carrying the νέκρωσις of Christ in himself (4.10). Hence Paul can say that, 'from now on we know nobody κατὰ σάρκα' (5.16).

The tradition about Moses' shining face receives so much emphasis in the midrash of 2 Corinthians 3 that Georgi locates its origin in the opponents' camp.[46] According to this interpretation the glowing faces are to be taken literally and we are asked to imagine that the super-apostles are really using their glowing faces as proof for their divinely inspired, charismatic leadership over the Corinthians. Whether that was in fact the case or not, the passage clearly shows that Paul's message of 1 Corinthians 1-2, where he insists that God's power is manifested in weakness and μωρία, has not been understood by the Corinthians.

We already noted above, with reference to Galatians, that Paul's whole focus and perception of the world changes with the death/ resurrection of Christ. His quarrel with the super-apostles centers on their seeming inability to comprehend the Christ event as utterly unique and definitive. If Christ is viewed as just another divinely empowered emissary in a long line of such characters, along with Moses and perhaps the super-apostles themselves, then Christ's cross was in vain. If the letter of the Law points to such an unending sequence of salvation-historical figures, viewed and judged κατὰ σάρκα, it kills. It is opposed to the Spirit of the Lord, that is freedom (3.17; see also Gal. 5.18).

In a sense, Christians can now read the Law 'from the same side of the veil as Moses'.[47] What Moses was granted during his periods of unveiling in the Tent, Christians are promised and now enjoy in incipient fashion. In Paul's view the super-apostles are still blinded by the veil in their reliance upon their own ecstatic experiences and 'in their failure to view the cross as the absolute epistemological watershed'.[48] Therefore they read Scripture κατὰ σάρκα and turn revelation into misperception. The true disciple, on the other hand, has been granted new eyes and with the help of the Spirit he can discern 'the marks of the new age. . . hidden *in* the old age'.[49] But this new vision can be enjoyed only by one who understands that life under the NC entails daily dying and making the cross of Christ one's own.[50]

(4) *Romans 9.4 and Romans 11.27*

When one turns to Romans one finds no mention of the NC and only two occurrences of διαθήκη. It is surely no accident that these are located in Romans 9-11, where Paul wrestles with the problem of his Jewish brethren and their rejection of Christ. Once again we notice that covenant terminology is not Paul's own preferred way of discussing the Christ event, but he employs it when forced to do so by his opponents and in relation to Israel. In Rom. 9.4-5 Paul lists the covenants[51] as one of the privileges granted to Israel, along with sonship, glory, the giving of the Law, worship, the promises and the patriarchs. Paul is speaking in summary fashion and we cannot be sure which covenants in the tradition he has in mind; it is noteworthy, however, that he does not exclude the Sinai covenant.

In the next paragraph Paul reiterates the argument that we encountered in Galatians, namely that only the descendants of Isaac—the children of the promise, not the children of the flesh—are to be reckoned among God's children (Rom. 9.7-8; see Gal. 4.28-29). This has to be read in light of the earlier description of Abraham in Romans 4, however, where Paul has nuanced the picture of Galatians 3.[52] Since the patriarch is presented as the model of faith and the father of all who share in that faith, both the circumcised and the uncircumcised (Rom. 4.9-16), we can surmise that Paul has primarily the *Abrahamic covenant* in view in Romans 9-11. Indeed throughout this section the Sinai covenant as such is never mentioned despite the discussion of the Law (in 9.30-10.13). Paul's focus is on God's election and call through his inscrutable mercy,[53] for which Abraham serves as a paradigm.

Having adduced numerous Scripture passages to account for the hardening of the majority Israel, Paul introduces the simile of the olive tree to warn the Gentiles against undue conceit and to explain that Israel can yet be saved—'grafted back into their own olive tree' (11.24). The second use of διαθήκη occurs in this context when Paul amalgamates two citations from Isa. 59.12 and Isa. 27.9. '. . . This will be my covenant with them, when I take away their sins' (11.27) may be based on parts of Jer. 31.33-34, like Heb. 10.16-17 which it resembles. But while Heb. is speaking about Christ's death as an event of the *past* that brought forgiveness—as indeed Paul does in other contexts—Paul is *here* referring to the *future* redemption of Israel,[54] which would be closer to the original thrust of the prophecy on the NC.

In paradoxical fashion Paul can assert that his Israelite brethren are 'enemies for your sake as regards the Gospel, . . . but beloved for the sake of their ancestors as regards election' (11.28). He appeals to the tradition of 'merit of the forefathers', which is frequent in Second Temple literature and thus provides another allusion to the covenant with Abraham. It is noteworthy that οἱ πατέρες are among the list of Israelite privileges with which we started our discussion of Romans (9.5). Paul echoes that list and clinches his argument by reasserting that 'the gifts and the call of God are irrevocable' (11.29). Yet it is our hunch that if pressed Paul would have had to admit that the χαρίσματα and the κλῆσις, which endure, do not include the Mosaic covenant nor its δόξα (see 2 Cor. 3).

We conclude that in Romans Paul never employs διαθήκη to describe the new order and therefore never contrasts the old covenant with the new one. Instead the focus is on Christ's death for all—even the ungodly (5.6)—which brought justificiation for all. From this vantage point Paul recognizes that all have sinned and all—whether they are circumcised or not—are in need of forgiveness (see Paul's use of Ps. 32.1-2 in Rom. 4.7-8) and reconciliation (Rom. 5.10; see 2 Cor. 5.18-19). Covenant terminology only arises when Paul is wrestling with the problem of Jewish rejection of Christ. The gist of Romans 9-11 is that the Patriarchal covenant and its promises are still valid. Paul argues—not altogether consistently, but passionately—that through the mysterious workings of God, and the mechanisms of universal sinfulness and of jealousy on the part of Israel, his brethren will ultimately partake of the prophetic covenant promise of forgiveness and will be saved in Christ along with the Gentiles.

(5) *Comparison between the NC Concept in Paul and in Hebrews*
We will now compare the salient points in the use of the NC idea in Paul and in Heb., bearing in mind that our brief remarks about the latter work will anticipate the more detailed discussion of our topic in Chapter 5. As in the case of the Last Supper accounts, which we will discuss later, we feel that a comparison to Heb. will help us to situate the epistle in its larger Christian context and to highlight some of its unique features.

(a) *Relationship to Jeremiah 31.31-34.* Unlike Heb., where Jeremiah's prophecy about the NC is quoted twice, once in full (8.8-12) and once in part (10.16-17), Paul never furnishes a quotation or even a direct allusion to this passage. Apart from the traditional reference in 1 Cor. 11.25, which will occupy us below,[55] there is a single *Pauline* usage of καινὴ διαθήκη in 2 Cor. 3.6. Commentators are uncertain as to whether this reference is based on Jeremiah's oracle. Van Unnik confidently[56] and Luz somewhat more tentatively[57] suggest a combination of themes from Jer. 31.31-34 and the new heart/heart of flesh-passages in Ezekiel. Grässer takes only the latter prophet into account and is entirely sceptical about any relationship to Jeremiah's prophecy on Paul's part, essentially because he interprets Jer. 31.31-34 as a *renewal* of Sinai, based on the *same Torah*, and detects a diametrical opposition to the Sinai covenant and its Law in Paul.[58]

Our own assessment is guided by the uniqueness of the *NC phrase* in Jeremiah's oracle within the OT. Above we concluded that in the absence of NC terminology, *similar ideas*, both in the OT and in early Judaism, are not sufficient to establish a direct relationship to Jeremiah.[59] On the other hand, we concur with Levin that 'Wo immer im NT vom 'neuen Bund', das bedeutet auch: wo vom 'besseren Bund', von den 'zwei Bünden' sowie vom 'ersten' oder 'alten Bund' die Rede ist, steht dieser Text im Hintergrund'.[60] It goes without saying that each such possible allusion to Jeremiah has to be analyzed in its own right and departures from the prophet's original intention are to be expected. But the Scriptures abound with examples of adaptations of old ideas, quoted or alluded to in new contexts and often undergoing radical transformation. That Jeremiah conceived of his NC in terms of the same Torah or that he failed to invoke a 'new Torah', let alone to abolish the whole concept of Law, does not seem to have deterred Paul (or the author of Heb.) from using Jeremiah's *Stichwort* (or from quoting his prophecy).

At first glance there appears to be a huge difference between Paul, in whom it is hard to find traces of Jeremiah, and Heb., where the oracle on the NC is accorded such a prominent place (κεπάλαιον 8.1) and so much space.[61] Yet upon inspection the approach of the two authors to the central ideas of this text turns out to be remarkably similar. While both authors are acutely aware of the people's sinfulness, neither pays any attention to Jer. 31.32, where the *human* rupture of the old covenant is discussed, since the fundamental problem with the old covenant lies at a deeper level. For both Paul and Heb. there is something *inherently* faulty about the old order which they have only come to realize through their encounter with Christ.[62] From the vantage point of the NC—the turn of the ages— which lay in the future for Jeremiah, the old is defined by opposition.[63]

Hence the vision of the prophet is radicalized and in light of the

Christ event only certain of its provisions retain validity. To use Levin's categories:[64] 1. The *Toraverheissung* (Jer. 31.33a) is problematic for both authors. In some cases (especially Heb. 7 and Gal. 3) νόμος has become virtually synonymous with old covenant. There are echoes of the element of a changed inner disposition of the heart (2 Cor. 3.3; 4.6; 5.12; Heb. 10.22; 13.9) which may be closer, however, to the above-mentioned Ezekiel passages.

2. The motif of the λαός τοῦ θεοῦ (see the *Bundesformel* of Jer. 31.33b) is more important to the author of Heb. than to Paul, and this is in keeping with his greater emphasis on covenant.[65]

3. *Erkenntnisverheissung* (Jer. 31.34a): Epistemological issues are of fundamental importance in 2 Corinthians and Heb. stresses the need for seeing beyond earthly realities; so both authors recognize the priority of knowledge from God. But their very works demonstrate their belief in the concomitant need for Christian teachers and correct human transmission of the tradition about Jesus Christ, unlike what Jeremiah envisaged.

4. Only the *Vergebungsverheissung* (Jer. 31.34b) is viewed by both Paul and Heb. as a consequence of the NC, since it was realized upon the death of Christ and is thus linked to the initiation of the NC. For Heb. this is the most important result of the NC, as can be seen from the quotation and the writer's conclusion in 10.16-18, whereas Paul uses forgiveness terminology only in traditional contexts: Rom. 3.21-26; 4.7-8; 11.27. In Paul's own radical formulation *justificatio impiorum* (Rom. 4.5) happened at Christ's death and brought the realization of universal sinfulness. Paul views himself as Christ's ambassador of reconciliation (2 Cor. 5.18-21).

Heb. combines Jeremiah's NC, which frames the central section 8.1-10.18, with the covenant blood-motif (Exod. 24), while Yom Kippur (Lev. 16) forms the background scene (see 12.24; 13.12, 20). The theme of purification for sins is already sounded in 1.3b. The τελει- word-group (see esp. 7.11; 12.2; 2.10; 5.9; 7.28; 10.14; 11.40) also speaks of the perfection/freedom from sin with which Christ was endowed and in which his followers share. For Heb., even more so than for Paul—for whom one would have to substitute justification by faith—'*Die Kraft zur Sündenvergebung ist das Wesen des Neuen Bundes*, macht seine *Neuheit* aus'.[66]

(b) *Relationship to the Hebrew Scriptures*. For both Paul and Heb. the problem of the NC is intimately bound up with the need to reflect on the function of the Scriptures. Of course this does not happen in a systematic fashion. Rather, the Scriptures are frequently employed to testify to the new reality in Christ and are freely adapted and modified in the process—sometimes to the point of being very different from what the original author intended. Both Paul and the author of Heb. are familiar with a wide range of exegetical techniques that were current in their day, and neither could dream of rejecting the Scriptures or of truncating them in a Marcionite fashion.

Allegory plays a minor role in both authors (e.g. Gal. 4.24; Heb. 9.8-9), but typological patterns are used extensively (e.g. Rom. 5.14, 18-19; 1 Cor. 15.21-22, 45-49; 2 Cor. 3.7-18; Heb. 3.2-6; 7.1-10; 9 *passim*; 12.18-29). *Negative* typology is characteristic of the way in which the two covenantal orders are defined by opposition to one another in Heb., Galatians and 2 Corinthians.[67]

Abraham is usually[68] viewed in positive terms, as a recipient of the promise which found its fulfillment in Christ; but Adam (in Paul) and Moses, as personification of the old order and the Law, function largely[69] as antithetical types of Christ. OT figures are used, not as historical persons, but as *exempla* of certain stances for paraenetic purposes or in theological exposition. Just as Moses can take on the functions of his ministry as covenant mediator, so Sarah and Hagar—and their two sons—can assume the traits of the two covenantal eras with which Paul associates them (Gal. 3.21-32).[70] In the philosophical terminology of Heb.—contrary to what one expects—the ἀντίτυπος (9.24) signals the old, while the τύπος (8.5) stands for the new order.[71]

From the vantage point of one convinced of the definitive salvific import of the Christ event, Paul and Heb. freely use the OT as a witness *both* to the inherent inadequacy of the old covenant recorded on its pages *and* to the infinitely superior NC initiated by Christ. In that process Scripture can be quoted against Scripture (something more characteristic of Paul[72] than of Heb.). But it is always assumed (and directly expressed by the way Heb. introduces quotations)[73] that the (same!) God/Holy Spirit who spoke to the ancestors still speaks in Scripture in the author's own time.

(c) *Problem of Salvation History*. The problem of Holy Writ is intimately connected with that of salvation history. We are confronted with the paradox that 'covenant' is a salvation-historical term in the

Bible and yet both Heb. and Paul (in Galatians and 2 Corinthians) can speak of *two* covenants in a way that no longer implies a sequence of covenant renewals. Instead they employ the term *new* covenant to signal a break in salvation history as previously understood and recorded in the Scriptures. Neither author displays an interest in retelling the past for its own sake and in reflecting on the significance of that past per se. As we stated repeatedly, the theological point of departure for the reflections of both writers must be sought in Christ's death and resurrection (Paul)/exaltation (Heb.), which function as a kind of lens through which Israel's past is viewed and judged.

Both authors are convinced of the inbreaking of the new age as a result of the Christ event and are concerned to demonstrate that God's word speaks to the NOW-time νῦν Gal. 4.25, 29; 2 Cor. 6.2; Rom. 13.11/σήμερον 2 Cor. 3.14-15; Heb. 3-4) in which God's judgment divides the lot of humanity. Thus the promise to Abraham is actualized and interpreted as having been addressed to the authors' own time. For Paul Christ is the 'seed' of Abraham in whom his followers inherit the promise (Gal. 3).[75] For Heb. the promise was foreshadowed in the lives of certain exemplary ancestors who could see beyond death by faith (e.g. Enoch 11.5; Abraham/Sarah 11.8-12, 19; Moses 11.25-27), but ultimately none of them truly received the promise, for 'God had foreseen something better for us, so that apart from us they should not be made perfect' (11.39-40 RSV).[76] In this manner the author of Heb. and Paul (at least in Galatians) come close to usurping ἐπαγγελία for the NC by incorporating the patriarchs into the Christian scheme.

The *Sinai* διαθήκη is the antithetical *old* covenant over against which Paul (in Galatians and 2 Corinthians) and Heb. choose to define the *new* covenant initiated by Christ (hence Heb. never calls the Abrahamic covenant a διαθήκη. Grässer recognizes the irony of this in relation to Paul, when he says 'Strenggenommen ist der *Neue* Bund der "ältere", der mit der Abrahamdiatheke gesetzt und in Christus erfüllt ist. Ihr gegenüber ist die Sinaidiatheke "jünger" und sachlich schon immer durch die ἐπαγγελία als die παλαιά διαθήκη qualifiziert, die zur Verheissungsdiatheke in einem diametralen Gegensatz steht'.[77] For Heb. this could not be said to the same extent, since ἐπαγγελία retains some of its traditional meaning and is not as central to the author's theological scheme as διαθήκη is (the reverse is of course true for Paul).

But the writers concur in their negative evaluation of the Sinai event. When the Law is delivered by angels, and through the mediatorship of Moses (Gal. 3.19; Heb. 2.2; 12.18-21) God seems left out of the picture.[78] Neither author dwells on the period of the old/ first covenant and the Law in its own right. Instead they are interested only in contrasting the Law with what they have come to recognize as the sole way of salvation in Christ. For Paul this means displaying the inherent impossibility of salvation by works of the Law and showing its limited, temporal function as a guardian until the coming of Christ (Gal. 3) and as a pointer to and ally of sin (Rom. 7) and ultimately of death (1 Cor. 15.56).

Similarly, Heb. speaks of the weak, useless commandment (Heb. 7.18), of the Law's fleshly, shadowy (10.1) character, its inability to perfect (7.19) and be anything but a perpetual reminder of sin (10.3), by virtue of its imperfect means of cleansing (9.13; 10.4, 11). Yet, despite these negative qualifications, the Law retains a severely limited positive function in Heb., which we find also in Romans, but not in Galatians. The Law, conceived of as the old Levitical order recorded by Moses, supplies the cultic language-framework by means of which the author of Heb. chooses to describe the NC.[79] 'High priest, tent, blood, sacrifice, covenant: every term here is old, yet each is transmuted. Each has become a way of asserting what happened in Christ.'[80]

Interpreters struggle hard in an attempt to reach a final verdict about the role of salvation history both in Paul and in Heb. While it is easy to agree about the great distance of both thinkers from someone like the author of Luke/Acts, it is much harder to decide where the ultimate differences between them lie. Some find more discontinuity in Paul than in Heb.,[81] some find the reverse.[82] In our opinion the author of Heb. goes further than Paul in his conscious articulation of the break which occurred with the *institutions* of Israel through the Christ event. But he imputes some limited value and function to this old cultic order because it is at once a reflection of eternal, heavenly realities and an adumbration of 'the good things to come'.

Both authors struggle with the problem of continuity and discontinuity, and this is reflected in their use of covenant language. Against Grässer[83] and Luz[84] we must assert that both Paul[85] and Heb.[86] can use διαθήκη as a label for the old *and* the new orders, even though they then proceed to describe them in antithetical fashion.

Despite their conviction that Christ's death initiated a new age and fulfilled the eschatological promises of old, neither writer dissolves the tension between what was already accomplished in Christ and what is yet to come, being enjoyed by his followers only in an incipient fashion. In 1 Thess. 4.14-17 and 1 Cor. 15.51-54 Paul depicts a sequence of events yet to come. Likewise the author of Heb. incorporates the *parousia* tradition (9.28) and envisages a final conflagration (12.26-27), while underlining throughout his work that the addressees—even though possessing access to the heavenly Tent—are still on a pilgrimage toward the heavenly city.[87]

(d) *Function of the NC in the Theological Framework*. In dealing with Paul and Heb. jointly we do not wish to brush aside the differences between their respective treatments of the NC concept. In Paul's letters covenant language occurs infrequently. While the midrashim in Galatians 4 and 2 Corinthians 3 play a pivotal role in the argument of those letters, Paul probably chooses covenantal terminology there in order to meet his opponents on their own ground. In Romans 9-11 the need to come to terms with the fate of Israel once again prompts Paul to use διαθήκη along with other traditional categories expressing Israel's elect status before God. In the Pauline corpus as a whole διαθήκη does not play a significant role.[88]

To Heb. on the other hand one can attribute a 'Bundes-Theologie' and an *original* rethinking and presentation of the Christ event as high priesthood of a new covenantal order.[89] Over and above the apocalyptic framework, which Heb. shares with Paul and which may be the traditional perception of the recipients of Heb.,[90] the author stresses abiding realities, probably under the influence of Greek metaphysics.[91] His covenantal theology functions in the interplay between these temporal and spatial dualisms.[92]

Given his readers' nostalgia for a cultic expression of their new faith and their familiarity with the Levitical order,[93] the writer of Heb. depicts Jesus as the new high priest, ministering in the heavenly Tent on their behalf. In a fusion of Jer. 31.31-34 and Exod. 24.8, Christ's death is portrayed as the initiation of the NC by superior blood and this covenant blood becomes the red thread, linking the ideas of heavenly priesthood, sacrifice and Tent.[94]

We may sum up our comparison between the use of the NC idea in Paul and in Heb. by employing the hermeneutical scheme of 'correspondence, contrast and superiority'.[95] In Paul the element of *correspondence* receives more weight in Romans than in Galatians where *contrast* is dominant. In Gal. 3.15-17 and 4.21-31 two *covenants* are being compared, but they are characterized antithetically by Law and promise and end up as two mutually exclusive realms, locked in combat. In 2 Cor. 3.7-11 different kinds of *doxa* are being compared in such a way that the old glory is very soon devalued and eclipsed by the infinitely *superior* new glory. Each is associated with a particular covenant mediator in the context of the whole chapter and once again the final verdict is incompatibility.

Whereas *contrast* is highlighted in the Pauline passges dealing with the *new* covenant, the same concept in Heb. encompasses all three elements of *correspondence, contrast and superiority* in a more balanced fashion. Having chosen to redefine 'covenant' as 'cultic order', the author of Heb. is able to retain the *form* and the linguistic categories that described the old covenantal relationship in his depiction of the NC. While Paul of course takes the continuity of God's word and promise for granted, Heb. spells it out more clearly.

But the balanced, majestic language of the proem of Heb., and the carefully structured comparisons between the old and the new, should not blind us to the huge difference in the *content* with which the author invests the ancient, familiar categories. If he sounds less combative than Paul does in Galatians and 2 Corinthians, the writer of Heb. nonetheless shows his polemical intent by his insistence on the recurring theme of κρείττων. His ultimate end is to demonstrate the definitive *superiority* of the NC, founded on Christ's death and exaltation. Paradoxically enough, Heb. manages to put new wine into old wineskins!

B. (1) *The NC in the Last Supper Accounts*

We will now discuss the concept of the NC in the Last Supper accounts and then attempt a brief comparison between the role of that concept there and in Heb. This will complete our survey of NC texts in the NT and will contribute to the matrix of possible backgrounds for the use of the NC idea by the author of Heb. The literature on the variety of textcritical, historical, *religionsgeschichtlich* and other problems surrounding the four parallel accounts of Jesus' Last Supper is abundant. For this brief survey the author has consulted mostly recent works.[96] Our discussion will focus mainly on the cup-word, to which the covenant (NC) motif is attached. The following schematic presentation[97] will serve as our point of departure:

MARK/MATTHEW	LUKE/PAUL

Context for BREAD-WORD

(1) εὐλογήσας	εὐχαριστήσας

Bread-word

(2)—	Expiation motif
(3)—	Repetition command

Context for CUP-WORD

(4) λάβων	ὡσαύτως
(5)—	μετὰ τὸ δειπνῆσαι
(6) εὐχαριστήσας	—
(7) ἔδωκεν αὐτοῖς	—
(8) Mk 14.23b	—
(in Matthew part of cup-word)	

Cup-word

(9) τοῦτο	τοῦτο τὸ ποτήριον
(10) τὸ αἷμά μου	ἡ καινὴ διαθήκη
τῆς διαθήκης	ἐν τῷ αἵματί (μου)

(11) Mark/Matthew: *parallel* structure of bread and cup words.
(12) Expiation: in Mark/Matthew: ὑπὲρ (περὶ)   πολλῶν
in Luke/Paul: ὑπὲρ ὑμῶν

Assumptions: Matthew is dependent upon Mark. Luke/Paul are from the same strand of tradition, but not dependent upon each other. Luke is closer to this strand than Paul, but shows traits explicable as secondary adaptations based on Mark.

In view of the complexity of the issues involved and the variety of solutions which have been proposed, we will content ourselves with stating those positions that seem most probable and coherent to us and will usually simply refer to the literature for the underlying reasons.

The table on the previous page has been put together in such a way as to highlight the shared elements in each of the two strands of the Last Supper tradition. The numerous attempts to reconstruct an *Urform*[98] or an *Ursprungsform*[99] from which these two strands could have developed need not detain us here. Likewise the complicated arguments in favor of the priority of either the Mark/Matthew or the Luke/Paul strand will be bypassed.[100] We will follow Grässer's opinion, that 'Mk und Paulus... bieten das Kelchwort jeweils in einer Form, die nicht voneinander ableitbar ist'.[101]

Scholars have isolated a variety of motifs within the forms of the Last Supper tradition that have been preserved for us, and have argued extensively about their respective origins (Palestinian or Hellenistic), age (from Jesus or later traditions) and original locus in the text (as interpretation of the bread-word or the cup-word). To cite three examples: Kuhn believes that (a) the motif of *vicarious, expiatory suffering* could be from Jesus himself; (b) the *eschatological expectation of the parousia* could also have come from a Palestinian context; whereas (c) the *covenantal interpretation* (impossible in Aramaic, following Jeremias) and (d) the *sacramental interpretation* (from the mystery cults) have to be located in a Hellenistic environment.[102]

Hahn detects five motif-complexes: (a) the βασιλεία imagery, (b) the *manna* and (c) the *passover* typologies all apply to the overall celebration of the meal, whereas the concepts of (d) *expiation* and (e) *covenant* are individual motifs, pertaining only to the words of institution.[103]

Lang emphasizes that all forms of the Last Supper accounts have three temporal dimensions: (1) they are grounded in the *past* event of Jesus' expiatory death and in his initiation of a new order of salvation in the resurrection (Christology); (b) they testify to the *present* celebration of κοινωνία with the risen Lord (see esp. Paul's phrase κυριακὸν δεῖπνον 1 Cor. 11.20, and 1 Cor. 10.14—22—ecclesiology); (c) they celebrate in incipient fashion the *future* banquet of the kingdom (see Mk 14.25 par.; 1 Cor. 11.26—eschatology).[104]

All of these conceptual schemes reveal important aspects of the Last Supper accounts. We will focus on the motifs of expiation and covenant, both of which occur in both branches of the tradition.[105] The majority of scholars regard the *expiation motif* as (one of) the oldest, since it seems most plausible as a possible interpretation of Jesus' death by Jesus himself or by his earliest followers. Its occurrence within the *bread*-word of the Luke/Paul strand (2) and within the *cup*-word of the Mark/Matthew strand (immediately attached to (10); but see (12) of the chart above p. 81), is viewed as a sign of its tenacity and indispensability.[106] For conceptual purposes we should note that expiation can occur without the elements of vicariousness and sacrifice, one or both of which are often thought to be secondary additions.[107]

The *covenant motif*—our central concern—is usually regarded as later than the expiation motif within the Last Supper tradition, but interpretations are by no means uniform. The spectrum of opinions ranges from the position that Jesus himself could have used ברית חדשה in a non-cultic sense of a qualitatively new order *à la* Jer. 31.31-34,[108] to the other extreme of the *Bundesschweigen Jesu*.[109] According to this latter view the NC ideas was not perceived as a suitable means of articulating the eschatological self-understanding in the oldest Christian community, because it had strong connotations of restitution/renewal of the *old* order both in Jeremiah's prophecy and at Qumran.[110]

Both these extreme positions can be criticized on the same grounds. They seem to assume that to have established what Jeremiah said and meant about the NC is to know what that concept means to future communities who employ it.[111] Thus interpretations that do not fit Wagner's understanding of the prophet's original intention are by that very fact judged to be secondary additions to the earliest version of the cup-word. Similarly, given Grässer's views of Jesus' and of Jeremiah's messages, Jesus (and the earliest Christians) are in some sense denied the freedom to use an ancient religious concept and to invest it with new meaning.[112]

For our purposes, we are not concerned with ascertaining which elements in the Last Supper tradition could derive from Jesus himself. We hold that Mk 14.24 makes it plausible that Jesus did in fact give an interpretation to his impending death at the last meal with his disciples.[113] The tradition about the meaning of that meal and of Christ's death—and the connection of both of these events to the Christian Last Supper praxis—could then develop from this nucleus.[114]

To return to the *covenant motif*, there are a number of interpreters whose views about the origins of this motif lie somewhere in between the two extremes which we just discussed. Merklein describes how, once Jesus' death had occurred and interpretations of it as an eschatological event were emerging under the impact of resurrection appearances, the NC motif could plausibly have arisen as the *first* post-Easter interpretation of the Last Supper.[115] The reserve expressed in Mark 14.25, where Jesus refrains from drinking until the coming of the βασιλεία, no longer applies once his death is thought of as ushering in the kingdom and hence the *present* drinking of the cup can be qualified as καινὴ διαθήκη.[116]

Hahn, admitting that all we can rely upon is guesswork, surmises: 'der Bundesgedanke... (hat) im Umkreis der Herrenmahlstradition *frühzeitig* seinen Platz gefunden'.[117] For Lang the very sparseness of occurrences of the *new* covenant motif in the remains of Hellenistic Christianity constitutes an argument for its *early Palestinian* origin. He postulates that this motif would have to have left more traces and been developed more extensively than is the case in Paul and Heb., had it only arisen on Hellenistic soil.[118] In Schweizer's view the covenant motif, while clearly secondary, represents a logical outgrowth of Jesus' radical call to repentance and new communion with the Father, and expresses well the eschatological fulfilment of that mission in death.[119]

Our own interest lies in the *association of motifs* exhibited by our present Last Supper texts:

a.　　death
b.　　blood
c.　　expiation/forgiveness
d.　　covenant

In keeping with their presuppositions illustrated in the theories above, scholars tend to *separate* these motifs from each other by their putative age and origin. If we examine the cup-word, it is clear that the Mark/Matthew strand emphasizes the *blood* and the Luke/Paul strand the *newness* of the covenant (see (10) on the chart, p. 81). The former is usually said to derive from Exod. 24.8[120] and the latter from Jer. 31.31-34.[121]

Even though the manuscript evidence clearly attests the presence of καινή in the Luke/Paul branch and only gives καινή weak, late attestation, favouring secondary harmonization, in the Mark/Matthew branch of the tradition,[122] we do not think too much ought to be made of this difference. While it is likely that the Luke/Paul version alludes to Jeremiah's prophecy and that the Mark/Matthew version refers back to the typology of the Sinai covenant and its initiation by a blood-ceremony (Exod. 24.3-8), in their final form *both* versions wish to present Jesus' death as an unprecedented eschatological event.

Lang reminds us of the second ceremony associated with the Sinai covenant (Exod. 24.1-2, 9-11). That somewhat mysterious covenant meal finds its counterpart in the tradition about the eschatological meal on Mount Zion which was to be a feast for all peoples (Isa. 25.6-8).[123] In the context of the Last Supper and given the close association of the cup-word and the so-called eschatological outlook (in Mk 14.24-25/Mt. 26.28-29) such an echo may not be as far-fetched as it first sounds.

In the final analysis even Grässer who, following Hahn,[124] stresses the *difference* between the two covenantal conceptions employed by the two versions—Luke/Paul claiming the realization of the *new* and Mark/Matthew pointing back to *old* covenant—ends up admitting the *closeness in their present meaning*.[125]

We conclude that despite numerous differences in detail, the two strands of the Last Supper tradition concur in associating the motifs of death, blood, expiation and covenant. These links can plausibly be assumed to have happened rather early in Christian thinking and *praxis* and hence it is artificial and purely conjectural to posit two originally separate Last Supper types in the manner of Lietzmann and Lohmeyer,[126] or to speculate endlessly about the respective origins of individual motifs.

Each of the four accounts has its *Sitz im Leben* in the cult[127] and each is thus influenced by the ongoing practice of communities celebrating their participation in the NC, initiated by the expiatory death of Christ. From their experience of communion with the risen Lord in the sharing of the bread and the cup[128]—understood as his σῶμα and αἷμα—they formulated their conviction that the promised eschatological covenant had begun and from this vantage point the Sinai covenant was implicitly judged to be old and outmoded. But an explicit verdict about the old covenantal era—such as we find in Heb. and in Paul—is lacking in the Last Supper texts.

The fluidity in early Christian thinking and the terse nature of the Last Supper accounts permits no exact assessment as to how they would have been understood by the different groups employing them at different times and places. We can surmise that the earliest communities probably understood 'new' in the NC formula in terms of a covenant renewal ceremony. Gradually—and by no means uniformly or progressively—a more radical view of newness would have developed and the Christ event would have been interpreted in terms of a break with the past and the inbreaking of a new aeon.

(2) Comparison between the New Covenant in the Last Supper Accounts and in Hebrews

The following remarks will be made in the awareness of the vast difference in genre and scope between the Last Supper accounts—essentially cult-aetiologies—and the λόγος τῆς παρακλήσεως which we call Heb. (13.22). The former cannot be expected to yield theological explanations of their content and are by their very nature compressed and evocative. The latter reveals an author skilled in theological exposition, who—if he chooses to say anything at all about eucharistic practice—is frustratingly vague and suggestive about it,[129] while he is rather explicit about his notions of covenant.

According to Grässer the only places where the NC is a central *theologoumenon* in the NT are the Last Supper tradition and Heb.[130] As in all of the NT texts which we studied, the point of departure is the new reality brought about by Christ and the only reason for discussing the old covenant is to underline the superior quality of the NC.

What is only implicit in the Last Supper accounts is made explicit by the author of Heb., who quotes both Jeremiah's prophecy (8.8-12; 10.16-17) and Exod. 24.8 (9.20). The Sinai typology is elaborated further in the context of the comparison between Moses as lawgiver and Christ as mediator of the NC (9.15-22; 12.18-29). While the exact meaning of the covenant ceremony in Exod. 24.3-8 may be debatable, there can be no question that the writer of Heb. views it as a covenant *sacrifice* and as such is able to fit it into his presentation of Christ's unique sacrifice against the backdrop of the typology of Yom Kippur. Given the author's cultic preoccupation, Heb. is closer to the Mark/Matthew strand of the Last Supper tradition, for in both Jesus' death is presented as 'das *eine* gültige Kultgeschehen. . ., durch das fernerhin jede Opferhandlung grundsätzlich aufgehoben ist. Jesu Tod begründet die Heilsordnung (Bund) der Endzeit'.[131]

The motif of *covenant-blood*, which appears in both of our present versions of the Last Supper accounts, is central to the concerns of the author of Heb. (9.19; 10.29; 13.20). 9.22 reveals that he regards forgiveness by blood as the basic axiom which governs chs. 9–10 of his text.[132] It is by the 'better blood'[133] of Christ that the new and better covenant is initiated, and the greater, more perfect Tent is dedicated as the place of access for all believers. In Heb. we are confronted with an expanded, paraenetically grounded[134] form of the same association of motifs that characterizes the Last Supper: death—blood—expiation/forgiveness—covenant.

It is notable that the absence of cultic motifs in general and of covenant-blood in particular in Jer. 31.31-34 does not keep the author of Heb. from quoting Jeremiah's oracle and from using it to frame his exposition about the *cultic* superiority of the NC. He knows nothing about a supposed incompatibility between notions of blood sacrifice and the NC.[135] Quite the reverse: he insists on the need for blood to effect purgation and demonstrates the infinite superiority of Christ's blood over animal blood, by its ability to effect lasting purification of the conscience (See 9.6-14 where blood is the very basis for the *qal-waḥomer!*).

From the believers' point of view, we implicitly assume as background for the Synoptic Last Supper accounts and explicitly read in Paul's exposition of κοινωνία that *participation in the NC* is celebrated at eucharistic meals in remembrance of Christ's death and in the knowledge of the presence of the risen κύριος.

In Heb. the concept of προσέρχεσθαι[136] provides the link between the theological exposition of Christ's high priesthood and the NC and the paraenetic appeal to his followers who are summoned to seize with boldness the hope lying before them (6.18) and to enter the heavenly Tent via the new and living way, opened for them by their forerunner, by means of his ἐφάπαξ bloody sacrifice (6.20; 10.19-20). The entire treatise is aimed at strengthening the readers' faith in their existence as people living in a new aeon, belonging to a new, infinitely superior cultic order. To this end they are being called to a pilgrimage toward unseen, heavenly realities which Christ secured for them by his death and exaltation to the right hand of the Father.

Thus both the Last Supper *paradosis* and Heb., while focusing on the expiatory death of Jesus as decisive event that initiated the NC, presuppose the experience of participation in that NC by his followers. Yet neither gives us a clear articulation of that eschatological self-understanding, such as we find at Qumran.[137] The NC motif is employed to explain the theological significance of Christ's death, but it does not function as a title for the community in a manner that would designate those characteristics that set it apart from other Jewish groups. If we knew more about contacts between Qumran and early Christianity, we might speculate that Christians wanted to avoid the sectarian connotations which were clearly attached to the NC idea in the DSS. In our present state of knowledge, however, this is mere guess-work.

We may conclude by stating that the element of *newness* in the NC idea is not elucidated in the Last Supper accounts and its meaning has to be derived there from the portrayal of Jesus and his work in the respective Gospel. In Heb. on the other hand, we are confronted with an explicit, highly developed articulation of the significance and quality of the NC which is at each step compared to and contrasted with the old covenant and its institutions.

C. Early Patristic Uses of the New Covenant Idea

The traditional use of διαθήκη in the sense of the OT ברית continues in the Apostolic Fathers and in the Apologists. Of the former only Barnabas shows a fondness for the term, but nowhere uses the phrase 'NC', even though it would have suited his enterprise very well.[138] The two uses in 1 Clement occur in OT quotations.[139] Among the Apologists only Justin's Dialogue with Trypho employs διαθήκη, apart from the one occurrence in Melito of Sardis which has been preserved for us by Eusebius in his *Historia Ecclesiastica* IV. 26, 14 and will be discussed below.[140]

In connection with the Montanist crisis in the last quarter of the second century CE, a new development seems to have occurred in which διαθήκη started being used as a designation for collections of books, first in relation to the Hebrew Scriptures as παλαιά διαθήκη and then in relation to the Christian ones as καινή διαθήκη.[141] In trying to trace the steps in this process, we are left with three rather obscure texts whose exact meaning has been debated.

The first is the above-mentioned passage from the proemium of Meilto's book of *Eklogai*. Around the year 170 CE this bishop from Asia Minor bothers to travel to Palestine to ascertain the exact list of the 'books of the old covenant'.[142] In his controversy with the Montanists it is evidently important to Melito to obtain the *Jewish* list of the Hebrew Scriptures, since certain differences of opinion exist among Christians and Jews with regard to what we would call the OT canon, and the polemical argument has to be fought out in terms of mutually agreed upon testimonies. Along with this rather unusual way of referring to the OT, Melito employs the traditional phrase 'the Law and the prophets', and also 'the old books'. Hence the references are still fluid and we have no evidence that Melito is thinking of the Christian Scriptures in analogous terms as a 'NC'.[143]

The other two texts that illustrate the process of formation of the 'NT' title, come from an anonymous Antimontanist quoted in Eusebius. He may have been another bishop who belonged to the same geographic area as Melito and wrote during the last decade of the second century CE.[144] In H.E. 5.16.3 this man speaks about his having hesitated about replying to his correspondent's request for a refutation of a certain sect lest someone might think that he was adding something to the 'wording (λόγος) of the NC of the gospel'.[145] He insists that nothing can be added to or taken away from this 'NC', yet in another passage in H.E. 5.17.3 the same author names a list of prophets κατὰ τὴν παλιάν and κατὰ τὴν καινήν that extends beyond the confines of our NT to include people of the author's recent past.[146] Thus the concept of a fixed list of books is beginning to emerge, yet this Anti-montanist still retains a much larger sense for διαθήκη in terms of an era and a reality of salvation.

'Though Irenaeus uses the word διαθήκη and the combination καινὴ διαθήκη and παλαιὰ διαθήκη many times, it is highly uncertain whether he had a book in mind'.[147] He retains the more inclusive idea of a salvation-historical, covenantal theology that he inherits from his predecessors in Asia Minor.[148] Irenaeus continues the use of 'NC' as a tool in polemics when he seeks to show the Gnostics that the same God is instrumental in both covenants and that his Spirit is still operative in the bishop's own time.[149]

From the time of the Alexandrians Clement and Origen, the 'book-sense' of old and new covenant is used extensively. Clement retains the meaning of two orders of salvation, along with the new meaning, while Origen takes the latter for granted, but is still somewhat surprised by its strangeness as a title, when he refers to the 'so-called' old and new covenants.[150]

From the beginning of the third century CE onward, while other traditional ways of referring to the Scriptures continue, there is a quick acceptance of the titles 'old and new covenant' in Christian usage. Soon the OT sense of 'covenant' is forgotten in both the East (where διαθήκη is understood in its profane sense of 'will') and in the West (where *testamentum* is employed to render διαθήκη). As Campenhausen points out, however, even in this much reduced sense, the new terminology for the Scriptures has the advantage of safeguarding both the unity of the 'testaments' (precluding a Marcionite solution), and their diversity as 'old' and 'new' (from a Christian viewpoint).[151]

Summary

In this chapter we examined the uses of the NC motif in the NT apart from Heb. Most attention was devoted to Paul's employment of the idea in Galatians and in 2 Corinthians. In Galatians 3 the covenant motif seems freely to have occurred to Paul in the context of his discussion of the Law and the promise. But in both Galatians 4 and 2 Corinthians 3 it appears likely that Paul's opponents are forcing him to deal with the Christ event in covenantal terms. Here the *new* covenant concept is employed in polemical manner to highlight the contrast with the old covenant of Sinai. In Romans 9–11 the covenants are listed among Israel's special privileges, but as the discussion unfolds only the Abrahamic promises retain significance for Paul. Thus the NC idea is not a central one in Paul, and where it occurs it is made to express Paul's primary concern of justification of the ungodly by faith.

Our comparison between the use of NC concept in Paul and in Heb. yielded a number of similarities. But in Heb. the concept occupies center stage and is used much more extensively and systematically in the author's theological framework. (Detailed discussion of Heb. will be given in Chapter 5.)

The Last Supper accounts are the other important place where the NC idea is found in the NT. We surveyed various scholars' opinions about the age and origin of this motif in this particular context. Given the close association of the motifs of death—blood—(vicarious) expiation/forgiveness and covenant in both strands of the Last Supper tradition, as it has been preserved for us, we found the similarities between these strands to be more significant than their differences. In comparing them to Heb., however, we detected a greater kinship to the Mark/Matthew strand with its emphasis on the blood of the covenant and expiation.

The comparison between the function of the NC motif in Heb. and in the rest of the NT prepared the way for our next chapter. Our principal observation, which we hope to substantiate further in Chapter 5, is that the element of newness in the NC is nowhere in the NT as explicit and systematically articulated as it is in Heb.

Finally we undertook a very brief survey of the NC idea in the early Fathers. The most important and noteworthy development is the gradual emergence of the notion of 'old and new covenant' as titles for collections of books. This process takes place in the latter part of the second century CE in Asia Minor during the Montanist crisis and gains surprisingly rapid acceptance from the early third century CE onward. Concomitantly the larger sense of 'covenant' as salvific order is lost in favour of the reduced notion of 'testament'.

Chapter 5

THE FUNCTION OF THE NEW COVENANT CONCEPT IN HEBREWS

We have now reached the point in our study where we can focus exclusively on the NC idea in Heb. In the first chapter we posited that the NC concept plays a prominent role in the structure of Heb. We argued that, given his comparative form of argumentation,[1] the author chooses the διαθήκη motif in order to express both the elements of continuity and discontinuity in the Christian story (vis-à-vis its Israelite precursor). In this presentation the Christ event, characterized by Christ's death and exaltation, entails a break in salvation history by initiating a NC.

In the second chapter we traced the major lines of OT covenantal traditions employed by Heb. Chapters 3 and 4 described the use of the NC concept by various Jewish and Christian predecessors and near contemporaries of our author in order to provide a background for the development of the NC concept in Heb. Specific comparisons between the way in which the NC functions in Heb. on the one hand, and in the DSS, in Paul and in the Last Supper accounts on the other hand, were designed to highlight the unique features of Heb.

In this chapter the various elements in the author's employment of the NC idea that we discovered earlier will be drawn together in a more systematic fashion. It appears that what is most distinctive and original about the writer's reworking of the covenant motif is his *cultic perspective*. We will see that the NC motif is implicitly linked to the author's treatment of revelation (section A) and explicitly shapes his exposition of priesthood (section B).

Then we will trace the influence of the NC idea in the paraenetic sections and analyze what consequences the author envisages for those belonging to the cultic community of the NC (section C). In trying to come to terms with the nature of NC cultus envisaged by the author (section D), we will touch upon the long disputed questions concerning the lack of clear references to baptism and to the Eucharist in Heb., for those rites were elsewhere becoming central in Christian cultic practice and were closely tied to covenantal theology.

Most interpreters of Heb. recognize the centrality of the idea of Christ's high priesthood in the epistle and many have stressed that it is connected to the notion of covenant, but usually the latter category is subsumed under the former.[3]

On the one hand, it is commonly recognized that the author's deliberate and fully developed portrayal of Jesus in priestly terms is unique in the NT, even though traces of such a conception are present in other NT works. On the other hand, few scholars note that the highly elaborate covenantal theology of Heb. and its pivotal role in the text are equally unique in the NT.[4]

It seems plausible that the author had a preference for cultic metaphors and believed that they would best meet the needs of his addressees.[5] Hence, in formulating his convictions about the Christ event, he seems to have developed his covenant conception largely from the so-called 'P' strand of the OT. In the final analysis Christ's sacrifice and the inauguration of the NC are coterminous events for him.[6] If it is understood that διαθήκη is reduced to its cultic dimensions in Heb., then one is justified in making 'covenant' the overarching category for conceptual purposes and in treating priesthood and sacrifice from a covenantal angle.[7]

Of the various explanatory schemes that we encountered, the one proposed by G. Vos[8] seems most faithful to the author's intent and best able to incorporate the major ideas of Heb. Vos recognizes the centrality of the covenant concept in Heb. and asserts that 'through its removal the inner organism of the Epistle's teaching would be injured and significant lines and shades of its doctrinal complexion obliterated from our view'.[9]

Hence he makes the *covenant idea* the linchpin in the work's structure and proceeds to trace its influence along the two lines of *revelation* (A) and *priesthood* (B). These lines are shown to represent two complementary movements, the former from God to human beings, the latter from human beings to God. 'Where both reach their perfection, there the ideal covenant is given.'[10] Vos correctly notes that a third element, namely the *conception of faith*, as it emerges particularly in ch. 11, but also in the paraenetic sections interspersed throughout Heb., is implicitly tied to the work's covenantal outlook, because the ancestors are portrayed as exemplars of the same traits that the NC community is supposed to bear.[11] In our own treatment below we will broaden the third element of Vos's scheme to include various *consequences of belonging to the NC community* (C).

Even though of unequal weight in the text, these three elements are interrelated and the strength of the covenantal theology of Heb. consists precisely in their interpenetration and in the author's ability to ground his expositions in paraenetic exhortations at each step of the argument. We have already encountered each of the three elements at various points in our study and will now deal with each in turn.

A. *Revelation*

In Chapter 1 we briefly discussed the centrality of the concepts of the Word and of revelation,[12] found especially in Heb. 1–4 and 12.18-29, but also in the multitude of scriptural quotations that are introduced as Word of God, Jesus or the Holy Spirit. G. Hughes suggests that starting from reflection on the question: 'how does God's Word have earlier and later forms?... (the author's) theology of the two covenants was created with their dialectical pattern of historical continuity and discontinuity, in which the forms of priesthood, sacrifice and cultic approach have been preserved...'[13] Hughes's exegesis of key passages from Heb. 1–7[14] confirms the intimate link between the ideas of revelation and covenant in Heb., a link that only becomes explicit once the author introduces covenantal terminology in 7.22.

The function of the series of comparisons between Jesus and other agents of revelation/redemption from the old dispensation in these opening chapters of Heb., and their interrelationship, has been hotly debated. We agree with Hughes that 'Jesus is consistently portrayed as a new form, and an eschatologically superior form, of God's 'Word'.[15] Thus the focus on Jesus' person in chs. 1–7 parallels the focus on Jesus' work in chs. 8–10, and all of Heb. can be described as an extended examination of the *relationship* between the old and the new covenantal orders and their representatives. The analysis of Hughes is inadequate, however, in its insistence on the predominance of the *historical*, horizontal relationship between the covenants. Hughes does not deny the presence of spatial/vertical thought patterns in Heb., but makes them ultimately subservient to the temporal/eschatological mode of comparison.[16]

The works by Dey, Thompson, Nomoto and Luck, among many others,[17] show clearly that the so-called Alexandrian vein of Heb. must be taken seriously and that the author works with a consistent metaphysic of abiding, heavenly, perfect realities, which is blended in a creative way with traditional eschatology.[18]

Dey's theory about the function of the series of comparisons between Jesus and angels, Moses, Levi/Aaron and Melchizedek in the overall scheme of Heb.[19] has the merit of showing that this sequence operates within a coherent pattern of thought. In this scheme there are two corresponding levels of existence and agents mediating between them which help people in their progression towards perfection.

Peterson may be right in saying that 'we have no real evidence that the writer's use of the terminology of perfection was part of a special polemic against a form of perfectionism being expounded to or by the readers'.[20] Dey's contribution, however, lies not so much in his discovery of a particular 'heresy' being combated in Heb., but rather in his description of a plausible *background* for the metaphysical assumptions of the author and his readers, and in his ability to explain the function of the paraeneses. Thus according to Dey the high-priestly ministry of Jesus is presented by the author as the only means of procuring perfection within the realm of the flesh. By his suffering and death Jesus won unmediated access to the heavens for himself. Thereby he became the supreme exemplar of perfection and enabled his followers to enjoy that same perfection in their present earthly existence, provided they have faith and hope and share in his trials.[21]

The theme of perfection, a major one in Heb.,[22] provides the link between the comparative scheme of revelatory agents and the NC idea. Perfection language[23] is another metaphor employed by the author to describe the blessings of the NC, since immediacy of access to God is the goal in both cases.[24]

While the cultic connotation of the idea of perfection may not be uppermost on the author's mind when he first employs it (2.10), the link to Christ's suffering and death is already established there. As the work progresses the concept of perfection acquires a deeper cultic significance. The author explicitly connects perfection to the salvific import of Christ's priesthood (5.9; 7.28) and to the sanctifying effect of the blood of his NC sacrifice upon his followers (chs. 9-10; 12.23-24; see 13.12).[25]

From these reflections it has become obvious that the oncept of revelation in Heb. can hardly be treated in isolation. If the Son is the new definitive form of God's 'Address',[26] he is likewise the unique and blameless high priest, and in both capacities he is perfected and becomes the source of eternal salvation/perfection.[27] These functions of Christ are both subsumed under the covenant motif. Starting from the principle of *Vielfalt gegen Einmaligkeit*[28] to distinguish the old covenant from the NC, the author parallels the uniform and undivided revelation in the Son[29] with the one, ἐφάπαξ, ever efficacious sacrifice by the single, eternal high priest. It is to this NC priesthood that we now turn.

B. *Priesthood*

Let us consider the central section, Heb. 4.14–10.18, which contains the core of the author's cultic argumentation,[30] from the standpoint of the hermeneutical scheme of 'correspondence, contrast, superiority'.[31] Against the backdrop of several interwoven OT scenarios, mainly the high priest's activities on Yom Kippur, but also Moses' actions at the inauguration of the covenant/Tabernacle,[32] the author depicts the NC cult analogously to the old covenant cult. In so doing he is able to highlight both the shared and the contrasting features and ultimately wants to persuade his readers of the infinitely superior worth of the NC.

What is at stake, however, is not simply historical typology, as we have seen above.[33] The author employs both a vertical, platonizing scheme and a horizontal temporal scheme. His very genius lies in the way in which these two ways of thinking intersect in his comparative framework. 'The writer of Heb. . . specifically (equates) the world to come with the new covenant, (and) is led to identify the first age with the first covenant'.[34] But while traditional eschatology presents the two ages as two chronologically successive stages with no overlap between them, in Heb. this view is merged with a 'distinction between two contemporaneous states or worlds'.[35] The author is probably no philosopher, but he deliberately employs Middle-Platonic categories[36] and places positive emphasis upon the 'primordial, constant, stable existence of the higher world, antedating and overarching and outlasting all temporal developments. . . '[37] By means of this scheme he can attribute some limited *positive* value to the old covenant,[38] because he views it as a God-given reflection in sketchy, 'embryonic form', of the 'celestial prototype'[39] of the NC. In this sense the latter existed from all eternity, but was fully revealed and realized only in Christ.

It is possible to structure the material according to the categories that seem to dominate in certain chapters. Both cultic orders are depicted in terms of the *shared* rubrics of *priesthood* (ch. 7), *covenant*[40] (ch. 8) and *bloody sacrifice offered in the Tabernacle* (chs. 9-10). But such a division is clearly superficial and imprecise, since there is considerable overlap and these categories are interwoven in the author's description.

The *corresponding features* of the author's description of priesthood and covenant are readily discernible. Christ's high *priesthood* resembles the Levitical priesthood in the following ways: he is compassionate, and able to sympathize with human weakness, since he—though sinless—is likewise tempted and suffers (2.17-18; 4.15; 5.7-8; 13.12). He is appointed by God (5.1, 4-6; 7.28), and intercedes for human beings before God (7.25; 9.24).[41] Like the priests of old, Christ must have something to offer (5.1; 8.3), and he enters the *Tent*[42] with a *bloody*[43] sacrifice that cleanses the worshippers (9.11-14, 24-26).[44] In both covenantal orders blood provides some access to God (9.7, 12, 25; 10.19), it sanctifies/consecrates and imparts some degree of perfection (9.9, 14; 10.14) and forgiveness (9.22).

In like manner, both the old *covenant* and Christ's NC are based on a sovereign act of God on behalf of his people (8.8-13) who are thereby summoned to become a cultic assembly bound by God's Word (12.18-24). Both are initiated/sealed by a bloody ceremony[45] involving the death of the victim (9.15-22). Both covenantal orders require allegiance and obedience to God on the part of their members who are otherwise punished,[46] and both are grounded in the promise of an inheritance (9.15).

The *contrasting features* can be represented schematically:

Cult under Old Covenant	Cult under NC
Many mortal priests with genealogy	One high priest lives forever
Appointment by fleshly commandment/Law, in weakness	By word of oath perfected forever
Offer for their own sins	Sinless, blameless
Daily earthly ministry	Superior heavenly ministry
Patterns of the heavenly things	The very heavenly things
Holy places made with hands	Heaven itself
Figures of the 'real'	God's presence
Many offerings	One ἐφάπαξ offering

Many (annual) entries	One entry
Continual services	Climax of ages
Limited access; barriers	Access to the 'real'
No final purgation	Sins definitively removed
Sacrifice of animals	Sacrifice of himself
Animal blood	Christ's own blood[47]

This table reveals how the author uses the corresponding features of both cults to draw out the contrasts between them and to highlight the infinite superiority of the new cult.

In sum, the following factors contribute to the superiority of Christ's high priesthood (and of the NC which it initiates/mediates) over the Levitical one: (1) *appointment* by oath, (2) *rule* by power of an indissoluble life, (3) infinite *duration*/no succession, (4) *nature* of the Son, made perfect forever, (5) *scene* in heaven, (6) *offering* of his *own* blood, (7) *completeness* of one offering, consummated in life and death, in submission to God's will.[48]

We will now deal separately with the Law and the Tabernacle, since these categories are rather complex. In the process, some additional *superior features* of the new order will emerge. Thereafter, we will analyze some of the concepts and argumentative techniques used by the author to cement his case for the infinite superiority of the NC.[49]

The category of *Law* is in many ways the most difficult one to assess. On the one hand, priesthood and Law can function as synonymous terms for the (old) cultic order (7.12) under which the people received the Law (νομοθετέομαι 7.11) and which was instituted at God's command (ἐντέλλομαι)[50] through the blood of the covenant (9.20). Even the NC is enacted/promulgated legally (νομοθετέομαι) on the basis of superior promises (8.6). Therefore one might be tempted to think that the NC 'can be represented as a new species of legislation'.[51]

On the other hand, the most negative remarks that the author makes about the old covenant are all connected to the (cultic) Law, which was fleshly (7.16), had weak and useless commandments (7.18), perfected nothing (7.19), appointed weak men (7.28) and was unable to perfect those drawing near (10.1-4).

In our previous discussions about the Law in Heb.[52] we concluded that despite the writer's use of legal terminology in connection with the new order, the NC is *not* perceived as a new Law and *nomos* ultimately belongs to the old order. When the author means Torah in the inclusive sense, he speaks of the 'Word' that endures as Scripture and reached its pinnacle in the Son. But unlike the rubrics of priesthood, covenant, bloody sacrifice and Tent, which the author borrows from the old legal order, the rubric of Law itself is not transferable from the old covenant to the new one.

The concept of the *Tabernacle* deserves closer examination at this stage. It is a further cultic element that is central to *both* orders and plays a crucial role in the author's comparison between the covenants. D'Angelo shows how the Tabernacle motif becomes a metaphor for the two ages/two covenants in Heb.: by shifting the discussion from the image of one divided Tent to two separate Tents, the writer unfolds his typology in a combination of spatial and temporal metaphors.[53]

The *second* (see 6.19; 9.3, 7, 12, 24)[54] Tent of the *earthly* sanctuary, its holy of holies, is the shadowy, anti-typical representation of the true,[55] heavenly Tent, not made with hands (9.11). Christ's passage through the heavens into the heavenly Tabernacle is the τύπος of which all prior cultic activity in the old order was the fragmentary reflection; the Christ event fills out the sketchy picture with perfection.[56]

But the puzzling thing is the *coexistence* and overlap between the ages which the Tabernacle idea is meant to convey. The first Tent does not simply stand for the *past* old covenant of Judaism,[57] but is called a παραβολή of the *present* age. 'The language of "first tent" has a clear eschatological purpose: it means the old covenant order now in process of dissolution by the καιρὸς διορθώσεως (9.10)'.[58] Through the Christ event the way into the sanctuary has been opened for his followers (10.19-20) and they enjoy proleptic access to the heavenly realities; yet the old age has not completely given way to the new.

It is plausible that in 9.8 the author is referring, not so much to the situation of contemporary Jews,[59] but to the yearnings of *some of* his addressees for a conservative form of *Jewish-Christianity* that included some kind of concrete replacement of Levitical worship.[60] Thus 'the way into the (*heavenly*) sanctuary is not yet open, while the first Tent (i.e. *earthly*/material-sacrificial ritual) is still in existence' (9.8) and while Christians forget that 'here (they) have no lasting city' (13.14). Life at the turning point of the ages entails tension and requires hope and endurance (2.8; 9.29; 10.36-39).

We may conclude that the motif of the two Tents is in many ways the best illustration of the writer's application of the hermeneutical scheme of 'correspondence, contrast and superiority', and of his simultaneous employment of spatial and temporal images. Throughout his presentation of the Tabernacle 'our author has clearly never lost sight of his original discussion of the covenant (8.13–9.1)...'[61] By means of the metaphor of the two Tents the author illustrates the similarities and differences between the first and second covenants, and their respective earthly and heavenly cultic orders.

Above we listed the corresponding, contrasting and superior features of the categories of priesthood and covenant.[62] In addition to the Tabernacle motif, Heb. uses various other concepts to highlight the *superior features* of the NC and its priesthood.

From Middle-Platonic philosophy the author borrows the categories of *stability* and *permanence* to undergird the definitive nature of Christ's high priesthood.[63] He emphasizes the absolute stability and trustworthiness[64] of God's promise realized in Christ. He assures his readers that Christ is forever ὁ αὐτός (1.12; 13.8). By an ingenious twist in typological argumentation, the person and τάξις of Melchizedek are made to function both as a reflection of the (preexistent) Son of God and as a prefiguration of his everlasting indestructible high priesthood (7.3, 8, 16b, 25). Unlike his many mortal predecessors in the old Levitical cult, Christ is unique and remains forever.[65] Hence he imparts those same characteristics to the new order that he initiates.[66]

Already in the ancient covenant ceremonies known to us from the OT and other ancient Near Eastern texts the concept of an *oath* played an important role[67] in confirming the validity of covenants. The author of Heb. resorts to this concept with much greater frequency than the rest of the NT.[68]

As stated above,[69] he has recourse to three Scripture passages mentioning oaths in order to underline the serious negative consequences of falling away (Ps. 95), the absolute trustworthiness of God's promise to Abraham (Gen. 22) and—most importantly—the authenticity and effectiveness of Christ's high priesthood (Ps. 110.4). While the Levitical priesthood is instituted without an oath and its concomitant legal order is unable to impart perfection (7.11, 19-20), the 'word of the oath'/the 'better promise' that initiates Christ's priesthood perfects him forever, and thereby brings a definitive μετάθεσις in the cultic system (7.12) and an ἀθέτησις of the former commandment (7.18) and of sin (9.26).[70]

In a similar vein, the author adopts the title 'guarantor' from the legal sphere as another means of strengthening a community living in the 'interim' between 'gegenwärtiger Erfüllung. . . und zukünftiger Vollendung'.[71] In his sharing of the human condition of suffering and death, and in his exaltation,[72] Jesus[73] becomes the 'ἔγγυος of a better covenant' (7.22) and his τελείωσις is a pledge for his ability to intercede for his 'brethren' and to lead them to their own perfection/salvation (2.10-11; 5.9; 7.25; 9.28).[74]

While ἔγγυος ('guarantor') is not strictly synonymous with μεσίτης ('mediator', see 8.6; 9.15; 12.24) in the secular sphere, in Heb. both titles are connected to the NC[75] and function analogously[76] to assure the addressees that Christ's person and work guarantee the superior effectiveness of the NC and make its blessings available to his followers.

Along with these specific concepts, the author enlists the support of a variety of *rhetorical techniques*[77] to make a convincing case for the superior worth and benefits of the NC.

It is immediately apparent that *terms of comparison* abound in Heb.[78] In addition to the author's frequent chracterization of the realities in the new order as κρείττων,[79] the comparative adjectives διαφορώτερος (1.4; 8.6), πλείων (3.3; see 11.4), μείζων/τελειοτέρος (9.11), περισσότερος (6.17; 7.15; see the adverb in 2.1; 13.19) are employed. *Qal-waḥomer*-argumentation[80] and past unreal conditions[81] are used to the same end.

On closer analysis, one is struck by the emphatic ways in which the author is determined to convince the reader of the *necessity and absoluteness* of his message. There is a stress on the impossibility of certain matters[82] and on the necessity of certain others.[83] It is inherently appropriate (ἔπρεπεν) that Jesus should be perfected through suffering (2.10) and that the recipients should have such a high priest (7.26). Without the slightest hesitation the writer asserts axiomatically that blessings involve a hierarchy (7.7) and that there can be no forgiveness without blood (9.22).

The author frequently uses rhetorical questions requiring a positive answer[84] and appeals to his readers' sense of logic.[85] He is obviously confident that his style of argumentation and manner of reasoning will be readily understood. 'In the majority of cases. . ., (he) uses terms of necessity to express an inner necessity, that is, a necessity of no outward ordinance but based only on the nature and the condition of the matter under discussion. . . In the final analysis

God's will stands behind this necessity, but (the writer) feels that the statements in themselves are convincing to every reader'.[86]

One does not have to be in full argreement with Grässer's diagnosis of the situation of the addressees[87] to concur with his judgment that—far from using a 'Schein-Argumentation'[88]—the author of Heb. is *forced* to be argumentative by the circumstances and has to challenge his readers to think about their relationship to Jesus' person and to his work of initiating a NC. Even if the modern reader has trouble following the logic at times, and does not share the metaphysical presuppositions upon which it is based,[89] the author himself must have believed in the persuasive appeal of his arguments and his style and cannot fairly be accused of circular reasoning.[90]

To sum up, the above-mentioned concepts and techniques are employed by Heb. to support the author's dualistic reading of the Hebrew Scriptures. By an ingenious cultic reinterpretation of διαθήκη the writer makes the covenant motif the organizing principle in the text, and employs the same cultic categories to describe the *contours* of the old and the new orders.[91] Their *content*, however, is depicted in strongly contrasting colors. But the argument moves beyond these contrasts and the main emphasis is placed, not on the shortcomings of the old, but on the superior and definitive nature of the new covenantal order and its priesthood.

While many interpreters would deny the polemical intent of Heb. and think that the OT functions simply as a foil for the writer's theological exposition,[92] we do not find such explanations adequate. It may not be possible to identify a particular group at which the author's treatise is aimed, but the whole tenor and tone of his work can be accounted for much better if one sees polemics at work.

Taken together, the above-mentioned 'weapons' in his crusade for the superiority of Christ and his NC overwhelmingly speak in favour of a dangerous situation among his addressees. They are certainly weary and aimless in their journey, and lacking in hope and παρρησία ('boldness').[93] But in addition to this 'malaise', and perhaps because of it, their faith is being threated by a group (or groups) of conservative Jewish-Christians from within (or from without) their number. It is plausible that these people are busy arguing from the OT that Christianity continues the Levitical heritage, and that they are hoping for (or already practising) a kind of visible replacement of Levitical cult.[94] Hence the author has to meet these opponents on the same ground and presents his own (prior) convictions about the Christ event by appealing to the OT and portraying Jesus as a priestly covenant mediator. Concomitantly, he calls his readers to an alternative form of cultic life in the NC. Let us now examine this alternative.

C. The Consequences of Belonging to the NC Community

Since the paraeneses in Heb. have received so much scholarly attention,[95] we will not discuss their function in detail. We shall begin with a schematic overview in which we have artificially separated negative and positive consequences of NC membership. In what follows we wish to call attention to four key concepts that occur predominantly in the paraeneses to which we shall return after the listing: ὁμολογία (rendered 'confession' below, 3.1; 4.14; 10.23); ἔ ειψχειν to express the privilege of special Christian possessions ('having'... 4.14; 6.9, 18-19; 8.1; 10.19, 34; 12.1, 28; 13.10, 14); προσέρχεσθαι ('draw near' 4.16; 7.25; 10.1, 22; 11.6; 12.18-24); παρρησία ('boldness' 3.6; 4.16; 10.19, 35).

Negative Consequences: Warnings

*2.1-4:	Call not to *drift away/neglect* so great a salvation.
3.12-13:	An evil, unbelieving heart/deceitfulness of sin might lead to a *falling away* from the living God.
4.11:	The desert generation is a ὑπόδειγμα of how one *falls* through disobedience.
6.6:	One who has *fallen away* (by again crucifying the Son of God and holding him up to contempt) cannot be restored to repentance.
5.11/6.12:	'Hebrews' have become hard of hearing/sluggish.
10.25:	Must not *neglect* to meet, as the Day approaches.
*10.28-31:	Greater punishment (than death under the Law) for one who *spurns* the Son of God, *profanes* the blood of the covenant and *outrages* the Spirit; vengeance belongs to the living God.
10.35:	Must not *throw away* confidence.
11.39:	*Shrinking back* leads to destruction.
*12.8-9:	Must be subject to the Father of spirits (as to an earthly father) to be a legitimate child/to live.
12.15-17:	Must not: *fail* to obtain grace/let 'root of bitterness spring up to *defile* many/be immoral like Esau, otherwise there is no repentance/no blessing.

*12.25:   Must not *refuse/reject* the warning Word from heaven—
no escape at Sinai, much less at Zion; God is a consuming
fire.

          (* = *qal-waḥomer*)

Positive Consequences: Exhortations

2.1:   Must *pay closer attention* to (superior) message.

3.1:   Sharers in a heavenly call must *consider* Jesus, the apostle
and high priest of their confession.

3.6:   Must *hold fast* the boldness/pride of hope.

3.14:   Sharers of Christ must firmly *hold on* to their first
conviction until the end.

4.11:   Must *strive* to enter the promised rest.

4.14:   Must *hold fast* to their confession, since they have a great
high priest/Jesus/Son of God.

4.16:   Can/should *draw near* to the throne of grace with
boldness, will find mercy/grace/help.

6.12:   Must become μιμήται of those who through faith/
patience inherit promises.

6.18-19:   There is strong encouragement to *seize* hope lying before
them;. sure, steadfast anchor *enters* inner shrine, where
Jesus went as forerunner/high priest.

10.19-25:   Having boldness to *enter* by blood/by new, living way,
and having a great priest, must *draw near* with true
heart/assurance of faith, must hold fast the confession of
hope, must *consider* how to *stir up* one another to love/
good works, not neglecting to *assemble*/to *encourage*.

10.34-39:   Having better, abiding possession/great reward, must *not
throw away* boldness; they need endurance/faith to do
will of God, to receive promise.

12.1-4:   Having cloud of witnesses, must *lay aside* all impediments/
sin, must *run* the race with endurance, *looking to* Jesus/
pioneer/perfecter of faith, who endured the cross. Must
consider him who endured hostility from sinners, in their
struggle against sin.

12.5-11:   As children of God, must *endure* his discipline.

12.28:   Having unshakable kingdom, must *offer* acceptable
worship, pleasing to God.

13.1-6:   Exhortations on: brotherly love, hospitality, kindness to
prisoners, sexual morality, generosity, based on the
assurance of the Lord's help.

13.7-8, 17:   Jesus is always ὁ αὐτός: must remember leaders/preachers
of God's Word, must *consider* the outcome of their life,
imitate their faith, *obey* them.

13.9-16:   Avoiding diverse, strange teachings, the heart should be
                  strengthened by grace, not foods.
                  Having (heavenly) altar, must *go forth* to Jesus, bearing
                  his shame.
                  Seeking city to come, must *offer* sacrifice of praise to God
                  through Jesus, must *not neglect* to do good/ to share, for
                  such sacrifices are pleasing to God.

The structure of Heb. shows that the author deliberately inserts paraenetic sections into his theological exposition in order to convince his readers of the intimate link between the reality of the new covenantal order and its effect upon their conduct and lives. At each step, the argument leads to a paraenetic conclusion, which in turn prepares the addressees for the next point in the argument.[96]

Even though negative and positive consequences of NC membership are joined together in the major paraenetic sections of Heb., we chose to separate them in our listing above in order to highlight the twofold pastoral intent of the author. The majority of the underlined verbs imply *movement*. On the one hand, the warnings are intended to prevent the danger of 'drifting away/shrinking back/falling away' from a stage that the readers had already reached (5.12; 6.10; 10.32-34).

On the other hand, the exhortations are formulated in the hope of moving the recipients beyond the status quo, beyond the 'first principles' (6.1-2) toward higher stages of Christian living, greater maturity/perfection (5.14–6.1),[97] and ultimately toward the destination of their pilgrimage. The heavenly realities, which have been won for them by Christ, are already proleptically possessed (see the ἔχοντεα/ ἔχομεν passages),[98] and celebrated/'confessed'[99] in the new cult at Zion and in works of love (12.28; 13.15-16).[100]

But these privileges can be lost, and so the readers are summoned to 'seize/hold fast/endure/strive/run the race/go forth'. This same goal is expressed cultically by the call to 'draw near/enter'.[101] As we saw above,[102] the superior nature of the NC entails greater responsibility on the part of its members. To borrow the language of ancient Near Eastern covenantal treaties,[103] as the negative consequences/ 'curses' for rejection of the NC are far more severe than under the old covenant, so the NC 'blessings' exceed those conveyed by the old order in quality, stability and duration.[104]

The covenantal perspective, while seldom explicit[105] in the paraeneses, is always upheld by the author. The recipients are addressed communally, as members of God's *cultic*[106] λαός,[107] who can of course individually fail or apostasize. 'Sünde ist Zurückbleiben hinter dem wandernden Volk; unbildlich gesprochen: Abfall, Preisgabe des Bekenntnisses und Glaubens, damit des Heils'.[108] Grässer holds that, as distinct from Paul's emphasis on the justification of the individual, the accent in Heb. falls on the eschatological sanctification of the community.[109]

In Sanders' terms,[110] the paraenetic appeals are never about 'getting in', but always about 'staying in' the NC, while the warnings are about the danger of 'dropping out', that is losing the elect status of κεκλημένοι/μέτοχοι that Christ won for the NC people.[111] Similarly, Peterson notes that even though Christ's life is presented as a pattern for Christian discipleship, Heb. nowhere suggests that the addresses must earn their own perfection through suffering, since Christ has already done this on their behalf.[112]

The elaborate theological expositions about the Christ event can be regarded as a kind of 'historical prologue' for the 'stipulations' governing life under the NC. Just as the Lord's action of 'taking the Israelites by the hand and leading them out of Egypt' (Jer. 31.32; Heb. 8.9) stands at the beginning of the Decalogue as the foundation for every commandment (see Exod. 20.2), so Christ's death and exaltation/session at God's right hand are presupposed by all the injunctions in Heb.

As in Paul's theology, so in Heb., the 'indicative' of the λόγος δικαιοσύνης (5.13), spoken in the Son (1.1-4), always precedes the 'imperative' of the λόγος τῆς παρακλήσεως (13.22).[113] If Laub is correct, the author reinterprets the community ὁμολογία of the Son in terms of the suffering/dying/exalted high priest.[114] In so doing, he is conscious that he is confronting his readers with a λόγος δυσερμήνευτος ('hard to explain' 5.11), but he regards this as the best (and perhaps only) means of moving their understanding and faith forward.

Regardless of what the original *Sitz im Leben* of the 'confession' might have been in the tradition,[115] the author of Heb. retains the formand terminology and infuses it with new life. It suits his emphasis on the process of oral transmission of the Gospel[116] to present ὁμολογία as proclaimed σωτηρία, which has to be repeatedly heard, understood, and confessed and which leads to λατρεία in worship and life.[117]

The central theological section on the NC cult is framed by the two paraeneses of 4.14-16 and 10.19-25. In both the summons to 'hold fast' (κρατέω—4.14/κατέχω—10.23)[118] to the ὁμολογία implies the need for παρρησία ('boldness'). The concepts of ὁμολογία and παρρησία both embody a mixture of objective reality of salvation and empowerment derived from the Christ event (ἔχοντες), with the subjective necessity of reaffirming, reappropriating and 'seizing' this reality in the act of 'drawing near'[120] with hope.[121]

The author wants to help his readers to sustain this tension between the 'already' and the 'not yet',[122] foremost by his presentation of Jesus, but also by recounting the stories about the ancestors. Jesus functions both as the subject and the interpreter of the ὁμολογί.[123] He has become the πρόδρομος ('forerunner' 6.20) for 'Christians', firstly by completing the race that they are now summoned to run, fully sharing and enduring their suffering, and secondly by opening the way into the heavenly Tent and procuring unlimited access and lasting perfection for them.[124] As ἀρχηγός ('pioneer') and τελειωτής ('perfecter'),[125] he can function at once as the ground of salvation (2.10) and faith (12.2), and as the supreme exemplar and goal of that faith.

In a much more limited, but likewise exemplary fashion, the patriarchs have the role of exemplars for the addressees. Unlike the Israelites in the desert, who are ὑποδείγματα of disobedience (4.11)/ unbelief and illustrate the fate of failure to the readers (3.7-4.11), Abraham[126] and the carefully selected group of ancestors in ch. 11 are portrayed as models of endurance/patience and faith in the promises of the unseen, heavenly world.[127] The cloud of witnesses proleptically belonged to the new covenantal order by foreseeing it and greeting it from afar (11.13). NC members are therefore enjoined to become μιμηταί of their qualities (6.12), even though the ancestors could never have attained perfection apart from that of the readers (11.39-40).

D. *The Nature of the NC Cult*

Without any doubt, the nature of the NC cult has been one of the most hotly debated questions concerning the 'riddle' of Heb.[128] It is intimately linked to the problem of how the cultic language in the theological sections is to be related to the cultic language in the paraenetic sections.[129]

Two extreme answers are found even in recent literature. On the one hand, there are those scholars who think that the sole purpose of the paraeneses is to inculcate steadfastness/endurance, faith and hope. In this reading the cultic terminology is employed strictly metaphorically and serves the purpose of proclaiming the inadmissibility and end of all earthly cultic worship. As a consequence the 'sacrifices' of Christ's followers are to be performed in their daily lives.[130] Most of the exponents of this view are unable to find any references to the Eucharist in Heb. and some would even detect an explicit or implicit polemic against this rite or against a sacramental understanding of it.[131] It is noteworthy that the division is not as clear-cut with regard to baptism, for even exponents of this 'non-cultic' position find allusions to this rite in the text.[132]

On the other hand, there are those interpreters who insist that the cultic language in Heb. works on several levels and has a cultic referent *in addition to* its more general descriptive function regarding faith and good works. They find a number of allusions to the Eucharist in the text,[133] and some would go so far as to place eucharistic worship at its core.[134]

In light of our findings so far, it should be obvious that neither of these extreme positions are satisfactory in our view. In trying to relate the different parts of Heb. to each other, the *transitions between theology and paraenesis* deserve special attention.[135] In these passages the term προσέρχεσθαι plays a prominent role, as we already noted.[136] While the 'non-cultic', general meaning of 'drawing near' in the sense of having faith and approaching God with boldness is generally recognized (4.16; 10.19-24; also 11.6), the question is whether this understanding exhausts the meaning intended by these passages,[137] or whether we have to probe deeper. Clearly the author knows the traditional cultic sense of the term when he uses it of Levitical worship in 10.1. In 7.25 he establishes the connection to Christ's intercessory priestly office on behalf of 'those drawing near'. But is there room in Heb. for regular communal worship, in which the individual's faith commitment can find concrete ritual expression?

In seeking further to specify the content of προσέρχεσθαι, Thüsing shows that the concept speaks first and foremost to the *present* situation of the worshipper.[138] By focusing on the present, ongoing, heavenly λειτουργία of Jesus (8.1-6), and on the power of his blood that initiated the NC,[139] the 'one drawing near' has the assurance that the way into the heavenly sanctuary stands wide open

(10.19; see 6.19) and that lasting purification/perfection has been won.

But the concept of προσέρχεσθαι also includes a *past* dimension. It is grounded in and derives its objective meaning from the Christ event, while subjectively the recipients are said to 'have drawn near' (12.22, perfect tense) at some decisive moment in the past that could refer to their baptism.[140]

Finally, προσέρχεσθαι reaches into the *future*, to which the worshipper is drawn, for it is connected to the eschatological journey of the people of God toward the heavenly sanctuary (4.16; 10.19)/ Zion (12.22)/city (13.14).[141] The readers may *already* 'draw near', 'because they are a cultic community, they are *now* 'clean', *now* have access to God, *now* have their consciences purged, *now* have Jesus as high priest'.[142] But they have *not yet* arrived and live as 'sojourners' (11.9), 'strangers/exiles' (11.13) who must keep 'drawing near', moving faithfully toward their goal lest they fail to reach it.

In this manner, προσέρχεσθαι encapsulates the two important metaphors of the *community of the NC* and *pilgrimage/migration*. Johnsson rightly notes that in joining these motifs in the picture of the 'cultic community on the move' the different parts of our document can be harmonized. Thus the former metaphor is dominant in the theological sections, in which the 'defilement-purification' conception is operative and the *past* high priestly achievement of Christ is in view, whereas the latter metaphor governs the 'unbelief-faithfulness' complex that is characteristic of the *future*-oriented paraeneses.[143]

But Johnsson's case for a holistic view of Heb. can be further strengthened, if it is recognized that the division is less clear-cut than he makes it out to be. On the one hand, both the λαός motif (4.9; 11.25; 13.12) and the covenant motif (10.29; 12.24; 13.20) are explicitly found in the paraeneses and are implicitly woven into the argument at many other points. On the other hand, the pilgrimage idea is implicitly sounded in the notion of cultic separation in the theological sections.[144]

As we saw above,[145] perfection-language, like προσέρχεσθαι, runs like a red thread through the different parts of the document and likewise has both general moral and specific cultic dimensions.[146] Similarly λατρεύω, while primarily used of Levitical worship (8.5; 9.9; 10.2; 13.10; cf. the noun is 9.1, 6), is paraenetically applied to Christians in two important passages about the cultic order of the

NC. In 9.14 the superior blood of Christ cleanses their consciences and frees them for service/worship of the living God, and in 12.28 the proleptic possession of the unshakable kingdom empowers them to offer acceptable service/worship to God.

In all these instances a strictly ethical, individualistic interpretation of the cultic terminology in Heb. will simply not do justice to its theocentric and communal orientation. 'Der Hebr treibt Kulttheologie, weil er in einer sehr konsequenten Weise theozentrisch denkt und es ihm auf die *Herstellung der Relation zu Gott* ankommt, ... —weil ihm die Kulttheologie geeignet erscheint, das Werk, bzw. die Funktion Christi als *Ermöglichung des Zugangs zum heiligen Gott* darzustellen. So will er Christen aufrufen, sich mit dem Opfer Christi zu vereinigen'.[147]

The marriage of covenant and cult, therefore, enables the author to express his vision of salvation as free approach to God and communion with him through Christ, the Son and high priest.[148] Even though it might embarrass the sensibilities of the modern reader, one must take seriously the writer's insistence that, both on the heavenly and on the earthly plane, the Christ event resulted in *communal ritual purgation*. The sacrifice of Christ's *flesh* is depicted as the removal of the curtain hiding the heavenly sanctuary (10.20; cf. 6.19), i.e. the removal of the ritual barrier of sin,[149] in fulfilment of Jer. 31.34 (Heb. 10.16-18). The cleansing effect of his *blood* extends to τὰ ἐπουράνια (9.23).[150]

At the heavenly Mount Zion there is a worshipping community (12.22-23), the 'household' of God (10.21),[151] to which the NC people have been proleptically admitted (3.6; 12.22) by that same ἐφάπαξ sacrifice. The initiation of the NC corresponds to the consecration of the heavenly Tent (10.20),[152] while the sprinkling and washing of the community of recipients mirrors priestly initiation (10.22).[153]

In our opinion all this cultic terminology is not simply to be taken figuratively as another way of expressing 'Glaubensparänese'.[154] 'Der Kultus wird nicht durch eine selbstevidente Moral ersetzt, sondern das *ganze Leben der Gemeinde* mit in den Kultus hineingenommen'.[155] Granted that there is a polemical edge in some of the author's indictments against the old Levitical cultic order, his starting point is not a rationalist critique against any form of cultus. He departs from the conviction that Christ *fulfilled and replaced* the old covenant by a new one and that the ἐφάπαξ, blameless, complete nature of Christ's heavenly sacrifice rendered all further earthly, material sacrifice obsolete. Christ's followers, however, are still engaged in a heavenly cult.

In what then does the 'gottesdienstliche Existenz'[156] of the addressees consist? Everyone agrees that over and above moral conduct (13.1-5), διακονία (6.10), κοινωνία (13.16) and endurance of public abuse and persecution (10.32-34; 12.4), acceptable service of the 'living God' (9.14) implies prayer, praise and confession (12.28; 13.15; cf. 5.7).[157] Thurén therefore interprets the NC cult in light of the *Shema*, as a covenantal confession of God that is intimately connected with neighbourly love and service.[158]

Furthermore it is clear that the NC people are called to regular gatherings (10.25). Most scholars assume that the community ὁμολογία played a role at these assemblies and was publically proclaimed/confessed there. But are we to imagine that their communal worship consisted only in a word-service?[159] The text furnishes no explicit connection between the ὁμολογία and baptism. Neither this rite nor the Eucharist are ever unambiguously mentioned in Heb.

Many of the difficulties in this matter stem from the fluid nature of these rites and the varied practices associated with them in early Christianity. In the case of baptism, the *water-rite* that some interpreters seem to have in mind when they use the term was only a part of the total conversion-initiation experience in NT times, namely the 'expression of the faith to which God gives the Spirit'.[160] Dunn's exegesis has convinced me that *Baptisma* or *Baptismos* in the NT means the water-rite pure and simple, whose cleansing efficacy reaches no further than the body'.[166] The case of the Eucharist is equally complicated since we know that it was at times and in some areas celebrated with an intervening meal.

Bearing this in mind, we will now briefly turn to the only four passages that may, in our view, shed light on the author's perception of these rites, namely 6.1-8; 9.20; 10.19-31; 13.9-16.[162]

(1) *Heb. 6.1-8*
As is often overlooked, this pericope should include the agricultural simile of 6.7-8, because its covenantal echoes of blessing and curse form a fitting conclusion to the previous verses.[163] I consider it plausible that some members of the community of addressees are converts from Judaism, so that 6.1-2 describes the 'area of overlap between Judaism and Christianity in terms common to both. . .

Βαπτίσμοι must then at least include a reference to Christian baptism...'[164] If Heb. 6.1-2 deals with basic baptismal instruction, in terms of repentance ('turning from') and faith ('turning to'), then 6.4-5 can then be regarded as the 'decisive differentia of Christianity'.[165] The parallelism of these verses, based on the two γευσαμένους-clauses, has been noted by several exegetes,[166] and prevents us from taking the 'heavenly gift' as a reference to the Eucharist. 'Tasting' is used metaphorically to express the experience of salvation, as *already* proleptically enjoyed, but *not yet* fully/completely attained. Against Schröger[167] and many others who believe that φωτισθέντας refers to Christian baptism, we agree with Williamson that this is a 'general characterization of the experience of the Christian', followed in 6.6 by 'the tragic annihilation of that experience which apostasy brings about'.[168] The serious implications of NC membership are graphically recapitulated as it were in the concluding simile of 6.7-8.

As noted by Williamson, there is a close connection between the images of light-speech and salvation in Heb.[169] Thus our passage resembles 2.1-4 in describing the work of salvation by the Son and the Spirit. There are three parties collaborating in the conversion-initiation experience: the *preacher* of the Gospel Word (2.3; 4.2, 12-13; 13.7), the *individual* who repents/receives faith and—in a process that is inseparable—hears the Word/is cleansed/sanctified/perfected by the Son, 'tastes' the Spirit and is baptized into the NC community (6.1-2; 10.22), and finally the *divine actions* of illumination/purgation by the Son/high priest and powerful signs/gifts of the Spirit (1.3; 2.3-4; 6.4-5).[170] Unfortunately the text nowhere states clearly that the Eucharist was a part, or the conclusion of this complex of experiences.

(2) Heb. 9.20
The change from the LXX of Exod. 24.8 ἰδού to τοῦτο in Heb. 9.20 has been frequently taken as an allusion to the eucharistic words of institution. As Schröger points out, however, there are some textual witnesses of the LXX. Exodus verse exhibiting the same change. Besides, the importance of the covenant-blood motif in Heb. as a whole would be sufficient to explain the author's preference for or change to this textual version, without having recourse to the Last Supper.[171] Loader's contention, 'Im Hb scheint der Begriff "Bund" in einem engen Zusammenhang mit eucharistischer Tradition zu stehen (vgl vor allem 9,20)',[172] is really no more than an interesting

speculation. At most one could say that the author might be acquainted with a tradition about Jesus' words at the Last Supper, but nothing can be deduced about eucharistic practice from this verse.

(3) *Heb. 10.19-31*

We have repeatedly come across this passage before, and the interpretation reached for the references to the blood (v. 19) and the flesh (v. 20) of Jesus[173] leaves no room for any allusion to the eucharistic elements. Even Thüsing, who is otherwise cautious in his assessment, has to resort to Jn 6.53-58 in order to sustain his theory that this passage has eucharistic overtones.[174] This procedure leaves much to be desired and cannot help us understand the author of Heb., who is after all usually not so equivocal when something is important to him.

As for baptism, I agree with most commentators that 10.22 alludes to this rite. As in 9.11-14, 18-22, the conjunction of sprinkling, inauguration and blood in 10.19-22 depicts the NC sacrifice of Christ against the background of the old covenant sacrifice, meshed with Yom Kippur typology. The 'sprinkling of hearts from an evil conscience' refers to the sanctification by Christ's superior blood (see 9.14), while the 'washing of the body with clear water' refers to the water-rite of baptism, viewed against the background of the ashy water from the red heifer ritual (see 9.13). The Levitical ceremonies once again partially and imperfectly prefigure the conversion-initiation experience of the recipients, of which their baptism constitutes a part.[175] Thus the two parts of 10.22 complement each other in synthetic parallelism.[176] In confirmation of my earlier remarks[177] the water-rite of baptism per se accomplishes the outer cleansing of body. Nonetheless it is inseparable from and points to the cleansing of the whole person and the very conscience itself[178] that only Christ's blood could effect.

As in the case of 6.1-8, the larger context of the pericope reminds the readers of the serious consequences of belonging to the NC community when judgment by the 'living God' (see 9.14) is evoked in heavily cultic terms (10.26-31). As already stated,[179] the passage deals with the NC cultus both in its individual and communal aspects. The writer reminds his addressees that in their baptismal conversion they turned from 'dead works' (6.1; 9.14) to 'good works' (10.24). He summons them to mutual encouragement, repeated assembly and (communal) exhortation in view of the approaching Day (of the Lord). But he nowhere explicitly calls them to eucharistic fellowship.

(4) *Heb. 13.9-16*

Without going so far as to claim that ch. 13 contains the 'key' to Heb.,[180] we concur with Lührmann's verdict: 'In dem Abschnitt 13.7-17 kommen... die wichtigsten Motive der Theologie des Hebräerbriefes noch einmal zur Sprache',[181] We have narrowed the pericope to 13.9-16, even though we accept that the references to the 'leaders' form an inclusio around it.

Few passages in Heb. have had so much ink spilled about them as this one and the disagreements are by no means settled in contemporary exegesis. For our purposes it suffices to present what we consider to be the most plausible interpretation. With Loader, we hold that the references to 'foods' in Heb.[182] are somewhat polemical and must contain clues for at least one of the temptations affecting the readers.[183] Typologically speaking, the most likely referent are Levitical sacrificial meals in light of the following quote from Lev. 16.27 that deals with the exceptional situation of the Yom Kippur sacrifice and the prohibition of eating it. What this may have meant concretely in the life of a (certainly overwhelmingly *lay*) diaspora community is indeed hard to tell and may be impossible to discover from the terse nature of the passage. Suggestions as to some kind of visible replacement for the Tabernacle, born of a nostaligia for the Levitical heritage,[184] and the need for concrete ritual expression of sacrifice are not altogether implausible.

What is clear, however, is that the author disapproves of these practices and appeals to grace[185] as an important alternative source of strength for the heart. καρδία is the place where a person's basic inner orientation vis-à-vis God is decided. The writer uses Ps. 95 to warn against an 'evil unbelieving heart' (3.12; cf. 3.8, 10, 15; 4.7) and Jer. 31.33 (8.10; 10.16) to describe God's action in transforming the heart of NC members, which transformation is effected by Christ's blood in Christian initiation (10.22).

Since ἔχομεν consistently refers to the proleptic possession of heavenly realities by the addressees, there can be no doubt that the 'altar' in 13.10 must be situated in the heavenly sanctuary, while the logic of the sentence demands that 'those who serve the Tent' must be Levitical priests.[186] The phrase could include Levitical worshippers and those 'judaizing' Christians tempted to join them. Once again we are dealing with figurative language, and therefore φάγειν (like γευσαμένους in 6.4) does not imply physical, literal eating, but rather the proleptic enjoyment of salvation.[187] We saw above that this involves 'drawing near',[188] and here we find the same summons expressed as 'going forth' to Jesus, bearing his shame. If it is true that the author is writing 'in einer Zeit, wo das Christsein mehr Schmach und Verfolgung einträgt als das Judesein',[189] then the threat of persecution may have led some of his readers to hide their identity by going to Synagogue services.[190]

According to the author such a stance is inadmissible for one who has been sanctified by Jesus' blood and belongs to his NC people (13.12). It is a question of unambiguously showing one's allegiance to Jesus and of participating in his suffering by moving 'outside the camp' of former loyalties to the Synagogue or indeed to any earthly πόλις (13.13-14). In sanctifying them through his ἐφάπαξ self-offering, Christ definitively abolished the first (cultic covenantal order) and established the second (10.9-10). Thereby his followers were decisively cleansed from sin (10.18), and so their offering can no longer be a sin offering (10.26) but a 'sacrifice of praise' (13.15). In Jesus the recipients have a model of what it means to do God's will (10.5-10, 36; 13.21) and to please him (13.16; cf. 11.5; 12.28).[191]

I concur with Reumann's cautious judgment concerning this passage that 'if brought into connection with Christ's sacrifice'—and the author does in fact establish that connection in 13.12—'these verses speak *at most* of our entering into and appropriating its benefits (for example, at the Lord's Supper, though the *sacrament is not mentioned*) and responding thereafter in the world with sacrificial service to others'.[192]

To sum up, while the text of Heb. as a whole does not allow us to rule out the possibility of eucharistic celebration among the addressees, we can at least say that the author does not seem interested in it. As Williamson recognizes, it is not as if the Eucharist would have been extraneous to his argument; on the contrary, it could have strengthened his case. Conceivably, he might have interpreted it as a foretaste of the heavenly realities, the proleptic possession of which he repeatedly emphasizes, or even as a remedy against 'falling away' and a stimulus to keep on striving.[193] 'It is almost incredible that the author of Hebrews should have believed what he did about the 'already' and the 'not yet', without relating those beliefs to the Eucharist. . . '[194] We have chosen to leave out the end of Williamson's sentence ('if in fact he did belong to a community in which that Sacrament was celebrated') because it is possible that the author simply passes the Eucharist over in silence and feels no need to emphasize it or to polemicize against it.[195] After all, baptism, which could have been exploited theologically (à la Rom. 6) in terms of Christ's ἐφάπαξ death, is scarcely mentioned.

Summary

In this chapter we found that the NC idea lies at the heart of the author's concern to relate the old (cultic) order to the new one. The concept is influential throughout Heb., even where it is not explicitly mentioned. It stands in the background of the treatment of revelation, while it explicitly shapes the theological exposition of Christ's high priesthood. We saw how the hermeneutical scheme of 'correspondence, contrast and superiority' is operative in the writer's dualistic reading of the Hebrew Scriptures. We showed that the comparison of cultic orders unfolds by means of the shared rubrics of covenant, priesthood, bloody sacrifice and Tent, and how these categories are then contrasted with the ultimate end of demonstrating the infinite superiority of the new covenantal order in the process.

Then we posited the implicit influence of the NC motif in the paraenetic sections by interpreting them as warnings against abandoning the NC, and as exhortations to embrace it and to continue on the journey of the NC people. We stressed that the author envisages a heavenly cultus in the NC which is grounded in the ἐφάπαξ Christ event. He pictures this new cult as a life of service through communal worship/praise/confession of God, and works of love, mutual support and sharing of suffering. Finally we saw that the author seems to include the rite of baptism in the experience of conversion-initiation into the NC community, but is strangely silent about—though not directly opposed to—eucharistic celebration.

Chapter 6

CONCLUSIONS

This study has sought to demonstrate that the author of Heb. has the remarkable ability to balance different factors that are often thought to be extremes or even contradictory elements. Many of his interpreters like to emphasize particular strands of his work to the point of ignoring or even denying the presence of others.[1]

Unlike them, the writer in fact manages to incorporate horizontal and vertical thought patterns to uphold the tension between realized and futurist eschatology and to portray the Christian story both from the vantage point of its continuity and of its discontinuity with its Israelite heritage. As MacRae shows, 'the rationale for the presence of [these different elements] 'lies in the literary genre of homily. The preacher supports the audience's views with his own'.[2] '... In the mixed congregations of the early church it is not unlikely that a preacher with an Alexandrian background should address an apocalyptically oriented [partially] Jewish-Christian community, not with a view to destroying its futurist eschatology, but with a view to shoring it up with his own Philonic perspective'.[3]

It has been my contention throughout that the NC concept plays an important role in this 'balancing act' in two ways. (1) By creatively reinterpreting the category of *covenant* from a cultic perspective the author is able to depict the Christ event in *continuity* with and as the perfect fulfillment of the cultic heritage of Israel. (2) By stressing the elements of *newness* and drawing a *contrast* to the former system, he succeeds in presenting Christ as the permanent, definitive, *superior* replacement of that same heritage.

Despite his philosophical bent, the author chooses the scriptural metaphor of covenant[4] as a suitable means of expressing his convictions about the person and work of Christ. He may be familiar with early Christian traditions linking the death of Jesus to the NC, but the text does not explicitly show literary connections to the use of the NC idea in Paul or in the Last Supper accounts. Nor do we have any clear evidence that the NC concept is important to the addressees, although it is possible that the writer adopts it from community tradition. Regardless of where he got the idea, however, he reworks it in an original manner that constitutes a departure from the other known NC texts that we examined in Chapters 3 and 4.

The author of Heb. infuses the NC metaphor, which bears no relationship whatsoever to the cult in Jeremiah's prophecy on the NC (31.31-34), with cultic content that is rooted elsewhere in the OT. In Heb. cultic imagery is used in a novel, deliberate way to characterize the utterly non-cultic event of Jesus' death on a cross and its consequences for his followers. In trying to understand the reasons for this transference of cultic terminology[5] and to grasp its peculiar force,[6] the usual approach of *Religionsgeschichte* is not very helpful. 'What is necessary is to search for the concrete situation and theological motives that. . . led to the transference of cultic language'.[7]

The rest of this concluding chapter will summarize this study's findings along these lines and show how the two elements of (1) covenant and (2) newness[8] meet the needs of the concrete predicament of the addressees and flow from the author's theological concerns.

With regard to the *situation faced by the recipients* our study has confirmed the plausibility of the following two problem complexes.

(A) On the one hand, the text furnishes hints of suffering and abuse, impounding of property and imprisonment, which point to official (state) persecutions (10.32-34).[9] This recurring 'external' threat is matched by the 'internal' problem of unclear allegiance to Christ and to his NC.[10]

(B) On the other hand, the internal longing for some kind of concrete replacement for the Levitical cult[11] may have been occasioned in part by the external charge of atheism, based on the absence of visible cultic institutions, officials and symbols,[12] and in part by the campaigning of conservative Jewish-Christians.[13] In this writer's view these factors are by no means mutually exclusive, as is sometimes thought. Simultaneous attacks and pressure from various sides would explain the tendencies to withdraw and fall away on the part of the embattled readers.

The combined weight of these factors, perhaps coupled with a disappointment over the delay of the *parousia*, seems to have produced spiritual lethargy and a lack of concrete acts of love and fellowship among the readers. Presumably the external threats would have been powerless to affect them if their faith had been firm and their understanding of the Christ event mature and unassailable. But to wonder which came first—waning faith or external harrassment— seems a moot point. Instead, it is important to pay heed to the polemical hints in the text. For they have convinced me that internal explanations alone are not sufficient to diagnose the predicament of the addressees nor to explain the author's mode of reply to which we shall now turn.

The *author's own theological motives* are combined with his diagnosis of the community's problems and needs in order to formulate his homiletical treatise. For conceptual purposes I will separate different responses by the author, bearing in mind that he has skillfully woven them into a unified whole.

Thus I would argue that when he has problem complex (A) in view he counters by appealing to Jesus' way of suffering. The recipients are called to look to Jesus who helps his persecuted followers as their πρόδρομος ('forerunner'), and cures their feeble faith as their ἀρχηγός ('pioneer/leader') and τελειωτής ('perfecter'), enabling them to see beyond the visible world and to anchor their security in the invisible heavenly realm that he opened for them.

The 'imperative' of these paraenetic appeals would not be very effective, however, if it were not grounded in the 'indicative' of the theological exposition of Christ as high priestly NC mediator. The writer wishes to solidify the readers' faith and rekindle their hope by reminding them that as members of the NC they already share in a heavenly cult and enjoy proleptic possession of heavenly realities, even if they have not yet arrived at their destination and must suffer trials on the way. In fact, he assures them that they can view their shame and abuse as cultic service in light of the shameful sacrifice of Christ (13.12-13; cf. 12.1-4).

When assailed they should remember that they are not suffering alone, but as members of God's *covenantal* λαός who are responsible for each other (element 1). But in contrast to the old covenantal people, to which some of their number might feel drawn, they participate in a *new* cultic assembly, which has drawn near to the heavenly Zion and has open access to the very heavens by the superior blood of the NC (12.18-24, element 2). As sharers in Christ (3.14) they share in a heavenly call (3.1) and must abandon earthly, 'fleshly' rulings and rituals. They must keep demonstrating their allegiance and reconfirming their self-identity through suffering and service.

In response to problem complex (B) the author portrays the scandal of Jesus' crucifixion in cultic terms as an ἐφάπαξ sacrifice that effected lasting purgation. To those who would charge the addressees with having no cult he replies with a resounding ἔχομεν: high priest, bloody sacrifice, Tent, and altar.[14] But this answer is aimed particularly at those who would chide the readers for breaking with their Levitical heritage and who would tempt them to seek some visible cultic replacement, for it is couched in the scriptural metaphor of *covenant* (element 1).[15] By reinterpreting 'covenant' as 'cultic order', the writer is able to reassure the recipients of his 'word of exhortation' that in one sense what happened in Christ continues the Levitical patrimony, because it can be pictured by means of the same cultic rubrics. The Hebrew Scriptures illuminate the Christ event by providing pointers and foreshadowings of it.[16] The very prediction of a NC in the OT is understood as implying the demise of the old (8.7, 13).

In another sense, however, the *newness* (element 2) in the comparison between the covenantal orders breaks the continuity.[17] For the NC is not only a 'second', but also a *heavenly* cultic order, which shares little more than the formal descriptive rubrics with its earthly counterpart. It functions in analogous, but infinitely superior ways to provide purgation/sanctification/perfection. The author presents Jesus as the one and only high priest who lives eternally to intercede for his brethren. Whatever the readers might hope to gain by earthly replacements of Levitical ritual, Jesus has already performed for them, once-and-for-all, by definitively fulfilling and replacing any such ritual by his self-offering on Calvary. Thereby he won for his followers whatever Jewish privileges they wrongly imagine they might be missing, privileges of an infinitely surpassing nature.

The author borrows Middle-Platonic categories and perfection terminology to undergird his convictions about the stability and trustworthiness of Christ's high priesthood and new cultic order. He impresses upon his readers that, as Son, Jesus stands above any scheme and cannot be viewed in line with other revelatory agents. In Jesus God spoke his definitive, final Word and the 'last days' were ushered in (1.1-4). Salvation history as previously known and experienced is no more, for Christ brought an 'unshakable kingdom' which will survive the final cataclysm of the entire created order. Correspondingly, the refusal to hear that Word and to respond by acceptable worship will be that much more perilous (12.25-29; cf. 10.24-29).

Thus we can say, by way of summary, that both problem complexes require the author to muster his entire register of thought patterns. While futurist eschatology/horizontal imagery may be said to dominate in the paraeneses where complex (A)—persecution/ unclear allegiance—is being addressed, there is likewise the assurance of Christ's having 'already' arrived in the heavens at the end of the path to be travelled by his followers.

On the other hand, realized eschatology/vertical imagery receives more emphasis when the writer engages in theological exposition to deal with complex (B)—the absence of visible cultic institutions—but even here he never allows the NC people to lose sight of the 'not yet', the need to persevere on the path and to keep 'drawing near' lest they fall.

In similar fashion, both sets of problems are countered with the help of the elements of *covenant* (1) and *newness* (2). In complex (A) the covenant concept is implicitly conveyed by the motif of the 'cultic λαός on the move' (1), but this people is explicitly differentiated from the old by its having been sanctified by the superior power of the *new* covenant blood (2). In complex (B) the covenant idea—cultically transposed—provides the overall framework and the categories for the argument (1). The author is at pains to make the Christ event intelligible by showing the ways in which it derives from these scriptural and Levitical roots. But he does this by looking back, as it were, from the vantage point of *newness* of which he wishes to convince his readers (2).

This strong emphasis on the element of newness is what sets the role of the NC idea in Heb. apart from its role in the DSS, in the Last Supper accounts and in Paul—near contemporaries of which our text betrays no explicit knowledge. Because of the obvious difference resulting from the conviction that Jesus is the Christ Heb. can go much further than Qumran in breaking with the past cultic order and in stressing realized eschatology and a definitive new revelation.

As a lengthy homiletical treatise, Heb. articulates much more fully what is only hinted at, but not explained, in the words of institution: the inbreaking of a new age of definitive purgation/forgiveness and salvation as a result of the bloody sacrifice of Jesus' death.

Despite some resemblances, Paul's use of NC terminology is not as original, deliberate and far-reaching in its implications as it is in Heb.

Paul's own proclamation of καινὴ κτίσις (Gal. 6.15; 2 Cor. 5.17) may have some of the same radical force as καινὴ διαθήκη does in Heb. The author of Heb., however, works from a cultic perspective quite foreign to Paul and hence goes much further in his conscious articulation of the break with the *cultic institutions* of Israel that happened in Christ.

In an environment of varied religious groups, the writer of Heb. chooses the NC concept as a vehicle for affirming the self-identity of his readers as members of a cultic group. While this identity is shaped by their roots in the cultic heritage of Israel, they proleptically participate in an utterly new, heavenly cult, which empowers them to concrete expressions of communal confession/prayer and neighbourly acts of service, endurance and suffering.

The struggle with Jewish tradition is omnipresent in the NT but nowhere do we find a clear rupture with Judaism. Paradoxically enough, it is the writer of Heb. who—while passionately arguing along Jewish lines—moves furthest in the direction of the breach with Judaism that was later to take place.

NOTES

Notes to Chapter 1

1. Monographs on our topic are rare: R. Schreiber, *Der Neue Bund im Spätjudentum und Urchristentum* (unpublished dissertation; Eberhard-Karls-Universität Tübingen, 1954), see pp. 108-29 on Heb.; V.R. Gordon, *Studies in the Covenantal Theology of the Epistle to the Hebrews in Light of its Setting* (Ph.D. Dissertation, Fuller Theological Seminary, 1979); E. Grässer, *Der Alte Bund im Neuen* (Tübingen: Mohr, 1985), pp. 95-115 on Heb. Articles usually deal with the NC within the OT (consult the bibliography); independent treatment of the concept as it reappears in the NT is rare: e.g. U. Luz, 'Der alte und der neue Bund bei Paulus und im Hebräerbrief', *EvT* 6 (1967) 318-37; D. Peterson, 'The Prophecy of the New Covenant in the Argument of Hebrews', *Reformed Theological Review* 36-38 (1977-78) 74-81. For specialized articles on Paul's treatment of the NC and on the Last Supper material see below Chapter 4, section B.

2. The first clear application of OT/NT in our sense dates back to Clement of Alexandria, but there are earlier traces in Melito of Sardis and in an Antimontanist, quoted in Eusebius, *Hist.* 5.16.3-5; see C. Levin, *Die Verheissung des neuen Bundes in ihrem theologiegeschichtlichen Zusammenhang ausgelegt* (FRLANT 137; Göttingen: Vandenhoeck & Ruprecht, 1985) 267 n. 4.

3. Questions of genre can be bypassed for our purposes. We are satisfied with the author's designation of his work as a 'word of exhortation' (13.22), so we could equally speak of 'hearers'. But since the document was handed down to us in writing and we regard it as a literary unit (including the epistolary ending) 'readers' or 'recipients' will be the preferred designation of the addressees.

4. W. Wrede, *Das literarische Rätsel des Hebräerbriefes* (Göttingen: Vandenhoeck & Ruprecht, 1906) 66.

5. An impressive number compared to only 16 other NT occurrences of διαθήκη: 8 in Paul, 4 in the Synoptics, 2 in Acts, 1 in Eph., 1 in Rev. I accept the conclusion of J.J. Hughes's thorough investigation ('Hebrews IX 15ff. and Galatians III 15ff.', *NovT* 21 [1979] 28-66; on Gal. see Chapter 4, below, where it is cited as 'Gal III 15ff.') and translate διαθήκη as *covenant* throughout Heb. For additional arguments see W.G. Johnsson, *Defilement and Purgation in the Book of Hebrews* (Ph.D. Dissertation, Vanderbilt University, 1973) 306-18.

6. E.g. in G. Hughes, *Hebrews and Hermeneutics* (Cambridge: Cambridge University Press, 1979) chs. 1-2; on the importance of revelation in Heb. see also below, Chapter 5, Section A.

7. R. Williamson, 'The Incarnation of the Logos in Hebrews', *ExpTim* 94 (1983-84) 4-8, makes an intriguing case for an incarnational Logos Christology in Heb. He goes beyond the arguments of H. Clavier, 'ὁ λόγος τοῦ θεοῦ dans l'epître aux Hébreux', in *New Testament Essays* (ed. A.J.B. Higgins; Festschrift T.W. Manson; Manchester, 1959) 81-93, who mainly appeals to semantic possibilities and to Origen's insights. Williamson compares the properties usually associated with the Logos in (Philo and) John to the Jesus of Heb., and finds many similar features in Heb., even though he can only locate one explicit reference in 4.13.

8. G. Hughes, *Hebrews* 8.

9. C. Spicq, *L'Epître aux Hébreux* (EBib; 2 vols.; Paris: Gabalda, 1952) 2.297.

10. Grässer, *Bund* 127 (emphasis mine).

11. See e.g. Grässer, *Bund* 96: 'Entsprechung/Andersartigkeit/Überbietung'. Also below, Chapter 5, note 31.

12. Grässer, *Bund* 129.

13. For an overview see e.g. D.J. McCarthy, 'Covenant in the Old Testament: the Present State of the Inquiry', *CBQ* 27 (1965) 217-40; W. Eichrodt, 'Covenant and Law: Thoughts on Recent Discussion', *Int* 20 (1966) 302-21.

14. Grässer, *Bund* 128-29.

15. See R. Bultmann, *Glauben und Verstehen* (4 vols.; Tübingen: Mohr, 1965-67) 2.174; for him this inconsistency is only removed in the NT, where the Christian community is regarded as the fulfilment of the prophetic promise but 'ist kein Volk als Gebilde der innerweltlichen Geschichte' (*ibid.*), as quoted in Grässer, *Bund* 131 n. 556a.

16. S.J.D. Cohen, 'Conversation to Judaism in Historical Perspective: From Biblical Israel to Postbiblical Judaism', *Conservative Judaism* 36 (1983) 36, cf. esp. notes 11-20.

17. *De facto* excommunication, even though we must not press some of the harsh rhetoric about 'enemies' to its last theological conclusion, which would mean denying people a share in the after-life.

18. See below on the Last Supper, Chapter 4, Section B.

19. See below, Chapter 3, Section D.

20. Spicq, *Epître* 2.294.

21. Mosaic covenant reinterpreted as perpetual covenant, with the sabbath as its sign (Exod. 31.16); legislation on cult, Tabernacle, Ark, foods, calendar, etc. is inserted into the old Epic tradition (Exod. 25-31; 35-40; Lev.; Num. 1-10).

22. See J.W. Thompson, *The Beginnings of Christian Philosophy: The Epistle to the Hebrews* (Washington, D.C.: Catholic Biblical Association,

1982) ch. 1, especially pp. 12-13, where he stresses the need for examination of the author's intellectual presuppositions and patterns of argumentation.
23. R.E. Brown and J.P. Meier, *Antioch and Rome* (New York: Paulist, 1983), introduction, pp. 2-8, where 'Group Two' is defined as not requiring circumcision, but insisting on *some Jewish observances*, notably food laws (p. 3), and 'Group Four' as those who required none of the above and *saw no abiding significance in Jewish cult and feasts* (p. 6). See below, Chapter 5, Section B.
24. See below, Chapter 5, Section D (4).
25. For a list of representatives of the 'Anglo-Saxon' viewpoint and for a confirmation of this 'cultural' division in the analysis of Heb, see F. Laub, *Bekenntnis und Auslegung* (Regensburg: Pustet, 1980) p. 3, n. 9. The 'German' view is too widespread to document here; see e.g. bibliographical entries under H. Braun, G. Fitzer, E. Grässer, B. Klappert, H. Koester, F. Laub, D. Lührmann, H. Zimmermann. For a recent attempt to recognize *both* kinds of threats affecting the readers, see W.R.G. Loader, *Sohn und Hoherpriester* (Neukirchen-Vluyn: Neukirchener, 1981) 256-60.

Notes to Chapter 2

1. Spicq, *Epître* 2.330-50; G.B. Caird, 'The Exegetical Method of the Epistle to the Hebrews', *CJT* 5 (1959) 44-51; S.G. Sowers, *The Hermeneutics of Philo and Hebrews* (Richmond: Knox, 1965); F. Schröger, *Der Verfasser des Hebräerbriefes als Schriftausleger* (Regensburg: Pustet, 1968); idem, 'Das hermeneutische Instrumentarium des Hebräerbriefverfassers', *TGl* 60 (1970) 344-59; J.C. McCullough, 'The Old Testament Quotations in Hebrews', *NTS* 26 (1980) 363-79; O. Michel, *Der Brief an die Hebräer* (MeyerK; 14th edn; Göttingen: Vandenhoeck & Ruprecht, 1984) 151-58, see further literature there.
2. Grässer, *Bund* 96.
3. See above, Chapter 1 note 13; also R. Martin-Achard, 'La signification de l'alliance dans l'ancien testament d'après quelques récents travaux', *RTP* 18 (1968) 88-102. J.J. Mitchell, 'Abraham's Understanding of the Lord's Covenant', *WTJ* 32 (1969-70) 24-48; H. Cazelles, 'Alliance du Sinai, alliance de l'Horèb et renouvellement de l'alliance', *Beiträge zur alttestamentlichen Theologie* (Fs. W. Zimmerli; Göttingen: Vandenhoeck & Ruprecht, 1977) 69-79.
4. P. Buis, 'La nouvelle alliance', *VT* 18 (1968) 12, n. 2: 'Pour P la théophanie du Sinai à partir de laquelle se constitue le peuple n'est que la première réalisation des promesses à Abraham; ce n'est pas une alliance distincte... Il est remarquable que dans le NT l'alliance devient souvent synonyme de promesse. La conception sacerdotale y est poussée à son extrême limite'.

5. See e.g. 7.23-24; 9.6-7, 9-13; 10.11-12. Also below, Chapter 5, Section A.

6. See Luz ('Bund' 334, n. 60), who distinguishes between the author's *Vorlage* (ἐπαγγελία = earthly goods) and the author's own reinterpretation (ἐπαγγελία = heavenly goods).

7. See below, pp. 26-27.

8. On p. 95 of 'The Figure of Moses as a Heuristic Device for Understanding the Pastoral Intent of Hebrews', *RevExp* 76 (1979) 95-107.

9. We cannot take into account the possibility of hidden allusions to Moses in chs. 1-2, which is postulated in the fascinating thesis of L.K.K. Dey, *The Intermediary World and Patterns of Perfection in Philo and Hebrews* (SBLDS 25; Missoula: Scholars, 1975). Dey believes that in the readers' Hellenistic milieu Moses functions as the supreme exemplar of perfection and therefore ranks above angels in the scheme of divine proximity (p. 123). Hence the figure of Moses stands in the background of the comparison between Jesus and the angels (chs. 1-2), and his mention in 3.2 comes as no surprise to initiates. See below, Chapter 5, Section A.

10. For an excellent recent treatment and for references to the literature see E. Grässer, 'Mose und Jesus: Zur Auslegung von Hebr 3 1-6', in *Bund* 290-311.

11. M.R. D'Angelo, *Moses in the Letter to the Hebrews* (SBLDS 42; Missoula: Scholars, 1979) 196.

12. *Ibid.*, 174. D'Angelo's thorough exegesis of Heb. 3.1-6, in chs. 2-4 of her book, appeals to extra-biblical traditions about Moses and gives due consideration to a variety of possible meanings for πιστός and οἶκος.

13. Grässer, *Bund* 310.

14. See *ibid.*, also, J.W. Thompson, *Beginnings* 13; U. Luck, 'Himmlisches und irdisches Geschehen im Hebräerbrief', *NovT* 6 (1963) 192-215.

15. On Heb. 7, see below pp. 26-27.

16. See e.g. Gen. 9.12 (Noah); Gen. 17.7 (Abraham); Gen. 17.19 (Isaac); Exod. 31.16 (Sabbath = sign of Sinai covenant); Num. 25.12-13 (Phineas and his priestly seed); 2 Sam. 23.5 (David).

17. D'Angelo, *Moses* 243-46; we can only present some of her striking conclusions in summary fashion here. On the NC priesthood in Heb. see below, Chapter 5, esp. Section on cultic Law.

18. See N. Dahl, 'A New and Living Way', *Int* 5 (1951) 404. See below, Chapter 5, Section D.

19. Unless otherwise specified, translations are mine.

20. For this contention see Johnsson, *Defilement* 222-27. 'Just as the preceding argument of the writer had established a better name, a better priest(hood), a better sanctuary and a better covenant, so here in the climax of the development we see the better *means* by which the new age has come about—the blood of Christ' (p. 222). See below, Chapter 5, Section B.

21. See J.W. Thompson, *Beginnings* 45.

22. Grässer insists that Heb knows of only *one* people of God (*Bund* 305). Likewise for A. Oepke, *Das neue Gottesvolk* (Gütersloh: Bertelsmann, 1950) p. 69, the only true people of God are the Christians. But according to E. Käsemann, *Das wandernde Gottesvolk* (FRLANT 37; Göttingen: Vandenhoeck & Ruprecht, 1939) p. 37, *two* peoples and two διαθῆκαι confront each other. See also above, Chapter 1, Chapter 5 Section C and Chapter 6.

23. Contrast Sir. 45.3-5 about Moses as *lawgiver*, but again note the absence of the word 'Sinai'. Most interpreters view ch. 11 in light of similar lists of moral exempla in Hellenistic paraenesis (for further examples and literature see D'Angelo, *Moses* 18-19) and regard large parts of this Chapter as traditional. Nonetheless the author employed his tradition selectively and provided us with editorial comments as a key to his intentions. For a cogent account of what all the witnesses have in common see J. Swetnam, *Jesus and Isaac: A Study of the Epistle to the Hebrews in Light of the Aqedah* (Rome: Biblical Institute, 1981) 86-89.

24. D'Angelo, *Moses* 63. But to call Moses a Christian martyr (*ibid.*, pp. 33, 258, and *passim*, as the argument develops) seems overstated on D'Angelo's part.

25. D'Angelo, *Moses* 64.

26. There can be no denying the presence of Platonic thought patterns in Heb., which may have reached our author through the Middle-Platonism current in his day.

27. For a good explanation for the revisions of the LXX version by the author, see D'Angelo, *Moses* 205-208.

28. See *ibid.*, 206; also Sowers, *Hermeneutics* 105-12.

29. See S. Nomoto, 'Herkunft und Struktur der Hohenpriester-vorstellung im Hebräerbrief', *NovT* 10 (1968) 19.

30. D'Angelo, *Moses* 225.

31. In contrast to a 'low' view (e.g. in Acts 7.20-40) of Moses as prophet-martyr, see D'Angelo, *Moses* 4 and 257.

32. Compare Exod. 33-34; Num. 12.6-8; and Deut. 34.5-10.

33. D'Angelo, *Moses* 249-54.

34. *Ibid.*, 254-58.

35. A great deal has been written about Melchizedek in Heb. We are convinced that he is not important to the author in and of himself, but only as a shadowy *Doppelgänger* of Christ. We can only cite a few references here: J. Fitzmyer, 'Now this Melchizedek. . . (Heb. 7.1)', *CBQ* 25 (1963) 305-21; M. de Jonge and A.S. van der Woude, '11QMelchizedek and the NT', *NTS* 12 (1965-66) 301-26; M. Delcor, 'Melchizedek from Genesis to the Qumran Texts and the Epistle to the Hebrews', *JSJ* 2 (1971) 115-35; E. Demarest, *A History of Interpretation of Hebrews 7.1-10 from the Reformation to the Present* (Tübingen: Mohr, 1976); F.L. Horton, *The Melchizedek Tradition: A Critical Examination of the Sources to the 5th Century A.D. and in the Epistle to the Hebrews* (Cambridge: Cambridge University Press, 1976).

36. D.M. Hay, *Glory at the Right Hand* (SBLMS 18; Nashville: Abingdon, 1973) 144-45. This does not imply our agreement with Hay's position that in Heb Jesus received sonship and priesthood only at the ascension.

37. 'Merciful covenant love/faithfulness'. See A. Stadelmann, 'Zur Christologie des Hebräerbriefes in der neueren Diskussion', in *Theologische Berichte* (ed. J. Pfammatter and F. Furger; Zürich: Benzinger, 1973) 2. 194: '. . . Das Bundesthema (wird) diskret vorbereitet'.

38. See Laub, *Bekenntnis* 88-90.

39. See pp. 22-23 above.

40. See D'Angelo, *Moses* 127-142; Sowers, *Hermeneutics* 116-18; Dey, *Intermediary* 174-77.

41. According to Hay, *Glory*, Ps. 110 was probably first used to legitimate a king of Judah in the pre-exilic period and was later applied to the Messiah and persons enjoying God's special favour (p. 33). Psalm 110 could be called the most important Scripture text in Heb. because it runs through much of the text like a red thread. But the author is only interested in two verses: *v. 1*: 1.3, 13; 8.1; 10.12-13; 12.2. . . always introduced at crucial junctures in the argument; *v. 4*: 5.6, 10; 6.20, 7.11, 7.17, 20-21, 24, 28. . . predominantly in ch. 7. Thus the thesis of G.W. Buchanan, *To the Hebrews* (AB 36; Garden City: Doubleday, 1972) to the effect that Heb. is an extended midrash on Ps. 110, is overstated.

42. The Scripture reads ἱερεύς, not ἀρχιερεύς, but this does not seem to bother the author of Heb.

43. See W.G. Johnsson, *Hebrews* (Knox Preaching Guides; Atlanta: John Knox, 1980) 48.

44. Hay, Glory 153.

45. *Ibid.*

46. See C.R. Koester, *The Tabernacle in the New Testament and Intertestamental Jewish Literature* (Ph.D. Dissertation, Union Theological Seminary, New York, 1986) 180-222. To appear in an enlarged form in the CBQMS in 1989-90.

47. This was stressed by Bernard Anderson in private conversation (October 1985).

48. See above, Chapters 2 Section B, 4 Section A (5), 5 Section B. Also J.W. Thompson, *That Which Abides: Some Metaphysical Assumptions in the Epistle to the Hebrews* (Ph.D. Dissertation, Vanderbilt University, 1974) esp. ch. 6 for the concept of 'abiding' in Heb.; also D'Angelo, *Moses* 229.

49. As Koester points out, the author is not consistent in his presentation of the features of the Tabernacle and one should not expect an exact correspondence between the earthly and the heavenly Tent. In fact the latter seems to lack the bipartite structure of the former (*Tabernacle* 203).

50. See below, Chapter 5 Section B.

51. See below, Chapter 5 Section C.

52. See C. Wolff, *Jeremia im Frühjudentum und Urchristentum* (TU 118;

Berlin: Akademie, 1976) 143-45; McCullough, 'Quotations' 364-67; F.F. Bruce, *The Epistle to the Hebrews* (NICNT; Grand Rapids: Eerdmans, 1964) 168-69, 237-38.

53. Caird, 'Method' 49. But Heb. never deals with the question (perhaps already implicit in Jeremiah) of how God could have given an inherently faulty covenant. As we saw above, the tension between this verdict, along with the affirmations that the Hebrew Scriptures are God's Word, and the belief that the old covenant was a God-given prefiguration of the NC is never resolved in Heb (see Loader, *Sohn* 258).

54. English translation by William L. Holladay, sent to me in private correspondence in the form of notes in preparation for his Hermeneia commentary on the book of Jeremiah. He distinguishes a prose and a poetry section and isolates several chiasms within each section (cf. my markings on the righthand side). I have followed his indentations of the text and have isolated the four occurrences of 'oracle of Yahweh'. The four categories of promise, which make up the NC, have been inserted into Holladay's text from Levin, *Verheissung* 268, for the purposes of subsequent discussion.

55. See W.L. Holladay, 'The Years of Jeremiah's Preaching', *Int* 37 (1983) 146-59.

56. J. Mejía, 'La Problématique de l'ancienne et de la nouvelle alliance dans Jérémie xxi 31-34 et quelques autres textes', *VTSup* 32 (ed. J.A. Emerton; Congress Volume Vienna 1980; Leiden: Brill, 1981) 272. W.E. Lemke, 'Jeremiah 31.31-34', *Int* 37 (1983) 183-87, lists elements of *continuity* and of *discontinuity* with the old order in the NC on p. 186. See also W.D. Davies, *Torah in the Messianic Age and/or the Age to Come* (JBLMS 7; Philadelphia: SBL, 1952) 21-28, for the view that Jeremiah's NC tries to preserve *both* the letter and the spirit of Torah and for a convenient summary of earlier scholars' opinions.

57. On the differences between Jeremiah's oracle on the NC and the priestly 'everlasting covenant', see B.W. Anderson, 'The New Covenant and the Old', in *The Old Testament and Christian Faith* (ed. idem; New York: Harper & Row, 1963) 230-31. On ברית עלם see above, note 16.

58. So e.g. Volz: 'neue Menschen, die nicht anders können als gut sein', quoted by Schreiber, *Bund* 22.

Notes to Chapter 3

1. G.W.E. Nickelsburg, *Jewish Literature Between the Bible and the Mishnah* (Philadelphia: Fortress, 1981) discusses the material chronologically under historical periods; in *Jewish Writings of the Second Temple Period* (CRINT 2; ed. M.E. Stone; Philadelphia: Fortress, 1984) the division is for the most part by genre, while Josephus, Philo and the DSS are singled out in special chapters; translations of most of the primary texts can be found in

Old Testament Pseudepigrapha (ed. J.H. Charlesworth; 2 vols.; Garden City: Doubleday, 1983, 1985; henceforth OTP). For primary and secondary literature on the DSS see below, note 45.

2. See indices under 'covenant' in the works cited in the previous footnote and in the following concordances: *Concordance to the Apocrypha/ Deuterocanonical Books of the RSV* (Grand Rapids: Eerdmans, 1983); *Index Verborum in Libris Pseudepigraphis Usurpatorum* (ed. J.B. Bauer; appended to *Clavis Librorum Veteris Testamenti Apocryphorum Philologica*, ed. C.A. Wahl; Graz: Akademische Druck- u. Verlagsanstalt, 1972); *A Complete Concordance to Flavius Josephus* (ed. K.H. Rengstorf; 4 vols.; Leiden: Brill, 1973); *Index Philoneus* (ed. G. Mayer; Berlin: de Gruyter, 1974).

3. *Paul and Palestinian Judaism* (Philadelphia: Fortress, 1977).

4. See Sanders, *Paul*, ch. 1 and pp. 419-20 for details and exponents of the old biased view.

5. *La notion d'alliance dans le Judaisme aux abords de l'ère chrétienne* (Paris: Le Seuil, 1963).

6. Levin, *Verheissung* 260. The authenticity of Jer. 31.31-34—as a whole or in parts—has been and continues to be debated endlessly. H. Graf Reventlow admits that the question of the redactional history of the prophetic books is one of the most intractable problems in OT studies, for the solution of which suitable criteria are largely absent. He cites Jer. 31.31-34 as a classic example of the most varied judgments by scholars and concludes: 'Auch hier wird man mangels zwingender Gegengründe vorerst an der jeremianischen Herkunft festhalten können, da sich das Stück genau in die Botschaft des Propheten einfügt', in *Rechtfertigung im Horizont des Alten Testaments* (München: Kaiser, 1971) 62; so also Anderson, 'New' 229.

7. Levin, *Verheissung* 56-59.

8. W.L. Holladay, in private correspondence, 23 January 1984, to which he appended a rough draft of the section on Jer. 31.31-34 from his Hermeneia commentary on Jeremiah. For Holladay's translation see above, Chapter 1 Excursus I.

9. This view is put forth by C. Wolff (in *Jeremiah*; on the NC, see pp. 116-47). He would deny any relationship to Jeremiah, whenever there are no clear quotations or references to the specific *content* of Jeremiah's prophecy, especially the *Torahverheissung* and the *Erkenntnisverheisswung* (for these labels see Levin, *Verheissung* 268 and above, excursus to ch. 2). In Wolff's opinion this is so at Qumran, in Paul and in the Last Supper accounts. We hold that the opposite view is much more plausible, namely that Jer. 31.31-34 stands in the *background* whenever the *NC phrase* occurs. For this position see Levin, *Verheissung* 266, quoted below, Chapter 4 Section A (5) (a).

10. Schreiber, *Bund* 24-32.

11. Schreiber, *Bund* 24. For selected references see above, Chapter 2 note 16.

12. See Schreiber, *Bund* 24-25 (my translation).

13. For a critique of this common bias in older scholarship, see G. Klinzing, *Die Umdeutung des Kultus in der Qumrangemeinde und im Neuen Testament* (Göttingen: Vandenhoeck & Ruprecht, 1971) 143-47; also Johnsson, *Defilement* 68-76.

14. See e.g. the famous new heart/heart of flesh; new spirit-passages in Ezek. 11.19-20; 16.60; 18.31; 36.28-38. S. Mandelkern (ed.), *Veteris Testamenti Concordantiae Hebraicae atque Chaldaicae* (Leipzig: Veit, 1896) 627-31 shows the abundance of phrases pertaining to the inner disposition/heart/seat if the will in the Hebrew Bible.

15. See C. Wolff, *Jeremiah* 117-19. For an insightful comparison between the return and restoration envisaged in Deut. 4.25-31; 30.1-14 and the completely new creation necessitated by the premises of Jer. 31.31-34, see A. Schenker, 'Unwiderrufliche Umkehr und neuer Bund', *Freiburger Zeitschrift für Philosophie und Theologie* 27 (1980) 93-106.

16. O.S. Wintermute, in *OTP* 2.35.

17. *Ibid.*, 2.37; in *Writings* (ed. Stone) *Jub.* is treated under 'The Bible Rewritten and Expanded' (97-104), not under 'Apocalyptic Literature'.

18. See *OTP* 2.47.

19. See *OTP* 2.38; Sanders, *Paul* 372-74, 385.

20. So labelled by R.H. Charles, quoted in *OTP* 2.44.

21. Jaubert, *Alliance* 115; but see Nickelsburg, *Literature* 79, who speaks of an 'unnamed sect', related to the authors of parts of Daniel and 1 Enoch.

22. See *OTP* 2.44; Nickelsburg, in *Writings* (ed. Stone) 103; Sanders, *Paul* 385.

23. Schreiber, *Bund* 26.

24. See Schreiber, *Bund* 26-28. In fact C. Wolff's analysis (in *Jeremia* 122-24) shows the absence of any influence, not merely of Jer. 31.31-34, but of the entire book of Jeremiah on *Jubilees* as a whole.

25. See Schreiber, *Bund* 28-29. Below, in Chapters 5-6 (*passim*), we shall see that Heb. combines Jeremiah's prophecy on the NC with *cultic* ideas. But the author envisages a *new* cult, bearing no relation to the old one.

26. Sanders, *Paul* 373.

27. *OTP* 2.46-47.

28. *Ibid.*, 48; Sanders *Paul* 372.

29. C. Wolff examines the same territory as Schreiber does in his discussion of the NC (in *Jeremia* 116-47). But while the other two passages in Bar. 2 and *Jub.* 1 are given due consideration by Wolff, *4 Ezra* 6 appears nowhere.

30. *4 Ezra* = chs. 3-14 of the Christian apocryphal book called 2 Esdras in Latin manuscripts. See *OTP* 1.516-17.

31. See *ibid.*, 1.520; Nickelsburg, *Literature* 287-88; Stone in *Writings* (ed. Stone) 412.

32. B.M. Metzger, in *OTP* 1.522, speaks of a growing consensus toward regarding *4 Ezra* as a literary unit.

33. Sanders, *Paul* 418 (his emphasis).

34. *Paul* 409.

35. 'Covenantal nomism' (defined by Sanders, *Paul* 422): '(1) God has chosen Israel and (2) given the law. The law implies both (3) God's promise to maintain the election and (4) the requirement to obey. (5) God rewards obedience and punishes transgression. (6) The law provides for means of atonement, and atonement results in (7) maintenance or re-establishment of the covenantal relationship. (8) All those who are maintained in the covenant by obedience, atonement and God's mercy belong to the group which will be saved. . . . Election and ultimately salvation are considered to be by God's mercy rather than human achievement'.

36. *OTP* 1.535.

37. See Schreiber, *Bund* 29.

38. Schreiber, *Bund* 30.

39. *OTP* 1.533.

40. Schreiber, *Bund* 31.

41. Schreiber, *Bund* 32.

42. Jaubert, *Alliance* 447.

43. Levin, *Verheissung* 266 (his emphasis).

44. For our own opinion about the original meaning of Jer. 31.31-34 see above, Excursus I.

45. For general accounts of the Qumran sect's life-style and its writings see pertinent sections in Nickelsburg, *Literature*; Stone (ed.), *Writings*; Sanders, *Paul*; F.M. Cross, *The Ancient Library of Qumran & Modern Biblical Studies* (rev. edn; Grand Rapids: Baker Book House, 1958, 1961); G. Vermes, *The Dead Sea Scrolls: Qumran in Perspective* (rev. edn; Philadelphia: Fortress, 1977); *idem*, *The Dead Sea Scrolls in English* (3rd edn; Sheffield: JSOT, 1987); For primary texts from cave I and a German translation, see *Die Texte aus Qumran* (ed. E. Lohse; München: Kösel, 1971); for CD see C. Rabin, *The Zadokite Documents* (2nd edn; Oxford: Clarendon, 1958) and P.R. Davies, *The Damascus Covenant* (JSOT Sup 25; Sheffield: JSOT, 1982); for further information, see J.A. Fitzmyer, *The Dead Sea Scrolls: Major Publications and Tools for Study* (Missoula: Scholars, 1977).

46. For different CD manuscripts see Lohse, *Texte* 66-107. We cannot here enter into the complicated question whether CD was composed at Qumran or appropriated by the sectaries from elsewhere. (For the latter view see P.R. Davies, *Damascus* 202-204). We know CD existed by the second century BCE.

47. M.P. Horgan, *Pesharim: Qumran Interpretation of Biblical Books* (CBQMS 8; Washington, D.C.: CBA, 1979) 13.

48. Fitzmyer, *Tools*, index p. 166. It is important to note that the book of Jeremiah is not nearly as popular in the DSS as some other prophetic works

such as Hab., Isa. Mic., Nah., Zeph. C. Wolff (*Jeremia* 130) concludes his survey of the DSS by saying that the only significant uses of Jeremiah (stemming mainly from the 'confessions') occur in 1QH, in the parts usually attributed to the Teacher of Righteousness. Both C. Wolff (*Jeremia* 125, 130) and R.F. Collins ('The Berith-Notion of the CD Covenant and its Comparison with the NT', *ETL* 39 [1963] 572-75) deny a relationship between the NC in CD and Jer. 31.31-34 on the grounds that (1) the Qumranites usually reveal their biblical sources and (2) the specific content of Jeremiah's prophecy is absent at Qumran and even partially contradicted by the insistence on instruction of Torah.

49. For references to these expressions see Sanders, *Paul* 241-42; K.G. Kuhn, *Konkordanz zu den Qumrantexten* (Göttingen: Vandenhoeck & Ruprecht, 1960) 36-37; for a good overview of OT covenant-types and expressions used in CD see Collins, 'Berith-Notion' 555-94.

50. Sanders, *Paul* 266-67.

51. For the text see below Chapter 3 Excursus II.

52. See below Chapter 3 Excursus II.

53. Vermes, *English* 106. See also the joining of columns 7-8 (MS A) and 19 (MS B) in Rabin's critical edition (*Zadokite* 26-36).

54. As translated by Vermes, *English* 106. Unless specified all translations are mine.

55. For a summary of his argument see Sanders, *Paul* 254-55. We have given a very simplified picture of the various groups of Qumran's enemies and cannot here enter into the complex historical questions—still debated among scholars—of their identity and of the different splinter groups which may at various times have joined and left the sect.

56. D. Flusser, 'The Dead Sea Sect and Pre-Pauline Christianity', in *Aspects of the Dead Sea Scrolls* (Scripta Hierosolymitana 4; ed. C. Rabin and Y. Yadin; Jerusalem: Magnes, 1958) p. 241.

57. Flusser, 'Sect' 237-38.

58. See e.g. Sanders, *Paul* 257-70; Stone (ed.), *Writings* 536-38.

59. Sanders, *Paul* 269.

60. See Chapter 3 section 2 (b) below.

61. See above, Chapter 2 section C.

62. V.D. Verbrugge, 'Towards a New Interpretation of Hebrews 6.4-6', *CTJ* 15 (1980) 61-73, finds echoes of Isa. 5.1-7 in Heb. 6.6-7, and interprets 6.4-6 in light of this covenant-community context (*ibid.*, 64-65).

63. Flusser, 'Sect' 236.

64. S.J.D. Cohen, 'The Significance of Yavneh: Pharisees, Rabbis, and the End of Jewish Sectarianism', *HUCA* 55 (1984) 47-48.

65. Flusser, 'Sect' 235-36.

66. Cross, *Library* 100-103; Klinzing, *Umdeutung* 41-43.

67. The impact of the unpublished 4QMMT remains to be seen. Announced for publication in 1988-89 by J. Strugnell, it seemingly lists some

136   *The New Covenant in Hebrews*

difficulties that the sectaries have with the procedures at the Jerusalem Temple.

68. Paul: 1 Cor. 3.16-17, 6.19; 2 Cor. 6.16; (see also Eph. 2.19-22; 1 Pet. 2.4-10; Mk 14.58). For 1QS see Klinzing, *Umdeutung* ch. 3, pp. 50-93.

69. John 2.21. We are not convinced by A. Vanhoye's exegesis of Heb. 9.11 ('Par la tente plus grande et parfaite. . . ', *Bib* 46 [1965] 1-28), according to which the Tent corresponds to the resurrected body of Christ.

70. See above, Chapter 2 section C and below, Chapter 5 section B.

71. On this see Klinzing, *Umdeutung* ch. 4, pp. 93-106.

72. See J. Thurén, *Das Lobopfer der Hebräer* (Åbo: Åbo Akademi, 1973). On Eucharist, see below, chapter 5 section D.

73. For C. Wolff the Qumran covenant is not a new one in Jeremiah's sense, but is rather understood in strict continuity with the Patriarchal covenant. The remnant at 'Damascus' withdrew from the old cultic center and renewed the old broken covenant on behalf of all Israel (see *Jeremia* 127, and *ibid.* n. 1, for other representatives of this view). Hillers calls the Qumran covenant the 'charter of a repristination movement', similar to the reforms under Josiah and Ezra (*Covenant* 178).

74. See our discussion above, Chapter 2 section B . But compare Mt. 5.17-19 for a Christian view closer to Qumran.

75. As Collins does in 'Berith-Notion' pp. 568, 575. He contradicts himself on p. 577. 'The community had a covenant renewed by God'.

76. Kuhn, *Konkordanz* 67; I was unable to locate his reference to 1QSb 5.5 anywhere. For special treatment of the ברית כהנת עלם, see N. Ilg, 'Überlegungen zum Verständnis von *berît* in den Qumrântexten', in *Qumrân: Sa piété, sa théologie et son milieu* (ed. M. Delcor; BETL 46; Leuven: Leuven University, 1978) 257-63.

77. Kuhn, *Kondordanz* 67-68, and above, chapter 3 section B.

78. Chapter 3 section B.

79. Collins, 'Berith-Notion' 577.

80. For this interpretation of 'Damascus' see Collins, 'Berith-Notion' 580-82. We are not convinced, however, by Collins' arguments against assuming that Jer. 31.31-34 lies in the background of CD's use of 'NC' (572-75); indeed he himself admits that 'most probably this expectation was ultimately based on the prophecy of Jer. 31, 31 . . . ' (p. 580).

81. 'Contrasting Notions of Covenant and Law in the Texts from Qumran', *RevQ* 8 (1972-75) 361-80.

82. Huntjens, 'Contrasting' 363-64, based on CD 6.14, 18-19a; 19.33-34a; 20.11-12.

83. *Ibid.*, 368.

84. *Ibid.*, 378.

85. Huntjens, 'Contrasting' 375.

86. *Ibid.*, 377.

87. See above, Chapter 2 section D.

88. R.A. Harrisville ('The Concept of Newness in the New Testament', *JBL* 74 (955) 69-79) shows that the meaning of the vernacular νέος and the literary καινός interpenetrate already in the LXX and that one cannot distinguish newness of quality καινός and of time νέος in the NT, the papyri and the early Fathers.

89. E.A.C. Pretorius, '*Diatheke* the Epistle to the Hebrews', *Neot* 5 (1975) 47-48.

90. A.F. Segal, 'Covenant in Rabbinic Writings', *SR* 14/1 (1985) 54.

91. W.D. Davies, *Torah* 85-86.

92. See W.D. Davies, *Torah* 86.

93. See Segal, 'Covenant' 54; Sanders, *Paul* 76.

94. W.D. Davies, *Torah* 53.

95. Cohen, 'Yavneh' 50.

96. W.D. Davies, *Torah* 53.

97. Segal, 'Covenant' 54.

98. See Sanders, *Paul* 12-13.

99. As noted by Sanders, *Paul* 13, as part of his plea for 'holistic comparison of patterns of religion' (12-21).

100. See Segal, 'Covenant' 54: 'she was only able to put together a short description of the use of the term covenant in rabbinic Judaism'; Sanders, *Paul* 50-51, criticizes Jaubert's approach: 'Thus we see that the traditional line of Christian scholarship on this point continues unchecked in Jaubert's work, even though Schoeps. . . had firmly shown that the supposed link of election with works is not anchored in the texts and that election depends on grace'.

101. Sanders, *Paul* p. 82.

102. See Sanders, *Paul* 233-38.

103. See *ibid.*, 93-94, 236-37.

104. Segal, 'Covenant' 55.

105. *Ibid.*

106. Segal, 'Covenant' 57, see also 62.

107. Schreiber, *Bund* 33-40; See Strack-Billerbeck 3.704.

108. W.D. Davies, *Torah* 71-72.

109. *Torah* 72.

110. *Torah* 69-70.

111. See Schreiber, *Bund* 39-40.

112. Schreiber, *Bund* 33, 39.

113. W.D. Davies, *Torah* 87-89.

114. As quoted in W.D. Davies, *Torah*, p. 90 (emphasis mine). See also J. Jeremias, *The Eucharistic Words of Jesus* (transl. from German 3rd edn; Philadelphia: Fortress, 1966) p. 195 n. 2.

115. C. Wolff, *Jeremia* 146 n. 3.

116. See Reventlow, *Rechtfertigung* 65.

117. See e.g. Schreiber, *Bund* 54: 'Es liegt im Wesen des neuen Bundes,

dass er nicht gebrochen werden kann'. Also above, Chapter 1 Excursus I.
118. See the questions raised above in section A.
119. See Levin, *Verheissung* 266 n. 2; Collins, 'Berith-Notion' 594.
120. CD translations by P.R. Davies, *Damascus* 249, 255, 261, 263 (emphasis mine). The 3 asterisks indicate 3 different warnings to 3 different groups in CD 19.33b–20.34 (see *Damascus* 121, 173).
121. Translation by Horgan, *Pesharim* 12-13 (emphasis and the three asterisks are mine; for the three groups of traitors see above, Chapter 3 section B (1) on 1QpHab).

Notes to Chapter 4

1. See e.g. Luz, 'Bund' 318; Pretorius, '*Diathēkē*' p. 37; Levin, *Verheissung* 267.
2. For the statistics on διαθήκη see above, Chapter 1 note 5; for references to the literary division OT/NT see above, Chapter 1 note 2.
3. 'Gal III 15ff.' 66-96; opposing interpretations and underlying arguments are given in the body of this article. On this passage see also Grässer, *Bund* 56-69, who translates 'Testament'.
4. See J.J. Hughes, 'Gal III 15ff.' 68.
5. 'Gal III 15ff.' 70.
6. J.L. Martyn's phrase, oral tradition.
7. J.J. Hughes, 'Gal III 15ff.' 82.
8. 'The Allegory of Abraham, Sarah, and Hagar in the Argument of Galatians', in *Rechtfertigung* (ed. J. Friedrich et al.; Käsemann Festschrift; Göttingen: Mohr, 1976) 1-16.
9. A.R. Brown, in a paper circulated informally in J.L. Martyn's Galatians Seminar, Union Theological Seminary, New York, Spring 1984.
10. Contra E. de W. Burton ('a supplementary argument') as quoted in Barrett, 'Allegory' 2; and A. Oepke ('Diktierpause?, nachträglicher Gedankenblitz?') as quoted in Luz, 'Bund' 319; and contra Luz's own 'Hilfsgedanke' ('Bund' 319).
11. On this expression for Paul's opponents in Galatia see J.L. Martyn, 'A Law-Observant Mission to Gentiles: The Background of Galatians', *Michigan Quarterly Review* 22 (1983) 221-36; and *idem*, 'Apocalyptic Antinomies in Paul's Letter to the Galatians', *NTS* 31 (1985) 410-24. The Teachers were Jewish-Christian missionaries insisting upon the need for circumcision and strict adherence to the Law for Gentile Christian converts. This is confirmed by F. Mussner, 'Gesetz—Abraham—Israel', *Kairos* 25 (1983) 206.
12. See Barrett, 'Allegory' 9.
13. Martyn, 'Antinomies' 419.
14. Martyn, 'Antinomies' 419.

15. Barrett, 'Allegory' 12.
16. M.C. Callaway, *Sing O Barren One: A Study in Comparative Midrash* (SBLDS 91; Atlanta: Scholars, 1986) 173-74.
17. *Sing* 175 (emphasis mine).
18. *Sing* 169-77.
19. See Barrett, 'Allegory' 9-10.
20. It is noteworthy, however, that Paul never uses the terms 'Jew' or 'Gentile' in this passage.
21. See Martyn, 'Antinomies' 419.
22. A.R. Brown, 'Seminar' 8-9.
23. See Martyn, 'Antinomies' 416-18.
24. 'Antinomies' 421.
25. On different attempts to characterize the nature of Paul's opponents in this section of 2 Cor., see S. Schulz, 'Die Decke des Moses', *ZNW* 49 (1958) 1-20; D. Georgi, *Die Gegner des Paulus im 2. Korintherbrief* (WMANT 11; Neukirchen-Vluyn: Neukirchener, 1964); G. Friedrich, 'Die Gegner des Paulus im 2. Korintherbrief', in *Abraham unser Vater* (ed. O. Betz et al.; O. Michel Festschrift; Leiden: Brill, 1964) 181-215. It seems that the super-apostles (2 Cor. 11.5; 12.11) are Jewish Christian itinerant preachers, related to circles of Hellenistic apologia and imitators of their techniques (i.e. speeches, scriptural exegesis, miracles, healings, visions under the influence of the Spirit). Jesus is probably viewed as one of a series of divine men—heroes of the past—in whose pneumatic power the super-apostles share during their transfigurations. Hence Jesus' suffering and death are deemphasized. On the concept of θεῖος ἀνήρ see 'Jesus als "Göttlicher Mensch"' in H. Koester and J.M. Robinson (eds.), *Entwicklungslinien durch die Welt des frühen Christentums* (Tübingen: Mohr, 1971) 201-204, and further literature there. Some would however question the applicability of this specific concept and label in the first century CE: see D.L. Tiede, *The Charismatic Figure as Miracle Worker* (SBLDS 1; Missoula: Scholars, 1972).
26. The extent of the *Vorlage* with which Paul is working is debated in the literature, but most interpreters believe that he is in fact reshaping exegetical traditions familiar to the Corinthians. See e.g. P. Vielhauer, 'Paulus und das Alte Testament', in *Studien zur Geschichte und Theologie der Reformation* (ed. L. Abramowski and J.F.G. Göters; E. Bizer Festschrift; Neukirchen-Vluyn: Neukirchener, 1969) 47. Luz ('Bund' 324) wants to deny the *polemical* character of 2 Cor. 3.4-18 and claims that Paul is in positive agreement with his *Vorlage*. With Friedrich ('Gegner' 184), Georgi (*Gegner* e.g. 266-73) and Grässer (*Bund* 78, 87) we are convinced about Paul's polemical intent in this chapter which prepares for the polemics of 2 Cor. 4 (see Georgi, *Gegner* 269, 279).
27. See J.L. Martyn, 'Epistemology at the Turn of the Ages: 2 Corinthians 5.16', in *Christian History and Interpretation* (ed. W.R. Farmer et al.; J. Knox

Festschrift; Cambridge: Cambridge University Press, 1967) 271-73. Georgi (*Gegner* 268) and Grässer (*Bund* 78) include 2.14-7.4 in this section.

28. συστατικός is a NT hapax legomenon in 2 Cor. 3.1, but συνίστημι is a favourite term in 2 Corinthians, and in the sense of 'commending oneself' it is confined to this epistle (see Luz, 'Bund' 323 n. 18). Seven of the eight occurrences are in 2.14-6.10; 10-13 where Paul is combating people who apparently had a habit of commending themselves and is trying to show that the only valid recommendation is from God.

29. With Luz ('Bund' 322) we prefer the reading ἡμῶν of p. 46. This antithesis is picked up in 5.12 where Paul distinguishes between his opponents' illegitimate boast ἐν προσώπῳ and his own/the Corinthians' legitimate pride ἐν καρδία.

30. See Georgi's word statistics and analysis, *Gegner* 268-69, and Martyn, 'Epistemology' *passim*.

31. Compare 2 Cor. 2.14-17 for a similar paradox.

32. Luz sees a problem in this transition: 'Wie kommt es zu dem unvermittelten Umschlag phänomenologisch-deskriptiver in heilsgeschichtliche Kategorien?' ('Bund' 323).

33. For this expression, see, R.W. Thurston, 'Midrash and "Magnet" Words in the New Testament', *EvQ* 51 (1979) 22-39.

34. For Grässer Exod. 31.18/Deut. 9.10 have been worked into the antithetical context of Ezek. 11.19; 36.26, while Jer. 31.31-34 is ignored (*Bund* 81). See also Prov. 3.3; 7.3.

35. Friedrich ('Gegner' 185-87) plausibly attributes the frequency of Paul's polemical use of the διακον- wordgroup in 2 Corinthians to his adoption of 'Schlagworte der Gegner' (186). The super-apostles exercises their διακονία through powerful pneumatic propaganda demonstrations, in aggressive competition with other missionaries.

36. W.C. van Unnik, 'La conception paulinienne de la nouvelle alliance', in *Littérature et théologie pauliniennes* (ed. A. Descamps et al.; Desclée de Brouwer, 1960) 119.

37. In his attempt to prove that vv. 4-18 are 'thetisch und lehrhaft', not polemical ('Bund' 324), Luz wavers in his assessment of Paul's intent. First, he claims that the glory of the Mosaic covenant is 'unbestritten' (even in Paul's eyes, p. 324), then he admits that this glory is swallowed up with the old covenant (pp. 325-26). (For a similar critique see Grässer, *Bund* 88, n. 366.) Georgi is more precise than Luz, when he stresses that the difference in *content* between the covenants is the basis for the proof of the superiority of the NC; *Gegner* 265, n. 1: '... Was zunächst noch den Anschein gemeinsamer Struktur erweckt hatte (die *doxa*) (ist) nicht nur von unterschiedlicher Stärke (3.10), sondern auch... von unterschiedlicher Funktion und Art (3.11ff.)'.

38. But Vielhauer ('Paulus' 47) exaggerates: 'der neue [Bund] bedeutet nicht die Wiederherstellung des obsolet *gewordenen* [his emphasis] alten—

denn dieser ist von Anfang an ein Dienst des Todes und der Verdammnis-
...' (Grässer, *Bund* 89 quotes this with approval). We would rather say that
Paul only reflects on the old covenant *in light of the NC*; he is not interested
in the beginning of the old covenant in its own right (see Luz, 'Bund' 326,
esp. n. 32; and pp. 335-36).
39. See Georgi, *Gegner* 274, and Vielhauer, 'Paulus' 47.
40. See Vielhauer, 'Paulus' 48, and Luz, 'Bund' 327.
41. This parallels the distinction between ἡ γραφή (Gal. 3.8, 22; 4.30)=ὁ
νόμος (in Gal. 4.21) that still speaks as ἐπαγγελία, and anarthrous νόμος (in
Gal. 4.21), which is abrogated.
42. The word νόμος is absent from this epistle, but Luz ('Bund' 325-26)
seems justified in his attempt to understand γράμμα as the negative, death-
imparting side of νόμος. We are reminded, once again, of the internal
antinomy within νόμος that we encountered in Gal. (see pp. 132-34 above),
and with which Paul would later wrestle in Rom. 7. See the discussion in
Grässer, *Bund* 83-85.
43. Vielhauer, 'Paulus' 48 (emphasis mine). Unlike his opponents, Paul
shows no interest in cataloguing the events of the past and its heroes.
44. See Martyn, 'Epistemology' 279-87.
45. On the tensions experienced by Paul as a consequence of the partial
inception of the new age, see also Van Unnik, 'Conception' 124-25.
46. See Georgi, *Gegner* 268-73; Martyn agrees in 'Epistemology' 28-84.
47. As D'Angelo (*Moses* 195) puts it, in her discussion of 2 Corinthians
3.
48. Martyn, 'Epistemology' 286.
49. *Ibid.*
50. See Georgi, *Gegner* 290 n. 2; 'Dadurch, daß Paulus weit mehr als seine
Gegner die Schwachheit Jesu betont, nimmt er das irdische Geschick Jesu
viel ernster als sie, so sehr, daß er es *als sein eigenes Schicksal zu übernehmen
wagt*' (emphasis mine).
51. With the majority of MSS. we would favour the reading αἱ διαθῆκαι,
even though ἡ διαθήκη is attested in p. 46.
52. See e.g. J.C. Beker, *Paul the Apostle* (Philadelphia: Fortress, 1980) 94-
100. Some recent attempts to grapple with the differences between Galatians
and Romans are: (1) development has occurred in Paul's thought between
Galatians (more discontinuity) and Romans (more continuity and more
positive statements about the Law)—see H. Hübner, *Das Gesetz bei Paulus*
(2nd edn; FRLANT 119; Göttingen: Vandenhoeck & Ruprecht, 1980); (2)
Paul has some basic convictions, is coherent, but not systematic and must be
interpreted contextually—see E.P. Sanders, *Paul, the Law and the Jewish
People* (Philadelphia: Fortress, 1983); (3) no development in Paul, inconsistency
between Galatians and Romans—see H. Räisänen, *Paul and the Law*
(WUNT 29; Tübingen: Mohr, 1983). While in our opinion Paul has to be
read contextually, we consider it plausible that Romans reflects Paul's
having 'learned' something from the Galatian controversy.

53. Apart from 1 Thess. 1.4, ἐκλογή occurs only here in Paul: Rom. 9.11; 11.5, 7, 28; while there are three other uses in Paul, κλῆσις is found only once in Romans (11.29); of the fourteen uses of the ἐλε- root in Paul, eight are found here: ἐλεέω- Rom. 9.15, 16, 18; 11.30, 31, 32, ἔλεος—Rom. 9.23; 11.31.

54. See Levin, *Verheissung* 268.

55. Section B of this chapter.

56. See 'Conception' 118-19.

57. 'Bund' 322; see n. 16 for references to Ezekiel.

58. Grässer, *Bund* 67-68 n. 284, n. 290; see also pp. 76, n. 320; 81, n. 335; 82, n. 338.

59. See above, Chapter 3 section A.

60. Levin, *Verheissung* 266. The same holds good for the Qumran texts, which, like Paul, fail to quote Jer. 31.31-34. For a contrary opinion see C. Wolff, *Jeremia* 116-47.

61. See our earlier remarks about the use of Jer. 31.31-34 in Heb. above, Chapter 2 section D.

62. See e.g. the parallel thought processes in the past unreal conditions of Gal. 3.21 and Heb. 7.11.

63. See sections (b), (c), (d) below. But in Romans 9-11 covenant language is used to underline continuity in God's relationship to Israel.

64. Levin, *Verheissung* 268, and above, Excursus I.

65. See below, Chapter 5 section C. On Paul's 'Individual-Prinzip des Heils' see Grässer, *Bund* 77.

66. Grässer, *Bund* 104 (his italics).

67. See Van Unnik, 'Conception' 119 for Paul, but the same holds true for Heb.

68. But in Heb. 7 Abraham becomes a representative of the *old* order, see above, Chapter 2 section A.

69. Whatever glory Moses had, is eclipsed by Christ's glory in 2 Cor. 3 and Heb. 3.2-6. For other limited *positive* functions of Moses in Heb. see above, Chapter 2 section B.

70. It should be noted, however, that he never explicitly identifies Sarah with the NC or Hagar with the old covenant.

71. For the metaphysical terminology of Heb. see above, Chapter 2.

72. See above, Chapter 4 section A (2).

73. See e.g. Heb. 5.5; 6.14 (God); 3.7; 10.15 (the Holy Spirit).

74. For Paul see: Luz, 'Bund' 327; Vielhauer, 'Paulus' 48; Grässer, *Bund* 91. For Heb.: Luz, 'Bund' 333; Grässer, *Bund* 97.

75. See above, Chapter 4 section A (1) (2).

76. See above, Chapter 2 section A on the Patriarchal covenant and *epangelia* in Heb. Luz ('Bund' 334) also detects certain inconsistencies in the author's treatment of the *epangelia*-motif which he allocates to tradition (realization on earth) and redaction (heavenly future gift).

77. Grässer, *Bund* 68 (his emphasis). But in *Romans* the continuity with Israel's history is affirmed by Paul's retelling of that history from a 'Christian' perspective and thus the 'NC'—as the earlier, Abrahamic one—would be part of that history if Paul had used that terminology there. As for the Decalogue, it remains binding after Christ (13.8-10).

78. See above, Chapter 2 section B.

79. On the Law see above, Chapter 2 section B.

80. D.R. Hillers, *Covenant: The History of a Biblical Idea* (Baltimore: Johns Hopkins, 1969) 180.

81. See e.g. D'Angelo, *Moses* 256: 'Hebrews' view of the law stresses the continuity between the two covenants, whereas Paul stresses the discontinuity'. Hillers, *Covenant* 182-83: 'In Hebrews the stress is on the new as foreshadowed in the old. The new covenant is better than the Sinai covenant, but it does not contradict it; it fulfils it and reveals its deepest meaning. In Paul... the two are contrasted so sharply that there is no apparent continuity left between the Sinai covenant and the new covenant,... the Sinai covenant is only an episode, an interruption in the history of faith'.

82. See e.g. Luz, 'Bund' 332: 'So scheint die Antithese zwischen altem und neuem Bund im Hebr. fast noch radikaler durchgeführt als bei Paulus, denn die überkommene typologische Antithese wird durch die... hellenistisch-jüdischen Denkkategorie ontologisch untermauert'.

83. *Bund* 62: 'διαθήκη wird also als gemeinsamer Oberbegriff für Verheissung und Gesetz von Paulus fallengelassen'.

84. 'Bund' 332: 'Nirgends... erscheint im Hebr. "Bund" als beiden Heilssetzungen gemeinsame Strukturbezeichnung'.

85. Gal. 4.24 δύο; 2 Cor. 3.6 καινῆς 3.14 παλαιᾶς.

86. Heb. 8.7, 13; 9.1, 18: ἡ πρώτη and δευτέραη (8.7), both implying διαθήκη.

87. See the ἔχομεν-ἔχοντες-passages 4.14; 6.9, 18-19; 8.1; 10.19, 34; 12.1, 28; 13.10, 14 for the incipient enjoyment of heavenly realities; and W.G. Johnsson, 'The Pilgrimage Motif in the Book of Hebrews', *JBL* 97 (1978) 239-51. See also below, Chapter sections C, D.

88. Hence the attempt by T.J. Deidun (*New Covenant Morality in Paul*, AnBib 89 [Rome: Biblical Institute, 1981]) to make the NC *the* central category of Pauline thought, from which both the theological indicative and the moral imperative flow, seems farfetched.

89. Contra Grässer (*Bund* 96), who asserts that because Heb. retains the LXX meaning for διαθήκη, the author uses the concept 'nicht in eigener theologischer Ausprägung'.

90. G.W. MacRae, 'Heavenly Temple and Eschatology in the Letter to the Hebrews', *Semeia* 12 (1978) 179-99; see below, Chapter 6 p. 119.

91. See above, Chapter 2 section B, section A and note 82 in this Chapter; J.W. Thompson, *Beginnings* 11-16, and *idem*, *Metaphysical passim*.

92. See D'Angelo, *Moses* 229-31; Nomoto, 'Herkunft' 17-19; MacRae's article ('Heavenly') shows how the *spatial* dimension is found both in apocalyptic eschatology and in Alexandrian eschatology. More on this below, Chapter 5 section A and Chapter 6.

93. See above, Chapter 1 and Chapter 2 section B.

94. See below, Chapter 5 section A; Chapter 6, *passim*.

95. On this see above, Chapter 1 p. 13; Chapter 5 pp. 122-23 and Chapter 6 below.

96. J. Betz, *Eucharistie in der Schrift und Patristik* (4.4a of *Handbuch der Dogmengeschichte*, ed. M. Schmaus et al. [Freiburg: Herder, 1979]); H. Feld, *Das Verständnis des Abendmahls* (Darmstadt: Wissenschaftliche Buchgesellschaft, 1976); Grässer, *Bund* 115-27; F. Hahn, 'Die alttestamentlichen Motive in der urchristlichen Abendmahlsüberlieferung', *EvT* 27 (1967) 337-75; J. Jeremias, *Eucharistic*; F. Lang, 'Abendmahl und Bundesgedanke im NT', *EvT* 35 (1975) 524-38; H. Merklein, 'Erwägungen zur Überlieferung der neutestamentlichen Abendmahlstraditionen', *BZ* (N.F.) 21 (1977) 88-101, 235-44; X. Léon-Dufour, 'Le mystère du pain de vie (Jean VI)', *RSR* 46 (1958) 481-523; J.H.P. Reumann, *The Supper of the Lord* (Philadelphia: Fortress, 1985); J. Roloff, *Neues Testament* (Neukirchener Arbeitsbücher, 2nd edn [Neukirchen, 1979]) 211-27; K.H. Schelkle, 'Das Herrenmahl', in *Rechtfertigung* (ed. J. Friedrich et al.; E. Käsemann Festschrift [Tübingen: Mohr, 1976]) 385-402; E. Schweizer, 'Das Herrenmahl im NT', in *Neotestamentica* (Zürich: Zwingli, 1963) 344-70; V. Wagner, 'Der Bedeutungswandel von *berît ḥădāšâ* bei der Ausgestaltung der Abendmahlsworte', *EvT* 35 (1975) 538-44. Many of these works contain a section on possible roots for the Last Supper; in addition see H. Gese, in idem, *Zur biblischen Theologie* (München: Kaiser, 1977), 'Die Herkunft des Herrenmahls', 107-27, and K.G. Kuhn, 'Über den ursprünglichen Sinn des Abendmahls und sein Verhältnis zu den Gemeinschaftsmahlen der Sektenschrift', *EvT* 10 (1950-51) 508-27.

97. From Merklein, 'Erwägungen' 89-90.

98. See e.g. Schweizer, 'Herrenmahl' 347-59; Feld, *Verständnis* 31-39; Lang, 'Abendmahl' 529.

99. Merklein's reconstruction ('Erwägungen' 92-98) seems rather plausible.

100. Priority of Luke/Paul seems more likely to us; see Grässer, *Bund* 117; J. Betz, *Eucharistie* 5-7; Merklein, 'Erwägungen' 94-98.

101. Grässer, *Bund* 116. See also Levin, *Verheissung* 271.

102. Kuhn, 'Sinn' *passim*. It should be noted that Kuhn, and Merklein's chart on p. 81, fail to differentiate vicariousness (e.g. 1 Cor. 11.24) and expiation (e.g. Rom. 3.25; 4.25).

103. Hahn, 'Motive' 358.

104. Lang, 'Abendmahl' 537-38. See also Schweizer, 'Herrenmahl' 363.

105. *Ibid.*, 528; See also Grässer, *Bund* 122-23.

106. Its original locus and possible direction of the shift between bread and cup-words are of no concern to us here.

107. See Hahn, 'Motive' 358-66; Merklein, 'Überlegungen' 91; Schweizer, 'Herrenmahl' 361-63.

108. Wagner, 'Bedeutungswandel' 544 and *passim*, for the argument: notions of blood-sacrifice are secondary intrusions, which could not have happened in Palestine, for in Palestine it was understood that the NC has no connection to blood; hence the priority of the Luke/Paul strand (where the blood theme is clearly *added to* the NC-predicate) over the Mark/Matthew strand (where blood *is* the predicate; see (10) on the chart above, p. 81).

109. Grässer, *Bund* 126.

110. Grässer, *Bund* 120-27. When the Christ event is nonetheless linked to the NC in the Last Supper accounts, not much more than the 'Begriff διαθήκη' remains from the OT (p. 126).

111. See our questions above, Chapter 3 section A, p. 42.

112. See n. 110 here above, where Grässer grudgingly admits that this is in fact what happens later; the implication seems to be that Hellenistic Christians did not know any better, while Palestinians knew their OT and avoided such blunders.

With regard to the Qumran sectaries, Grässer's use of their example seems rather problematic in relation to Christian self-perception. What little we can surmise of possible contacts of groups of 'Christians' through and around the person of John the Baptist with groups in the Dead Sea area suggests a contest in terms of the *shared* biblical heritage and rival attempts at self-definition and articulation of one's faith by appeal to the familiar patrimony. Among these shared religious institutions and concepts were the Temple/Tabernacle, descent from Abraham and also the covenant relationship to the God of Israel.

The fact is that the NC idea appears only in the literary remains of two first century groups and we have suggested in the previous chapter that this is probably not mere historical accident. Neither the Qumranite nor the Christian *literature* use the NC concept with great frequency and in both collections there are large segments which never employ the term, but the literary remains may not give us the complete picture of community attitudes and self-perception. From our present vantage point, we can ascertain some of the differences between the views of these groups. For conceptual purposes we can conclude that the Qumranites probably thought more in terms of *renewal of the old Sinai covenant*, while at least some Christians must have meant something *wholly other, qualitatively new and definitive* by 'NC'. But since the NT usage of 'covenant' is by no means univocal, we cannot imply, as Grässer does, that the use of the phrase 'NC' is more appropriate and legitimate in the DSS than in the NT.

113. For an explanation see Merklein, 'Erwägungen' 235-38. (It would go beyond our scope to discuss the nature of that meal. See references above, note 96).

114. By simply positing these links we do not mean to suggest that the processes involved were simple or uniform.

115. Merklein, 'Erwägungen' 240-43.

116. Merklein, 'Erwägungen' 237; in this connection the logion about the erection of the kingdom (διατίθεμαι/διέθετό βασιλείαν) in Lk. 22.28-30 deserves attention for establishing the links (1) between Jesus' death and the initiation of the NC and (2) between the NC and the Last Supper tradition (see Hahn, 'Motive' 367-68). It is also noteworthy that John's Gospel, even though it does not report the words of institution, has its own version of the eucharistic formula in 6.51-58. If R.E. Brown is right in positing that this part of the Bread of Life discourse has been moved from the Last Supper context/the farewell discourse (see *The Gospel according to John* [AB 29; Garden City, N.Y.: Doubleday, 1966] 286-87), then the mention of καινὴ ἐντολή (Jn 13.34; see 1 Jn 2.7-9; 3.23; 4.21; 5.2-3; 2 Jn 5) in that Last Supper context is significant. The new commandment of love may be John's way of implicitly showing the link between Last Supper and the NC (see R.E. Brown, *John*, 612-14). If John is independent of Mark (see 2.22 'no one puts new wine into old wineskins'), as Brown thinks, then John might be another witness to the association of the Last Supper with motifs of newness and covenant.

117. Hahn, 'Motive' 368.

118. Lang, 'Abendmahl' 528-29. He thinks that the silence in the Pastorals, Catholic epistles, and Johannine corpus means that the idea was subsequently dropped.

119. Schweizer, 'Herrenmahl' 360-61.

120. But a number of scholars view the covenant motif as secondary in Mark/Matthew, because of its awkward grammatical position, impossible in Aramaic (e.g. Levin, *Verheissung* 271; Roloff, *NT* 223-25, following Jeremias, *Eucharistic*). The association posited is a–b (blood shed in death), *later:* b–d (via Exod. 24), and b–c (via traditions like the 'blood-rule' of Heb. 9.22), and/ or c–d (via Jer. 31.34), see Merklein, 'Erwägungen' 240. Scepticism about the c–d link: in Hahn, 'Motive' 366; Grässer, *Bund* 120.

121. Most scholars insist on this derivation: Merklein, 'Erwägungen' 240; Hillers, *Covenant* 187; Levin, *Verheissung* 273 (who thinks that there is also an echo of *Exod.* 24 in 1 Cor. 11.25); Schweizer ('Herrenmahl' 360) is emphatic, yet vague: 'Die Vorstellung *musste* sich anbieten, nicht nur von Ex 24 und Jer 31, sondern auch von den spätjüdischen Strömungen her. . . ' (my emphasis).—Grässer is sceptical (*Bund* 120): 'Jedenfalls wäre ohne das Stichwort "Neuer Bund" im Zusammenhang mit der liturgischen Abendmahls- überlieferung sicher niemandem Jer 31 als paralleler Text eingefallen'.

122. See A. Huck, *Synopsis of the First Three Gospels* (Oxford: Blackwell, 1972) 186.

123. See Lang, 'Abendmahl' 533; Levin, *Verheissung* 273; and W.G. Morrice, 'New Wine in Old Wine-Skins: XI. Covenant', *ExpTim* 86 (1974/ 75) 135.

124. Hahn ('Motive' 370-71) regards Jeremiah's oracle as a promise of

universal dimensins, while the primary referent of the Sinai covenant is of
course Israel. But in conjunction with the expiation motif of Isa. 53.12 (in
Mk 14.24) even the boundaries of the old covenant are expanded.

125. See Grässer, *Bund* 116, 124-125.

126. '1. Eschatologisches Freudenmahl ohne Deuteworte, 2. Totengedächt-
nismahl ohne eschatologischen Ausblick'; as summarized and criticized by
Lang, 'Abendmahl' 535.

127. Therefore we felt justified in treating the pericopes in isolation from
their contexts, as is customarily done. We have likewise taken for granted
that Paul is quoting from tradition. Since he fails to interpret the NC motif
in 1 Cor. 11, we did not give his voice separate hearing.

128. We have purposely disregarded the various forms of celebration—
with or without an intervening *Sättigungsmahl*.

129. We will refrain from discussing this issue at this stage and reserve it
for Chapter 5 section D below.

130. Grässer, *Bund* 127.

131. Grässer, *Bund* 124 (his emphasis); see also Hahn, 'Motive' 371-72;
Lang, 'Abendmahl' 536-37.

132. Of the 21 occurrences of αἷμα in Heb., only seven occur outside of
9.1-10.39. See Johnsson, *Defilement* 222-379.

133. See above, Chapter 2 section B and below, Chapter 5 section B.

134. After the long central section of theological exposition, paraenesis
resumes in 10.19-39.

135. On this see Wagner, 'Bedeutungswandel' 542-44.

136. 4.16; 7.25; (used negatively of the Law in 10.1); 10.22; 11.6; 12.18-24;
cf. ἐγγίζω 7.19. See below, Chapter 5 section D.

137. See Grässer, *Bund* 126, who detects in Paul the same absence of an
articulated Christian self-perception via the NC concept.

138. Six of his fourteen uses of διαθήκη are in ch. 14, where he contrasts
the Mosaic covenant with that brought by Christ, and where he quotes from
Exod. 24.18, but not from Jer. 31.31-34. The latter prophecy does not appear
elsewhere either.

139. See διαθήκη in *Clavis Patrum: Concordance to the Apostolic Fathers*
(ed. Kraft) 102.

140. See διαθήκη in *Index Apologeticus Sive Clavis Iustini Martyris
Operum Aliorumque Apologetarum Pristinorum* (ed. E.J. Goodspeed [Leipzig:
Hinrichs, 1912]) 71.

141. It was A. von Harnack (in *Die Entstehung des Neuen Testaments und
die wichtigsten Folgen der neuen Schöpfung* [Leipzig, 1914]) who first
suggested that the need to combat Montanism was instrumental in this
development. For this see pp. 215-16 of W.C. van Unnik, *'He kainē
diathēkē*—a Problem in the Early History of the Canon', *Studia Patristica* 4
(Berlin: Akademie, 1961) 212-27.

142. The passage is quoted in the Greek original in van Unnik, 'Problem'
219 n. 2.

143. See H. von Campenhausen, *Die Entstehung der christlichen Bibel* (Tübingen: Mohr [Siebeck], 1968) 306-7; and van Unnik, 'Problem' 219.
144. See Campenhausen, *Entstehung* 307.
145. Greek original in *ibid.*, 269 n. 115.
146. Greek original in *ibid.*, 308 n. 293.
147. Van Unnik, 'Problem' 219.
148. See Levin, *Verheissung* 267.
149. See Van Unnik, 'Problem' 225.
150. See Campenhausen, *Entstehung* 309, esp. n. 300.
151. Campenhausen, *Entstehung* 310.

Notes to Chapter 5

1. For a convenient list of the major comparative assertions in Heb., see Dey, *Intermediary* 121.
2. But it is inaccurate to regard this break as having occurred at the 'midpoint in history,... (having) broken the *Heilsgeschichte* into two halves' (Sowers, *Hermeneutics* 92). This ignores the definitive, abiding, heavenly character of the NC age.
3. See e.g. the quote from Spicq above, p. 15, but then the headings in his commentary 2.441-42. Also A. Nairne, *The Epistle of Priesthood* (Edinburgh: Clark, 1913); J. Smith, *A Priest Forever* (London: Sheed & Ward, 1969); Loader, *Sohn*; Zimmermann, *Die Hohepriester-Christologie des Hebräerbriefes* (Paderborn: Schöningh, 1964) and *idem*, *Das Bekenntnis der Hoffnung* (Köln: Hanstein, 1977), where the author's high-priest theology is portrayed as a redactional corrective of traditional material, notably the NC prophecy in Heb. 8; see further the headings in the outlines of the commentaries by R.H. Fuller, *Hebrews* (Proclamation Commentaries; Philadelphia: Fortress, 1977) and Johnsson, *Hebrews*.
4. See quote from Spicq above, p. 13; Grässer, *Bund* 95: '... unter allen... NT... Schriften (vertritt) allein der Hebr so etwas wie eine "Bundes-Theologie"'; Morrice, 'Wine-Skins' 134, calls Heb. the 'Letter of the NC'.
5. See above, Chapter 1.
6. See above, Chapter 2 section B, and below Chapter 5 section B.
7. Compare Grässer (*Bund* 100), who admits that the NC motif is a *Schlüsselwort* after 7.22, but treats it as an 'interruption' of the unfolding motif of priesthood.
8. 'Hebrews, Epistle of the *Diathēkē*', *PTR* 13 (1915) 587-632; *PTR* 14 (1916) 1-61.
9. Vos, 'Hebrews', *PTR* 13: 592.
10. Vos, 'Hebrews', *PTR* 14: 52; also *ibid.*, 43.
11. See Vos, 'Hebrews', *PTR* 14: 52.

12. See Laub (*Bekenntis* 46-50) on the 'Wort-Theologie' of 1.1-4.12.
13. See G. Hughes, *Hebrews* 73.
14. *Ibid.*, ch. 1.
15. G. Hughes, *Hebrews* 24.
16. G. Hughes, *Hebrews* 45, 63, and *passim*. See also C.K. Barrett, 'The Eschatology of the Epistle to the Hebrews', in *The Background of the New Testament and its Eschatology* (ed. W.D. Davies and D. Daube; Cambridge: Cambridge University Press, 1956) 363-93.
17. Dey, *Intermediary*; Thompson, *Metaphysical*, and *idem*, *Beginnings*; Nomoto, 'Herkunft'; Luck, 'Geschehen'; See also most German exegetes, e.g. H. Braun, 'Die Gewinnung der Gewissheit in dem Hebräerbrief', *TLZ* 96 (1971) 321-30; Grässer, *Bund*; Luz, 'Bund'.
18. See above, Chapter 4 section A (5) (d). See also Vos, 'Hebrews', *PTR* 14: 5-19.
19. Dey, *Intermediary* shows that in Heb., Philo and other Hellenistic Jewish works (in contrast to the OT and the DSS) these agents have *synonymous* titles and *interchangeable* functions, and that there is a correlation between levels of perfection and immediacy of access to God. Accordingly, Hughes would be wrong in speaking of 'three elaborate, *descending* convolute circles of comparison' (*Hebrews* 24), because he—and many other commentators—argue from the OT that angels are above Moses, and Moses is above priests. In fact Heb. may be polemicizing against traditions that rank Moses highest, as the supreme exemplar of perfection (see above, Chapter 2 note 9 and section B for the role of Moses; the role of angels in Heb. cannot be pursued here—see commentaries on Heb. 1-2).
20. D. Peterson, *Hebrews and Perfection* (Cambridge: Cambridge University Press, 1982) 187.
21. Dey, *Intermediary* 218-26, and ch. 8.
22. Peterson, *Hebrews* 187: 'The teaching about the perfecting of Christ and the perfecting of believers is clearly *more central to the argument of Hebrews than many commentators have allowed*' (his emphasis).
23. The τελειο- root is used 14 times: *negatively* of the old cult: 7.19; 9.9; 10.1; *positively* of Christ and his new cult: 9.11 (Tent); 2.10; 5.9; 7.28; 12.2; and of 'Christians': 5.14; 6.1; 10.14; 11.40 (ancestors/NC people); 12.23.
24. Vos, 'Hebrews', *PTR* 14: 33-34, 38, 41-43; Peterson, *Hebrews* 149-56; 166-67. Dey's phrase 'unmediated access' (*Intermediary* 124) is not felicitous when the perfecting of believers is in view, since Christ is expressly called a NC μεσίτης ('mediator') for his followers (Heb. 8.6; 9.15; 12.24). On this concept see below, Chapter 5 section C.
25. On covenant-blood see below, p. 98. Despite the overlap in meaning ἁγιάζω and τελειόω are not completely synonymous in Heb. (Peterson, *Hebrews* 150-53). Peterson argues convincingly that one must interpret each use of perfection language in its context (*ibid.*, p. 48). His careful exegesis proves that Christ's perfecting involves a unified sequence of

events in Heb., from Christ's suffering through his death to his exaltation (= what we have been calling the Christ event). Perfection includes a range of vocational, moral and cultic shades of meaning and ultimately signifies the fulfilment of the promises of Jeremiah's oracle through Christ's definitive consecration. It provides 'facilitation of mankind's approach to God' (*ibid.*, p. 166), while concomitantly requiring a life of whole-hearted obedience to God patterned after Christ (see *ibid.*, p. 187).

26. See G. Hughes, *Hebrews* ch. 1, section 1.

27. See 2.10, and especially 5.5-10, where the titles and functions are joined together. We hold that in Heb. *sonship* belongs to Jesus from his preexistence, while *priesthood* is conferred to him through the Christ event. (Laub [*Bekenntnis* 59] correctly notes that Heb. is not interested in 'when', but only in 'how' Jesus acquired his present status). It is important to stress that the cultic note of purgation for sins is already sounded in 1.3b in the proem (a fact often overlooked or explained away as secondary addition, see Johnsson, *Defilement* 8-9, 82, 251). Heb. 1.1-4, while containing traditional phrases, has been shaped into a unified, programmatic prologue by the author. Following the acclamation of the *Son's* role in creation, 1.3b implicitly announces the theme of Christ's *high priestly* inauguration of the NC.

28. See Grässer, *Bund* 96.

29. Vos, 'Hebrews', *PTR* 13: 627.

30. As stressed repeatedly, however, the cultic theme is not confined to this section: see e.g. 1.3b; 2.17; 10.29; 12.24; 13.10-12, 20. See Laub, *Bekenntnis* 87: 'Hebr 1-2 als Grundlegung für das Hohepriesterverständnis des Autors'.

31. See above, Chapter 1. The applicability of this scheme for interpreting Heb. is widely recognized also by non-German scholars, e.g. Vanhoye: 'le triple rapport. . . ressemblance- différence- supériorité' ('Tente' 3-4).

32. For the fusion of these ceremonies see above. See also Johnsson, *Defilement* 228-29, and D'Angelo, *Moses* 231-49.

33. See above, Chapter 2 section B and Chapter 4 section A (5) (d). See also Grässer, *Bund* 96.

34. Vos, 'Hebrews', *PTR* 14: 6. Vos points out that the OT largely thought in terms of consecutive, historical covenants, while the scheme of two ages became dominant in the II Temple Period. We would add that Jeremiah's prophecy contains the seeds, but not the full development of the idea that the NC is coterminous with the new age.

35. *Ibid.*, 8. But see MacRae ('Heavenly') on the spatial dimension in apocalyptic eschatology.

36. See the excellent discussion in J.W. Thompson, *Beginnings* ch. 10; also above, Chapter 2 section B.

37. Vos, 'Hebrews', *PTR* 14: 11.

38. Thus we disagree with Grässer's exaggerated focus on the *antithetical*

features of the two covenants: 'Die positive Bedeutung des Alten Bundes [erschöpft sich] zuletzt doch darin, das *negative* Gegenbild des Neuen zu sein' (*Bund* 114, his emphasis). D'Angelo (*Moses, passim*), Käsemann (*Gottesvolk* 35-37), and Oepke (*Gottesvolk* 20; 70-71) are better able to account for the elements of *continuity*. Vos rightly criticizes the repeatedly found view (e.g. in Braun, *Gewissheit* 326) that the old covenant is '*only*' a shadow of the NC in Heb. Instead the author wishes to stress that it *is* a shadow of the 'good things to come' (See 'Hebrews', *PTR* 14: 17).

39. Vos, 'Hebrews', *PTR* 14: 12-13.

40. For proof that *both* the old and the new order are characterized as διαθήκη see above, Chapter 4 section A (5) (c).

41. These qualities have been discussed so often (see above p. 148, note 3), that further elaboration is not required here.

42. The corresponding and contrasting features of the two Tents are so interwoven, that we will deal with them jointly below.

43. Johnsson (*Defilement* 222-35) makes an important contribution to a better understanding of the role of blood in Heb. by treating it from a phenomenological viewpoint.

44. On the need for bloody sacrifice in *both* orders see e.g. Stadelmann, 'Christologie', 201. We disagree with those who negate the need for sacrifice in the NC, e.g. G. Fitzer, 'Auch der Hebräerbrief legitimiert nicht eine Opfertodchristologie', *KD* 15 (1969) 294-319, esp. 310-11; or E. Grässer, 'Rechtfertigung im Hebräerbrief', in *Rechtfertigung* (ed. J. Friedrich et al.; E. Käsemann Festschrift; Tübingen: Mohr, 1976) 88 n. 30: '... den "Opfertod"- ... lässt er... mitsamt dem Kult, dem er angehört, erloschen sein....' *Christ's* sacrifice *is* important to the author; although it calls an end to all *further* earthly bloody sacrifice (10.18, 26), the NC 'sacrifice(s) of praise' (13.15) are grounded in it.

45. On covenant-blood see above, Chapter 2 section B esp. note 20; pp. 86-87 and nn. 43-44 immediately preceding. The OT employs *dam (ha)berît* only twice; Exod. 24.8 (articular); Zech. 9.11 (anarthrous).

46. See 2.2-3; 10.28-29; 12.25-29; also 3.12; 12.15-17; more on the consequences of membership in the NC in section C below.

47. Table adapted from Johnsson, *Defilement* 292, 337.

48. See B.F. Westcott, *The Epistle to the Hebrews* (2nd edn; London: Macmillan, 1892) 210.

49. See below, pp. 101-103.

50. ἐνετείλατο instead of διεθέτο in LXX Exod. 24.8.

51. Vos, 'Hebrews', *PTR* 13: 621. See above, p. 26.

52. See above, pp. 22, 26-27, 78.

53. D'Angelo, *Moses* 225-29.

54. In Vanhoye's exegesis the *first* Tent is the symbol of Christ's resurrected body ('Tente' 22, 25), because the bipartite structure is strictly carried over to the heavenly realities. Thus there is a correspondence: first

Tent = both the old order with its curtain/barrier, *and* its removal by the sacrifice/transformation of Christ's flesh, giving access ('Tente' 24); second Tent = earthly *and* heavenly sanctuary into which the high priests or Christ enter(s). Contra Vanhoye's insistence on *distinction* between 'tent' and 'sanctuary' in Heb., see P.E. Hughes, 'The Blood of Jesus and His Heavenly Priesthood in Hebrews', *BSac* 130 (1973) 314. For our other disagreements with Vanhoye, see reasons below, p. 152 nn. 56-57. For a thorough treatment of the curtain motif see O. Hofius, *Der Vorhang vor dem Thron Gottes* (Tübingen: Mohr, 1972); his underestimation of the parallels between Heb. and Philo. and his overestimation of the parallels between Heb. and *4 Ezra* are criticized by J.W. Thompson, *Beginnings* 6-7.

55.   In the sense of 'veritable'/fully real, see Vos, 'Hebrews', *PTR* 14: 14-15.

56.   See D'Angelo, *Moses* 225-231. Many have noted the seeming inconsistency between 4.14 ('passed through the heavens'), 7.26 ('exalted above the heavens'), 9.2-3 (first/outer Tent = ἅγια; second/inner Tent = ἅγια ἁγίων, 9.11 ('through the great. . . Tent. . . entered. . . into the ἅγια') and 9.24 ('entered, not into the hand-made ἅοια, but into heaven itself'), e.g. C.R. Koester, see above, Chapter 2 section C and note 49. In response, D'Angelo's remarks are instructive: 'The metaphor cannot be consistently applied. The earthly sanctuary provides a metaphor that is at every point interrupted by the exchange: Christ traverses the (created?) heavens, crosses the curtain of his flesh, crosses the greater. . . tent. . . in order to enter into the true holy of holies. . . *These crossings cannot be arranged in sequence, for they are all a single crossing*:. . . All of these metaphors for the prelude of his appearance across the veil before the face of God. This less than perfect consistency of the metaphor's application. . . reveals it to be a metaphor and *not a cosmological theory*. . . ' Despite the metaphorical language, however, 'the true focus of Hebrews' desription and interpretation of the tabernacle is the *service* done in it by the priests. . . ' (*Moses* 230-31, emphasis mine). This is confirmed by the exegesis of Loader, *Sohn* 162-68.

57.   Paradoxically, in the writer's figurative scheme, the first Tent embraces the whole sanctuary ritual, both *annual* (entry by the high priest into the earthly holy of holies—5.1; 9.7; 10.1-3) and *daily* (into the fore-tent by priests—9.6; by the high priest—7.27 sic!), see N.H. Young, 'The Gospel According to Hebrews 9', *NTS* 27 (1981) 201. Thus the actual OT data on Levitical ritual are not very helpful, since Heb. reworks them creatively (*ibid.*, 209).

58.   Young, 'Gospel' 302.

59.   As often suggested, e.g. Sowers, *Hermeneutics* 94-95.

60.   In R.E. Brown rightly insists on the (often neglected!) possibility of *different outlooks* among the addressees (see *Rome* 152-56). Most interpreters who deny the old 'relapse-into-Judaism-theory' jump to the opposite conclusion that *all* the readers must be Gentiles.

61. Young, 'Gospel' 205 n. 52.

62. See above, pp. 98-99.

63. J.W. Thompson, *Metaphysical, passim.*

64. βεβαιο-root: 2.2-3; 3.14; 6.16, 19; 9.17; 13.9.

65. μένω (7.3, 24; cf. 1.11; 10.34; 12.27; 13.14). αἰών = for ever (5.6; 6.20; 7.17, 24, 28; cf. 1.8; 13.8).

66. With the exception of 6.2, αἰώνιος is always used to signal the special, superior quality of the NC blessings: salvation (5.9), redemption (9.12), spirit of Christ's blameless offering (9.14), inheritance (9.15), blood of the eternal covenant (13.20).

67. As N.H. Thompson points out, oaths seem to have been used in most, but not all, covenants of which records survive; see 'The Covenant Concept in Judaism and Christianity', *ATR* 64 (1982) 504-505.

68. See Grässer, *Bund* 102; Braun, 'Gewissheit' (321-22: God's swearing (ὀμνύω is mentioned five times (3.11, 18; 4.3; 6.13; 7.21—twice in the rest of the NT); the noun ὁρκωμοσία occurs four times (7.20, 21, 28); ὅρκος once (6.17—twice elsewhere in the NT).

69. P. 21.

70. The Law and sin are not allies in Heb. as they are in Rom. 7, but Heb. 9.26 resembles the Pauline understanding with its singular ἁμαρτία; see Grässer, 'Rechtfertigung' 88.

71. Grässer, *Bund* 103, n. 425.

72. Laub (*Bekenntnis, passim*) demonstrates the pastoral purpose of presenting Christ's work as a *unified path* to glory. See e.g. p. 95 (about Heb. 2.9-10): '. . . Im Nachweis der unlöslichen inneren Zusammengehörigkeit und Einheit von irdischem und himmlischem Geschehen in der Christologie des Hebr (wird) die Niedrigkeitsaussage neu akzentuiert ins Blickfeld der gefährdeten Gemeinde gerückt'.

73. Commentators rightly stress the simple use of 'Jesus' here and in 12.2. See e.g. Laub, *Bekenntnis* 66.

74. For the way in which Heb. connects the perfecting of Jesus and of his 'brethren' see above, p. 96; also Peterson, *Hebrews* ch. 8; and Laub's penetrating exegesis (*Bekenntnis* 66-104).

75. For the opposition to Moses, whom Heb. avoids calling a μεσίτης see above, pp. 22, 23-25.

76. See Vos, 'Hebrews', *PTR* 13: 621: '. . . the person who vouches for the execution of engagements made; in this sense μεσίτης becomes synonymous with ἔγγυος'. So also Grässer (*Bund* 103, n. 427), and Loader (*Sohn* 249), who rightly connects these titles to the whole work of Jesus, not just to a particular function.

77. Unfortunately few investigations of the author's rhetorical skills and of his way of reasoning exist. See W.C. Linss, 'Logical Terminology in the Epistle to the Hebrews', *CTM* 37 (1966) 365-69, and references there.

78. For the statistics consult Linss, 'Terminology' 368.

79. The importance of this adjective in Heb. is universally recognized, see e.g. Johnsson, *Hebrews* (*passim*); Dey *Intermediary* 121, furnishes a convenient list of all occurrences; Linss, 'Terminology' 368: 13 instances in Heb. compared to 6 in the rest of the NT; see above, Chapter 4 section A (5) (d).

80. Greater responsibility corresponding to greater salvation: 2.2-3; 10.28-29; 12.9, 25 (see below, p. 104); superior potency of Christ's blood 9.13-14.

81. The argument is remarkably parallel: no new priesthood (7.11), covenant (8.7), or sacrifice (10.2) would have been required, *if* the old had been effective (see also 11.15-16).

82. ἀδύνατον to restore one who has fallen away—6.4; for God to lie—6.18; for animal blood to remove sin—10.4; to please God without faith—11.6; οὐδέποτε δύναται: for Levitical sacrifices to perfect (10.1)/to remove sin (10.11).

83. δεῖ: pay greater attention to greater salvation—2.1; ἔδει: Christ would have had to suffer repeatedly—9.26; ὀφείλω: Christ had to become like his brethren—2.17; high priest must offer for his own sins—5.3; ἀνάγκη: death must be established/brought forward—9.16; necessity of better sacrifices for cleansing τὰ ἐπουράνια—9.23; ἐξ ἀνάγκης: simultaneous change of priesthood and Law—7.12; ἀναγκαῖον: Christ must have something to offer—8.3.

84. See examples listed in Linss, 'Terminology' 367-68.

85. See Linss, 'Terminology' 365, for the abundance of logical particles and connectives.

86. *Ibid.*, 367.

87. See e.g. *Bund* 105, where he denies the polemical thrust of Heb. See below pp. 103-104, for our opinion.

88. This is Braun's accusation (in 'Gewissheit' 327), to which Grässer responds critically: 'Zur Christologie des Hebräerbriefes', in *Neues Testament und Christliche Existenz* (ed. H.D. Betz and L. Schottroff; H. Braun Festschrift; Tübingen: Mohr/Siebeck, 1973) 195-206.

89. In response to Braun's criticism of the epistle's semphasis on the *superiority of Jesus* as the basis for his power to save, Grässer shows the ubiquity of this type of argumentation in early Christianity, and notes that it tends to be expressed via metaphysical concepts and titles ('Christologie' 201).

90. See Grässer, *ibid.*, 195-99.

91. See above, Chapter 2 section B, and below, Chapter 6.

92. E.g. H. Windisch, *Der Hebräerbrief* (HNT 14; 2nd edn [Tübingen: Mohr, 1931]) 123; and above, Chapter 1 note 25.

93. The preferred 'German diagnosis'.

94. See above, Chapter 1, esp. note 23, Chapter 5 esp. note 60, and below, Chapter 6. We are using 'Jewish-Christians' as a short formula but are aware that such groups may have included their Gentile converts of the same conservative bent. As R.E. Brown notes (*Rome* 2, n. 2) factors other than the

attitude to the Levitical patrimony, such as differences in Christology, might also have separated the author from (some of) his readers.

95. We can only list some works that have informed our discussion: J.W. Thompson, *Beginnings* chs. 2-4, 9; Johnsson, *Defilement* ch. 5; Peterson, *Hebrews* 153-87; Dey, *Intermediary* ch. 8; F.J. Schierse, *Verheissung und Heilsvollendung* (München: Zink, 1955) 166-96; G. Theissen, *Untersuchungen zum Hebräerbrief* (Gütersloh: Mohn, 1969) 53-114; Laub, *Bekenntnis*, esp. part 3, 167-272; Vos, 'Hebrews'; J.V. Dahms, 'The First Readers of Hebrews', *JETS* 20 (1977) 365-75; J.C. Adams, 'Exegesis of Hebrews VI. 1f.', *NTS* 13 (1966-67) 378-85; Verbrugge, 'Interpretation'; Dahl, 'New'; W. Thüsing, 'Lasst uns hinzutreten (Heb 10, 22): Zur Frage nach dem Sinn der Kulttheologie im Hebräerbrief', *BZ* 9 (1965) 1-17; Swetnam, *Jesus*; Thurén, *Lobopfer*; V.F. Filson, *Yesterday* (London: SCM, 1967); H. Koester, 'Outside the Camp', *HTR* 55 (1962) 299-315; D. Lührmann, 'Der Hohepriester ausserhalb des Lagers (Heb 13, 12)', *ZNW* 69 (1978) 178-86; F. Schröger, 'Der Gottesdienst in der Hebräerbriefgemeinde', *MTZ* 19 (1968) 161-81.

96. See e.g. Oepke, *Gottesvolk* 19, 69: Thüsing, 'Kulttheologie' 4; Dahl, 'New' 401. A. Vanhoye's literary structure may be overly artistic and artificial in some of its details, but is widely accepted by scholars: *La structure littéraire de l'épître aux Hébreux* (StudNeot 1; 2nd edn [Paris, 1976]); also W. Nauck, 'Zum Aufbau des Hebräerbriefes', in *Judentum Urchristentum, Kirche* (ed. W. Eltester; J. Jeremias Festschrift; Berlin: Töpelmann, 1960) 199-206.

97. See 'Hebrews 5.11-15 and Greek *Paideia*' = ch. 2 of J.W. Thompson, *Beginnings*, who analyzes the athletic metaphors in Heb. and emphasizes the connection between παιδεία and suffering (see. 12.1-11); Adams, 'Exegesis'; Peterson, *Hebrews* 176-86, argues cogently that the seeming inconsistency between positive and negative statements about the addressees (e.g. 6.9-10 versus 5.11-12) can be explained by positing a spectrum of 'mature' and 'immature' members and fluctuations among the group, under the impact of threatening persecution.

98. See above, p. 143, esp. n. 87.

99. See 13.15: ὁμολογούντων; on the importance of 'confession' see below, pp. 107-108, 112.

100. More on the twofold service in worship and life see below, pp. 111-12.

101. See above, Chapter 4 section B.

102. On sharp condemnations of back-sliders, see above, Chapter 3 section C (2) (a).

103. See e.g. McCarthy, 'Covenant' 221. We are not implying any resemblance between Heb. and the Hittite treaties in form; of the six characteristic features that Mendenhall isolated, only (2) 'historical prologue', (3) 'stipulations' and (6) 'curses'/'blessings' are relevant for our analysis; so also Reumann, *Supper* 41.

104. As stressed by Braun, *Gewissheit* 325; Vos, 'Hebrews', *PTR* 13: 628-29.

105. διαθήκη only appears in 10.29; 12.24; 13.20—always in connection with the superior effect of Christ's blood.

106. See Vos 'Hebrews', *PTR* 14: 50-51, and the cultic references underlined in the next footnote.

107. Of the 12 occurrences in Heb., 6 are linked to the old Levitical *priesthood/covenant* (5.3; 7.5, 11, 27; 9.7, 19); 4 cover the 'people of God' under both orders (4.9; 8.10; 10.3; 11.25) and 2 refer to the expiatory (2.17)/sanctifying (13.12) *NC sacrifice* of Christ, the new *high priest*.

108. H. Conzelmann, quoted with approval by Grässer, in 'Christologie' 205.

109. Grässer, 'Rechtfertigung' 91: 'der Akzent... (liegt) auf der eschatologischen "Heiligung" der Gemeinschaft'.

110. Sanders, *Paul passim*.

111. See above, Chapter 3 section C (1). On the need to persevere in following Jesus, see below, pp. 108, 120-21, 122.

112. Peterson, *Hebrews* 175, 187.

113. This is not to deny that *all* of Heb. can aptly be described as a λόγος τῆς παρακλήσεως. On 'indicative/imperative' see Grässer, 'Rechtfertigung' 92; *ibid.*, 'Christologie' 206.

114. Laub, *Bekenntnis* e.g. 41, and *passim*.

115. Laub, *Bekenntnis* 42, lists some of the suggestions that have been made, mostly related to Baptism and/or liturgy.

116. See Heb. 2.1-4; 4.1-2, 12-13; 13.7.

117. Laub, *Bekenntnis* 45-47; Vos, 'Hebrews', *PTR* 14: 46-51.

118. See also κατέχω in 3.6 (boldness/hope), 3.14 (conviction); κρατέω in 6.18 (hope).

119. On the dual character of παρρησία, see e.g. Grässer, 'Christologie' 202-4.

120. Laub (*Bekenntnis* 265-72) interprets the προσέρχεσθαι of the recipients as a consequence of Jesus' high-priestly εἰσέρχεσθαι (13.13).

121. On ελπίς in Heb. see K.M. Woschitz, *Elpis—Hoffnung* (Wien: Herder, 1979) 615-35. On the distinction between faith and hope in Heb., see MacRae, 'Heavenly' 190-95.

122. See above, p. 100, and below, p. 110.

123. Luck ('Geschehen' 215): 'Jesus (ist)... 'Gegenstand' dieses Bekenntnisses (und) selber zugleich sein 'Interpret',... der durch seinen Weg... das Bekenntnis auslegt'.

124. On perfection, see above, pp. 96-97.

125. See Laub, *Bekenntnis* 69-77, 154-61.

126. See above, Chapter 2 section A.

127. On ἐπαγγελία see above, Chapter 2 section A. On the list of witnesses in ch. 11, see above, Chapter 2 section B (note 23); and also Barrett, 'Eschatology'.

128. See Wrede's famous title: *Rätsel*.

129. Even though we have been referring to 'theological/espository sections' (often termed 'cultic sections', as if that terminology were confined to them!) and 'paraeneses'/'exhortations' throughout our study, we realize that they are sometimes inseparable in Heb.; e.g. 12.18-24 and esp. 13.9-16 contain the gist of Heb. in a nutshell.

130. E.g. Laub, *Bekenntnis*; H. Koester, 'Camp'; Lührmann, 'Hohepriester'; Schröger, 'Gottesdienst', who provides a large catalogue of views from both camps.

131. R. Williamson, quoting T.H. Robinson, in 'The Eucharist and the Epistle to the Hebrews', *NTS* 21 (1974-75) 311: 'The author of Hebrews does not mention the Eucharist, because he disapproved of "the celebration of the Supper as a special ritual"'. Theissen (*Verheissung* 76-79) thinks that Christian sacraments are on the same footing as the Law in Heb.

132. E.g. Schröger, 'Gottesdienst' 178 (about 10.22); Laub, *Bekenntnis* 269 n. 256 (10.22; 12.22).

133. E.g. O. Moe, 'Das Abendmahl im Hebräerbrief', *ST* 4 (1950) 102-108; P. Andriessen, 'L'Eucharistie dans l'Epître aux Hébreux', *NRT* 94 (1972) 269-77; also Schierse, *Verheissung* 166-210, who regards Heb. as a 'liturgical homily', and takes 13.9-10 as a warning against false reliance on eating the Eucharist (p. 195); for further views see Williamson, 'Eucharist' (*passim*), and Laub, *Bekenntnis* 266 n. 249.

134. J. Betz, whose position is summarized by Thüsing, 'Kulttheologie' 2-3, thinks that the unity of covenant and cult in Heb signifies that the Eucharist is the focal point of the letter.

135. See Dahl, 'New' 401.

136. See above, Chapter 4 section B and Chapter 5 section C.

137. Laub (*Bekenntnis* 269) rightly says: 'Die Aufforderung zum Hinzutreten und die Glaubensparänese gehören. . . engstens zusammen'. But he is unduly restrictive, in regarding this as the only admissible understanding of 'drawing near' in Heb.

138. Thüsing, 'Kulttheologie' 7-9.

139. While carefully avoiding talk about 'heavenly sacrifice', Thüsing ('Kulttheologie' 8-9) reminds us that the Yom Kippur typology of Heb. is applied to the point where Christ carried his blood into the heavenly Tent. To stay within the epistle's prudent metaphorical language, we can say that the NC blood—even though shed only once in the ἐφάπαξ sacrifice on the cross—still 'speaks' decisively (= 'better than the blood of Abel' 12.24; cf. 11.4) on behalf of the worshippers in the *present* (see also Johnsson, 'Pilgrimage' 248). Those interpreters who absolutize the ἐφάπαξ idea restrict the meaning of 'blood' to Calvary and understand 'drawing near' strictly non-cultically as an appropriation of the benefits of that *past* sacrifice in daily Christian endurance and service (e.g. Laub, *Bekenntnis* 266-69).

140. Thüsing, 'Kulttheologie' 9.

141. *Ibid.*, 10-11. Like Laub Thüsing equates ἔρχεσθαι (in 13.13) with προσέρχεσθαι in its substance. The virtual equivalence of the various pictures for the heavenly goal (rest, possession, etc.) in Heb. is commonly acknowledged, e.g. Dahl, 'New' 402.

142. Johnsson, 'Pilgrimage' 249.

143. Johnsson, 'Pilgrimage' 248-50. We agree with Johnsson's contention that the *religious* character of Heb. has often been overlooked, especially by those scholars who try to reduce the cultic terminology of the work to its ethical implications (for more detail, see Johnsson, *Defilement, passim*). On the importance of the phenomenological approach, see also below, Chapter 6 note 6.

144. Building on the work of Käsemann (*Gottesvolk*), Johnsson ('Pilgrimage' *passim*) is able to show convincingly that the phenomenological characteristics of the pilgrimage motif (derived from other religious literature) illuminate our understanding of Heb. The element of *separation* is found both in the theological and in the hortatory sections ('pilgrimage', p. 245 n. 33), while the other three elements of *journeying*, with a *purpose*, and the experience of *hardships* are confined to the paraeneses (*ibid.*, p. 248).

145. Above, pp. 96-97.

146. See Thüsing, 'Kulttheolgie' 16 n. 58.

147. Thüsing, 'Kulttheologie' 16, emphasis mine. On the importance of the two-way covenantal relationship between God and his people see also Vos, 'Hebrews', *PTR* 13: 619-20; *PTR* 14: 47-48, 52, 57.

148. See Dahl, 'New' 401.

149. For this interpretation see Dahl, 'New' 404-405.

150. 'New' 404; this *objective* benefit of Christ's self-offering is explained by Johnsson, *Defilement* 329-37.

151. Dahl, 'New' 406: 'The expression "house of God" seems to include the things and persons related to the sanctuary'.

152. See above, Chapter 2 section B and Chapter 5 section B.

153. See Dahl, 'New' 406-407. This insight should not be extended to the point where a full-fledged theology of the 'priesthood of believers' is claimed for Heb. See the criticism by Laub, *Bekenntnis* 266 n. 250.

154. As Laub (*Bekenntnis* 268) would have it.

155. Klinzing, *Umdeutung* 146 (emphasis mine), referring to Qumran, but this applies equally to Heb. The phenomenon of *reinterpreting* prayer, good works, meals and other non-bloody 'spiritual' or 'material' (see the criticism of this terminology in Klinzing, 'Umdeutung', 143-47) means of service in cultic terms *as equivalence and/or replacement of bloody sacrifice* took many forms in the ancient world. For Judaism see e.g. V. Nikiprowetzky, 'La spiritualisation des sacrifices et le culte sacrificiel au Temple de Jérusalem chez Philon d'Alexandrie', *Sem* 17 (1967) 97-116; S.J.D. Cohen, 'The Temple and the Synagogue', in *The Temple in Antiquity* (ed. T.G. Madsen [Provo: Brigham Young University, 1984]) 151-74; for *Hellenism* and

Christianity see e.g. F.M. Young, 'Temple Cult and Law in Early Christianity', *NTS* 19 (1972-73) 325-38; E. Schüssler-Fiorenza, 'Cultic Language in Qumran and in the NT', *CBQ* 38 (1976) 159-77. On the danger of misunderstanding the dichotomy of outer/inner as worthless/true in Heb., see Grässer (following Käsemann, in 'Rechtfertigung' 89): bad conscience can also lead to 'dead works', and perfection of conscience means more than moral renewal, since it affects the whole person (*ibid.*, 90).

156. So Grässer, 'Christologie' 206; similarly Käsemann (*Gottesvolk* 155) speaks of 'echter Gottesdienst' for which the addressees have been freed by Christ.

157. In Dahl's view 'worship is hope in action, and endurance in hope is the approach to worship' ('New' 409). Thus there is a 'mutual interdependence of worship and hope' in Heb. 'New' 411).

158. Thurén, *Lobopfer* 234-46.

159. M. Dibelius, 'Der himmlische Kultus nach dem Hebräerbrief', in *Botschaft und Geschichte* (Tübingen: Mohr, 1956) 2. 174, compares the author to an 'old Calvinist'. Following him, Schröger ('Gottesdienst' 174) believes that—like Synagogue services—the services of the addressees were restricted to prayer, Scripture reading, homily, warning/exhortation, discussion of community concerns, and public reading of letters.

160. J.D.G. Dunn, *Baptism in the Holy Spirit* (SBT 15; London: SCM, 1970) 227, and 205-14 (on Heb.).

161. *Baptism* 227, based on Mt. 3.7; Mk 7.4; Lk. 3.3; Jn 3.25; Eph. 4.5; Heb. 6.2; 9.10; 10.22; 1 Pet. 3.21. βαπτίζω is used *either* literally (water), *or* metaphorically (Spirit, suffering/death), never in both senses simultaneously.

162. It would be redundant to cover the same ground as Schröger ('Gottesdienst') and Williamson ('Eucharist') have done in their thorough investigations of possible allusions to the Eucharist (and to Baptism). I reject other suggestions by Moe, Andriessen and others regarding such passages as 2.14; 3.14; 9.1-14; 10.2. I have purposely deferred discussion of specific allusions until now, in order to place these passages in their larger cultic context. (See the criticism of atomistic exegesis in Laub, *Bekenntnis* 267 n. 252, which is, however, unfair to Williamson, 'Eucharist'.)

163. See above, pp. 12, 48.

164. Dunn, *Baptism* 206-207. According to Dunn (p. 207), Baptism and 'laying on of hands' should be thought of as a single rite (cf. Acts 8.19; 19.1-7).

165. *Baptism* 210.

166. Williamson, 'Eucharist' 302-303 (following Theissen); Dunn, *Baptism* 209, interprets the 'tasting'-clauses as conversion 'in both its inward and outward aspects: the ῥῆμα and the δυναμείς being what they heard and saw, the δωρέα and the πνεῦμα ἅγιον being what they experienced in their hearts'.

167. 'Gottesdienst' 167, further references there.

168. 'Eucharist' 303.

169. Williamson, *loc. cit.*

170. Adapted from Dunn, *Baptism* 209-10, whose scheme neglects the cultic-priestly dimension of the process in Heb.

171. Schröger, 'Gottesdienst' 168-69. On covenant-blood see above, p. 98.

172. Loader, *Sohn* 249.

173. See above, esp. p. 111; also pp. 110-12.

174. Thüsing, 'Kulttheologie' 11-13.

175. For this interpretation see Dunn, *Baptism* 213.

176. *Baptism* 211-12, and Dahl, 'New' 407.

177. See above, pp. 112, 113.

178. Dahl ('New' 408) aptly speaks of freedom from 'an evil attitude of mind, a consciousness full of evil inclination'.

179. Above, pp. 109-12.

180. As postulated by Filson, *Yesterday* (*passim*), and Thurén, *Lobopfer* 246-47.

181. Lührmann, 'Hohepriester' 186; see also above, note 129.

182. 9.10, as part of 'fleshly cultic regulations'; 12.15-17, the story of Esau's selling of his birthright for a meal; here in 13.9, connected to 'diverse and strange teachings'.

183. See Loader, *Sohn* 257-58.

184. R.E. Brown, *Rome* 152-54.

185. χάρις appears in key passages elsewhere, most of which are hortatory: 2.9; 4.16; 10.29; 12.15, 28; (13.25).

186. So also Williamson, 'Eucharist' 307-309; Schröger, 'Gottesdienst' 171-72; Oepke, *Gottesvolk* 72-74.

187. See Williamson, 'Eucharist' 309, cf. 304.

188. See above, pp. 108-10.

189. Oepke, *Gottesvolk* 73.

190. *Ibid.*, and also Loader, *Sohn* 258.

191. For more on 13.15-16 see above, pp. 110-12.

192. Reumann, *Supper* 13 (emphasis mine).

193. See Williamson, 'Eucharist' 311-12.

194. Williamson, 'Eucharist' 312.

195. Thus we disagree with those who see evidence of the latter stance in 13.9 (e.g. Schröger, 'Gottesdienst' 172, and further references there). While it is difficult to imagine a Christian community without the Eucharist, O. Kuss is right to stress that the writer's focus is so clearly on Christ's *unique* highpriestly service that any earthly cultic representation of it may be consciously avoided; see *Auslegung und Verkündigung* (Regensburg: Pustet, 1963) 1. 321-28, for a balanced discussion and exhaustive references.

Notes to Chapter 6

1. See the convenient overview by W.G. Johnsson, 'The Cultus of Hebrews in Twentieth-Century Scholarship', *ExpTim* 89 (1977-78) 104-108. In our view, MacRae's article ('Heavenly') is a good example of the holistic approach advocated by Johnsson, whereas Zimmermann's reconstruction (*Hohepriester-Christologie*) dissects the text much too neatly into 'tradition' and 'redaction'. Ironically, Zimmermann ends up with the opposite conclusions from what we regard as MacRae's more plausible ones by assigning realized eschatology to the readers (a focus on the exalted, heavenly high priest, antithesis/discontinuity, e.g. 8.8-12; 10.5-10), and futurist eschatology to the writer (a focus on the path of the suffering/dying Jesus, his continuity with/fulfillment of the old order, e.g. 5.5-10; 9.11-22). To mention but two problems with this interpretation: 1. how can some κρείττων passages belong to one strand, and others to the other strand of the text? 2. Most scholars regard the cultic presentation as the *author's* original contribution; its focus is clearly on the 'ἔχομεν'/the 'now' available access to God.

2. MacRae, 'Heavenly' 179 (insertion mine). This holds good, regardless of whether one prefers to think of Heb. as a *written* homily from its inception or not (see above, Chapter 1 note 3).

3. MacRae, 'Heavenly' 196 (insertion mine).

4. A non-philosophical category that rarely occurs in Philo, see J.J. Hughes, 'Hebrews IX 15ff.' 93, for an exhaustive list. In traditional OT manner, διαθήκη (συνθήκη) in Philo usually points to God's steadfast love/ grace and to Israel as his special portion.

5. Schüssler-Fiorenza ('Cultic' 159-61) suggests the term 'transference' in order to avoid the problematic category of 'spiritualization', and she points to the limits of the *religionsgeschichtlich* method in trying to account for the differences between transference at Qumran and in the NT. See also above, Chapter 3 section A and note 13.

6. Johnsson advocates a phenomenological approach to supplement the findings of *Religionsgeschichte*, since the latter can only establish historical links, while the former can muster comparative cross-cultural data with a view to probing the 'internal logic of cultic argumentation' ('Cultus' 108), its 'direct and irreducible [force], not to be simply equated with theological expression' (*ibid.*, 107). Johnsson's dissertation (*Defilement*) proceeds along these lines and has convinced us that—even though there is clearly a conscious use of figurative/symbolic language in Heb. in relation to the cult (e.g. 9.8-9, 11; 10.19-22; 13.10, 12, 15)—purely theological (e.g. Laub, *Bekenntnis*), ethicizing/existentialist (e.g. Käsemann, *Gottesvolk*; H. Koester, 'Outside') interpretations will not do justice to the author's intent in employing that language.

7. Schüssler-Fiorenza, 'Cultic' 161.

8. See above, p. 119.

9. The references in the text are so oblique that various scenarios are possible. Some scholars (e.g. Oepke, Loader) consider it plausible that some of the readers were trying to hide under the cover of Judaism from Roman persecution, but there is no evidence for such occurrences before the III-IV centuries CE. C.F.D. Moule's theory of 'private Jewish antagonisms' is not very likely; see 'Sanctuary and Sacrifice in the Church of the NT', *JTS* (1950) 40-41. We accept his criticism of the common habit of dating texts by known official Roman persecutions (*ibid.*, 41).

10. See above, pp. 16, 116. While it is unlikely that Heb. was addressed to an elitist intellectual clan, some of Nairne's other views regarding its milieu (in *Priesthod* ch. 1) are still worth pondering. He posits a rise of patriotic fervour and a longing for concrete national symbols among diaspora Jewish-Christians, occasioned by the outbreak of the Jewish War. There is of course no reference to this war or to (the destruction of) the Temple in the text. We have so far refrained from discussing the problem of the *date of Heb.*, but in the course of our work we found that most of the arguments usually advanced for a late dating (e.g. 85-95 CE) can be countered. (1) 2.3 could hold true for any Pauline community and is no proof that 50-60 years have elapsed since the crucifixion; (2) if 13.7 speaks of the death of leaders, that also could have occurred even before 70; (3) about trials and persecutions see note immediately preceding above; (4) highly developed christological/sustained theological argument is found even in Paul; (5) on the issue of Jewish vs. Gentile Christianity, see above, p. 00; (6) If a Roman group of Christians is addressed, some wealthy members are possible even in the late sixties; see J.A.T. Robinson, *Redating the New Testament* (London: SCM, 1976) 212. I favour a date in the seventies/early eighties CE for Heb.

11. See Westcott, *Hebrews*, introduction liv; also above, pp. 16, 104.

12. For the phenomenon of this charge against Christianity by pagans and Jews alike, see F.M. Young, 'Temple' (*passim*); Moule, 'Sanctuary' 38-39.

13. See above, pp. 100, 104, 115.

14. See Moule, 'Sanctuary' 39.

15. Hence an unsuitable apologetic to Gentiles (contra Moule, 'Sanctuary' 38).

16. See e.g. Barrett, 'Eschatology'; also above, Chapter 2 section B and Chapter 5 section B.

17. See above, Chapter 3 section C (2) (c).

SELECTED BIBLIOGRAPHY

Adams, J.C., 'Exegesis of Hebrews VI. 1f.', *NTS* 13 (1966-67) 378-85.

Anderson, B.W., 'The New Covenant and the Old', *The Old Testament and Christian Faith* (ed. B.W. Anderson; New York: Harper & Row, 1963) 225-42.

Andriessen, P., 'L'Eucharistie dans l'Epître aux Hebreux', *NRT* 94 (1972) 260-77.

Barr, J., *Old and New in Interpretation: A Study of the Two Testaments* (London: SCM, 1966).

Barrett, C.K., 'The Eschatology of the Epistle to the Hebrews', in *The Background of the New Testament and its Eschatology* (ed. W.D. Davies and D. Daube; C.H. Dodd Festschrift; Cambridge: Cambridge University Press, 1956) 363-93.

—'The Allegory of Abraham, Sarah, and Hagar in the Argument of Galatians', in *Rechtfertigung* (ed. J. Friedrich et al.; E. Käsemann Festschrift; Göttingen: Mohr [Siebeck], 1976) 1-16.

Bauer, J.B. (ed.), *Index Verborum in Libris Pseudepigraphis Usurpatorum*, appended to *Clavis Librorum Veteris Testamenti Apocryphorum Philologica* (ed. C.A. Wahl; Graz: Akademische Druck- u. Verlagsanstalt, 1972).

Behm, J., *'haima, haimatekchysia'*, *TDNT* 1.172-77.

—and G. Quell, *'diatithemi, diathēkē, TDNT* 2.104-34.

Beker, J.C., *Paul the Apostle* (Philadelphia: Fortress, 1980).

Betz, H.D., 'Zum religionsgeschichtlichen Verständnis der Apokalyptik', *ZTK* 63 (1966) 391-409.

—'Jesus as Divine Man', in *Jesus and the Historian* (ed. F. Trotter; E.C. Colwell Festschrift, 1968) 114-33.

—*Galatians* (Hermeneia; Philadelphia: Fortress, 1979).

Betz, J., *Eucharistie in der Schrift und Patristik* (vol. 4.4a of *Handbuch der Dogmengeschichte*; ed. M. Schmaus et al.; Freiburg: Herder, 1979).

Bickerman, E., 'En marge de l'écriture', *RB* 88 (1981) 19-41.

Boehmer, S., *Heimkehr und neuer Bund: Studien zu Jeremiah 30-31* (GTA 5; Göttingen: Vandenhoeck & Ruprecht, 1976).

Bourke, M.M., 'The Epistle to the Hebrews', *NJBC* 2. 60.1-69.

Braulik, G.P., *Psalm 40 und der Gottesknecht* (Würzburg: Echter, 1975).

Braun, H., *Qumran und das Neue Testament* (2 vols.; Tübingen: Mohr, 1966).

—'Die Gewinnung der Gewissheit in dem Hebräerbrief', *TLZ* (1971) 321-30.

—*An die Hebräer* (HNT 14; Tübingen: Mohr, 1984).

Bright, J., 'An Exercise in Hermeneutics: Jeremiah 31.31-34', *Int* 20 (1966) 188-210.

Brown, R.E., *The Gospel According to John* (2 vols.; AB 29, 29A; Garden City, N.Y.: Doubleday, 1966, 1970).

—and J.P. Meier, *Antioch and Rome* (New York: Paulist, 1983).

Bruce, F.F., '"To the Hebrews" or "To the Essenes"?', *NTS* 9 (1962-63) 217-32.

—*The Epistle to the Hebrews* (NICNT; Grand Rapids: Eerdmans, 1964).

—'Recent Contributions to the Understanding of Hebrews', *ExpTim* 80 (1969) 260-64.

164   *The New Covenant in Hebrews*

—'The Kerygma of Hebrews' *Int* 23 (1969) 3-19.
Brueggemann, W., 'The Kerygma of the Priestly Writers', *ZAW* 84 (1972) 397-413.
Buchanan, G.W., *To the Hebrews* (AB 36; Garden City: Doubleday, 1972).
—'The Present State of Scholarship on Hebrews', in *Christianity, Judaism and Other Greco-Roman Cults* (Studies for M. Smith; Leiden: Brill, 1975) 1.299-330.
Buis, P., 'La nouvelle alliance', *VT* 18 (1968) 1-15.
Bultmann, R., *Glauben und Verstehen* (4 vols.; Tübingen: Mohr, 1965-67).
Caird, G.B., 'The Exegetical Method of the Epistle to the Hebrews', *CJT* 5 (1959) 44-51.
—'Son by Appointment', in *The New Testament Age* (ed. W.C. Weinrich; B. Reicke Festschrift; Mercer University, 1984) 1.73-81.
Callaway, M.C., *Sing O Barren One: A Study in Comparative Midrash* (SBLDS 91; Atlanta: Scholars, 1986).
Campbell, K.M., 'Covenant or Testament? Hebrews 9.16, 17 Reconsidered', *EvQ* 44 (1972) 107-11.
Campenhausen, H. von, *Die Entstehung der christlichen Bibel* (Tübingen: Mohr [Siebeck], 1968).
Carlston, O.C., 'The Vocabulary of Perfection in Philo and Hebrews', in *Unity and Diversity in New Testament Theology* (G.E. Ladd Festschrift, ed. R.A. Guelich; Grand Rapids, Michigan, 1978) 133-60.
Carroll, R.P., *From Chaos to Covenant: Prophecy in the Book of Jeremiah* (New York: Crossroad, 1981).
Cazelles, H., 'Alliance du Sinai, Alliance de l'Horèb et Renouvellement de l'Alliance', *Beiträge zur alttestamentlichen Theologie* (W. Zimmerli Festschrift; Göttingen: Vandenhoeck & Ruprecht, 1977) 69-79.
Charlesworth, J.H. (ed.), *The Old Testament Pseudepigrapha* (2 vols.; Garden City: Doubleday, 1983, 1985).
Clavier, H., 'Ho logos tou theou dans l'épître aux Hébreux', in *New Testament Essays* (ed. A.J.B. Higgins; Essays in Memory of T.W. Manson; Manchester, 1959) 81-93.
Clavis Patrum: Concordance to the Apostolic Fathers (ed. Kraft).
Cody, A., *Heavenly Sanctuary and Liturgy in the Epistle to the Hebrews* (St. Meinrad, Indiana, 1960).
Cohen, S.J.D., 'The Destruction: From Scripture to Midrash', *Prooftexts* 2 (1982) 18-39.
—'Conversion to Judaism in Historical Perspective: From Biblical Israel to Postbiblical Judaism', *Conservative Judaism* 36 (1983) 31-45.
—'The Temple and the Synagogue', in *The Temple in Antiquity* (ed. T.G. Madsen; Provo: Brigham Young University, 1984) 151-74.
—'The Significance of Yavneh: Pharisees, Rabbis, and the End of Jewish Sectarianism', *HUCA* 55 (1984) 27-53.
Collins, R.F., 'The Berith-Notion of the Cairo Damascus Document and its Comparison with the NT', *ETL* 39 (1963) 555-94.
Concordance to the Apocrypha/Deuterocanonical Books of the RSV (Grand Rapids: Eerdmans, 1983).
Coppens, J., 'Les affinités qumrâniennes de l'épître aux Hébreux', *NRT* 84 (1962) 128-41.
—'La nouvelle alliance en Jer 31, 31-34', *CBQ* 25 (1963) 12-21.
Cross, F.M., *Th, Ancient Library of Qumran and Modern Biblical Studies* (rev. edn; Grand Rapids: Baker Book House, 1958, 1961).

Dahl, N.A., 'A New and Living Way', *Int* 5 (1951) 401-12.

Dahms, J.V., 'The First Readers of Hebrews', *JETS* 20 (1977) 365-75.

Daly, R.J., *Christian Sacrifice* (Studies in Christian Antiquity 18; Washington, D.C.: Catholic Biblical Association, 1978).

D'Angelo, M.R., *Moses in the Letter to the Hebrews* (SBLDS 42; Missoula: Scholars, 1979).

Davies, J.H., 'The Heavenly Work of Christ in Hebrews', *Studia Evangelica* (Berlin: Akademie, 1968) 4.384-89.

Davies, P.R., *The Damascus Document* (JSOTS 25; Sheffield: JSOT, 1982).

Davies, W.D., *Torah in the Messianic Age and/or the Age to Come* (JBL Monograph Series 7; Philadelphia: SBL, 1952).

Deidun, T.J., *New Covenant Morality in Paul* (AnBib 89; Rome: Biblical Institute, 1981).

Delcor, M., 'Melchizedek from Genesis to the Qumran Texts and the Epistle to the Hebrews', *JSJ* 2 (1971) 115-35.

Delorme, J. (ed.), *The Eucharist in the NT: A Symposium* (Baltimore, 1964).

Demarest, E., *A History of Interpretation of Hebrews 7.1-10 from the Reformation to the Present* (Tübingen: Mohr, 1976).

Dey, L.K.K., *The Intermediary World and Patterns of Perfection in Philo and Hebrews* (SBLDS 25; Missoula: Scholars, 1975).

Dibelius, M., 'Der himmlische Kultus nach dem Hebräerbrief', in *Botschaft und Geschichte* (Tübingen: Mohr, 1956) 2.160-76.

Dunn, J.D.G., *Baptism in the Holy Spirit* (SBT 15; London: SCM, 1970).

Eichrodt, W., 'Covenant and Law', *Int* 20 (1966) 302-21.

Ellis, E.E., 'Paul's Use of the Old Testament' (Edinburgh: Oliver & Boyd, 1957).

Feld, H., *Das Verständnis des Abendmahls* (Darmstadt: Wissenschaftliche Buchgesellschaft, 1976).

Filson, V.F., *Yesterday: A Study of Hebrews in the Light of Chapter 13* (London: SCM, 1967).

Fitzer, G., 'Auch der Hebräerbrief legitimiert nicht eine Opfertodchristologie', *KD* 15 (1969) 294-319.

Fitzmyer, J.A., 'Now This Melchizedek ... (Heb. 7.1)', *CBQ* 25 (1963) 305-21.

—*The Dead Sea Scrolls: Major Publications and Tools for Study* (Missoula: Scholars, 1975, 1977).

Flusser, D., 'The Dead Sea Sect and Pre-Pauline Christianity', in *Aspects of the Dead Sea Scrolls* (Scripta Hierosolymitana 4; ed. C. Rabin and Y. Yadin; Jerusalem: Magnes, 1958).

Freedman, D.N., 'Divine Commitment and Human Obligation: the Covenant Theme', *Int* 18 (1964) 419-31.

Friedrich, G.,'Die Gegner des Paulus im 2. Korintherbrief', in *Abraham unser Vater* (ed. O. Betz et al.; O. Michel Festschrift; Leiden: Brill, 1963) 181-215.

Fuller, F.H., *Hebrews* (Proclamation Commentaries; Philadelphia: Fortress, 1977).

Georgi, D., *Die Gegner des Paulus im 2. Korintherbrief* (WMANT 11; Neukirchen-Vluyn: Neukirchener, 1964).

Gerstenberger, E., 'Covenant and Commandment', *JBL* 84 (1965) 38-51.

Gese, H., 'Die Herkunft des Herrenmahls', in *idem, Zur biblischen Theologie* (München: Kaiser, 1977) 107-27.

Goodspeed, E.J. (ed.), *Index Apologeticus Sive Clavis Iustini Martyris Operum Aliorumque Apologetarum Pristinorum* (Leipzig: Hinrichs, 1912).

Goppelt, L., *Christentum und Judentum im 1. und 2. Jahrhundert* (Gütersloh: Bertelsmann, 1954).

Gordon, V.R., *Studies in the Covenantal Theology of the Epistle to the Hebrews in light of its Setting* (Ph.D. Dissertation, Fuller Theological Seminary, 1979).

Grässer, E., 'Der Hebräerbrief 1938-63', *TRu* 30 (1964) 138-236.

—*Der Glaube im Hebräerbrief* (Marburg: Elwert, 1965).

—'Zur Christologie des Hebräerbriefes', *Neues Testament und christliche Existenz* (ed. H.D. Betz and L. Schottroff; H. Braun Festschrift; Tübingen: Mohr, 1973) 195-206.

—'Rechtfertigung im Hebräerbrief', in *Rechtfertigung* (ed. J. Friedrich, et al.; E. Käesemann Festschrift; Tübingen: Mohr, 1976).

—*Der Alte Bund im Neuen* (Tübingen: Mohr [Siebeck], 1985).

Greer, R.A., *The Captain of Our Salvation: A Study in the Patristic Exegesis of Hebrews* (Tübingen: Mohr, 1973).

Hahn, F., 'Die alttestamentlichen Motive in der urchristlichen Abendmahlsüberlieferung', *EvT* 27 (1967) 337-75.

Hanson, P.D., 'Apocalypse, Apocalypticism', *IDBSup* 27-34.

—'Old Testament Apocalyptic Reexamined', *Int* 25 (1971) 454-79.

Harrisville, R.A., 'The Concept of Newness in the New Testament', *JBL* 74 (1955) 69-79.

Hay, D.M., *Glory at the Right Hand: Psalm 110 in Early Christianity* (SBLMS 18; Nashville: Abingdon, 1973).

Hillers, D.R., *Covenant: The History of a Biblical Idea* (Baltimore: Johns Hopkins, 1969).

Hofius, O., 'Das "erste" und das "zweite" Zelt', *ZNW* 61 (1970) 271-77.

—*Katapausis* (WUNT 11; Tübingen: Mohr, 1970).

—*Der Vorhang vor dem Thron Gottes* (Tübingen: Mohr, 1972).

Holladay, W.L., 'The New Covenant', *IDBSup* 623-25.

Horgan, M.P., *Pesharim: Qumran Interpretation of Biblical Books* (CBQMS 8l; Washington, D.C.: Catholic Biblical Association, 1979).

Horton, F.L., *The Melchizedek Tradition: A Critical Examination of the Sources to the 5th Century AD and in the Epistle to the Hebrews* (Cambridge: Cambridge University Press, 1976).

Huck, A., *Synopsis of the First Three Gospels* (Oxford: Blackwell, 1972).

Hübner, H., *Das Gesetz bei Paulus* (2nd edn; FRLANT 119; Göttingen: Vandenhoeck & Ruprecht, 1980).

Hughes, G., *Hebrews and Hermeneutics* (Cambridge: Cambridge University Press, 1979).

Hughes, J.J., 'Hebrews IX 15ff. and Galatians III 15ff.: A Study in Covenant Practice and Procedure', *NovT* (1979) 27-96.

Hughes, P.E., 'The Blood of Jesus and His Heavenly Priesthood in Hebrews', *BSac* 130 (1973) 195-212, 305-15; 131 (1974) 26-33.

— *A Commentary on the Epistle to the Hebrews* (Grand Rapids: Eerdmans, 1977).

Huntjens, J.A., 'Contrasting Notions of Covenant and Law in the Texts from Qumran', *RevQ* 8 (1972-75) 361-80.

Ilg, N., 'Überlegungen zum Verständnis von *berît* in den Qumrântexten', in *Qumrân: sa piété, sa théologie et son milieu* (ed. M. Delcor; BETL 46; Leuven: Leuven University, 1978) 257-73.

Jaubert, A., *La notion d'alliance dans le Judaïsme aux abords de l'ère chrétienne* (Paris: Le Seuil, 1963).

Jeremias, J., *The Eucharistic Words of Jesus* (Translation from 3rd German edn, 1960; Philadelphia: Fortress, 1977).

Johnsson, W.G., *Defilement and Purgation in the Book of Hebrews* (Ph.D. Dissertation, Vanderbilt University, 1973).

—'Issues in the Interpretation of Hebrews', *AUSS* 15 (1977) 169-87.

—'The Cultus of Hebrews in Twentieth-Century Scholarship', *ExpTim* 80 (1977-78) 104-107.

—'The Pilgrimage Motif in the Book of Hebrews', *JBL* 97 (1978) 239-51.

—*Hebrews* (Knox Preaching Guides; Atlanta: Knox, 1980).

Jones, P.R., 'The Figure of Moses as a Heuristic Device for Understanding the Pastoral Intent of Hebrews', *RevExp* 76 (1979) 95-107.

Jonge, M. de and A.S. van der Woude, '11Q Melchizedek and the NT', *NTS* 12 (1965-66) 302-26.

Käsemann, E., *Das wandernde Gottesvolk* (FRLANT 37; Göttingen: Vandenhoeck & Ruprecht, 1939).

—*Paulinische Perspektiven* (Tübingen: Mohr, 1972).

Klappert, B., *Die Eschatologie des Hebräerbriefes* (München: Kaiser, 1969).

Klinzing, G., *Die Umdeutung des Kultus in der Qumrangemeinde und im Neuen Testament* (Göttingen: Vandenhoeck & Ruprecht, 1971).

Kobelski, P., *Melchizedek and Melchiresa* (CBQMS 10; Washington, D.C.: Catholic Biblical Association, 1981).

Koester, C.R., *The Tabernacle in the New Testament and Intertestamental Jewish Literature* (Ph.D. Dissertation, Union Theological Seminary, New York, 1986). To be published in CBQMS in 1989-90.

Koester, H., 'Outside the Camp', *HTR* 55 (1962) 299-315.

— and J.M. Robinson, *Entwicklungslinien durch die Welt des frühen Christentums* (Tübingen: Mohr [Siebeck], 1971).

Kosmala, H., *Hebräer, Essener, Christen: Studien zur Vorgeschichte der frühchristlichen Verkündigung* (Leiden: Brill, 1959).

Kuhn, K.G., 'Über den ursprünglichen Sinn des Abendmahls und sein Verhältnis zu den Gemeinschaftsmahlen der Sektenschrift', *EvT* 10 (1950-51) 508-27.

—*Konkordanz zu den Qumrantexten* (Göttingen: Vandenhoeck & Ruprecht, 1960).

Kuss, O., 'Der theologische Grundgedanke des Hebräerbriefes', in *Auslegung und Verkündigung* (Regensburg: Pustet, 1963) 1.281-328.

—'Der Verfasser des Hebräerbriefes als Seelsorger', *ibid.* 1.329-58.

—*Der Brief an die Hebräer* (RNT Kommentar; Regensburg: Pustet, 1967).

Kutsch, E., *Verheissung und Gesetz: Untersuchungen zum sogenannten 'Bund' im Alten Testament* (BZAW 131; Berlin: de Gruyter, 1973).

Lang, F., 'Abendmahl und Bundesgedanke im Neuen Testament', *EvT* 35 (1975) 524-38.

—'Gesetz und Bund bei Paulus', in *Rechtfertigung* (ed. J. Friedrich et al.; E. Käsemann Festschrift; Tübingen: Mohr, 1976) 305-20.

Laub, F., *Bekenntnis und Auslegung: die paränetische Funktion der Christologie im Hebräerbrief* (Regensburg: Pustet, 1980).

Lemke, W.E., 'Jeremiah 31.31-34', *Int* 37 (1983) 183-87.

Léon-Dufour, X., 'Le mystère du pain die vie (Jean VI)', *RSR* 46 (1958) 481-523.

Levin, C., *Die Verheissung des neuen Bundes in ihrem theologiegeschichtlichen Zusammenhang ausgelegt* (FRLANT 137; Göttingen: Vandenhoeck & Ruprecht, 1985).

Linss, W.C., 'Logical Terminology in the Epistle to the Hebrews', *CTM* 37 (1966) 365-69.

Loader, W.G., *Sohn und Hoherpriester* (Neukirchen-Vluyn: Neukirchener, 1981).

Lohse, E. (ed.), *Die Texte aus Qumran* (München: Kösel, 1971).

Luck, U.,'Himmlisches und irdisches Geschehen im Hebräerbrief', *NovT* 6 (1963) 192-215.

Lührmann, D., 'Der Hohepriester ausserhalb des Lagers (Heb 13, 12)', *ZNW* 69 (1978) 178-86.

Luz, U., 'Der alte und der neue Bund bei Paulus und im Hebräerbrief', *EvT* 6 (1967) 318-37.

McCarthy, D.J., 'Covenant in the Old Testament: The Present State of Inquiry', *CBQ* 27 (1965) 217-40.

—*Treaty and Covenant* (new edn; Rome: Biblical Institute, 1978).

McCullough, J.C., 'The Old Testament Quotations in Hebrews', *NTS* 26 (1980) 363-79.

—'Some Recent Developments in Research on the Epistle to the Hebrews', *IBS* 2 (1980) 141-65; 3 (1981) 28-45.

MacRae, G.W., 'Heavenly Temple and Eschatology in the Letter to the Hebrews', *Semeia* 12 (1978) 179-99.

Mandelkern, S. (ed.), *Veteris Testamenti Concordantiae Hebraicae atque Chaldaicae* (Lipsiae: Veit, 1896).

Manson, T.W., 'The Problem of the Epistle to the Hebrews', in *Studies in the Gospels and Epistles* (ed. M. Black; Manchester, 1962) 242-58.

Manson, W., *The Epistle to the Hebrews* (London: Hodder & Stoughton, 1951).

Martin-Achard, R., 'La nouvelle alliance, selon Jérémie', *RTP* 11-12 (1961-61) 81-92.

—'La signification de l'alliance dans l'ancien testament d'après quelques récents travaux', *RTP* 18 (1968) 88-102.

Martyn, J.L.,'Epistemology at the Turn of the Ages: 2 Corinthians 5.16', in *Christian History and Interpretation* (ed. W.R. Farmer et al.; J. Knox Festschrift; Cambridge: Cambridge University Press, 1967) 269-87.

— 'A Law-Observant Mission to Gentiles: the Background of Galatians', *Michigan Quarterly Review* 22 (1983) 221-36.

—'Apocalyptic Antinomies in Paul's Letter to the Galatians', *NTS* 31 (1985) 410-24.

Mayer, G. (ed.), *Index Philoneus* (Berlin: de Gruyter, 1974).

Mealand, D.L., 'The Christology of the Epistle to the Hebrews', *Modern Churchman* 22 (1979) 180-87.

Mejía, J., 'La problématique de l'ancienne et de la nouvelle alliance dans Jérémie XXXI 31-34 et quelques autres textes', *VTSup* 32 (Congress Volume Vienna 1980; ed. J.A. Emerton; Leiden: Brill, 1981) 263-77.

Merklein, H., 'Erwägungen zur Überlieferungsgeschichte der neutestamentlichen Abendmahlstraditionen', *BZ* (N.F.) 21 (1977) 88-101, 235-44.

Michel, O., *Der Brief an die Hebräer* (MeyerK; 14th edn; Göttingen: Vandenhoeck & Ruprecht, 1984).

Mitchell, J.J.,'Abram's Understanding of the Lord's Covenant', *WTJ* 32 (1969-70) 24-48.

Moe, O., 'Das Abendmahl im Hebräerbrief', *ST* 4 (1950) 102-108.

Moffatt, J., *A Critical and Exegetical Commentary on the Epistle to the Hebrews* (ICC 16; Edinburgh: Clark, 1924).

Montefiore, H., *A Commentary on the Epistle to the Hebrews* (London: Black, 1964).

Morrice, W.G., 'New Wine in Old Wine-Skins', *ExpTim* 86 (1974-75) 132-36.

Moule, C.F.D., 'Sanctuary and Sacrifice in the Church of the New Testament', *JTS* 1 (1950) 29-41.

Murray, N., *The People of the Covenant* (New York: Abingdon, 1962).

Mussner, F., 'Gesetz—Abraham—Israel', *Kairos* 25 (1983) 200-22.

Nairne, A., *The Epistle of Priesthood* (Edinburgh: Clark, 1913).

Nauck, W., 'Zum Aufbau des Hebräerbriefes', *Judentum, Urchristentum, Kirche* (ed. W. Elteste; J. Jeremias Festschrift; Berlin: Töpelmann, 1960) 199-206.

Nickelsburg, G.W.E., *Jewish Literature Between the Bible and the Mishnah* (Philadelphia: Fortress, 1981).

Nikiprowetzky, V., 'La spiritualisation des sacrifices et le culte sacrificiel au Temple de Jérusalem chez Philon d'Alexandrie', *Sem* 17 (1967) 97-116.

Nomoto, S., 'Herkunft und Struktur der Hohenpriestervorstellung im Hebräerbrief', *NovT* 10 (1968) 10-25.

Oepke, A., *Das neue Gottesvolk* (Gütersloh: Bertelsmann, 1950).

Peterson, D., 'The Prophecy of the New Covenant in the Argument of Hebrews', *The Reformed Theological Review* 36-38 (1977-78) 74-81.

—*Hebrews and Perfection* (Cambridge: Cambridge University Press, 1982).

Pretorius, E.A.C., *'Diathēkē* in the Epistle to the Hebrews', *Neot* 5 (1971) 37-50.

Rabin, C., *The Zadokite Documents* (Oxford: Clarendon, 1954).

Räisänen, H., *Paul and the Law* (WUNT 29; Tübingen: Mohr, 1983).

Rengstorf, K.H. (ed.), *A Complete Concordance to Flavius Josephus* (4 vols.; Leiden: Brill, 1973).

Reumann, J.H.P., *The Supper of the Lord* (Philadelphia: Fortress, 1985).

Reventlow, H., *Rechtfertigung im Horizont des Alten Testaments* (München: Kaiser, 1971).

Robinson, J.A.T., *Redating the New Testament* (London: SCM, 1976).

Roloff, J., *Neues Testament* (Neukirchener Arbeitsbücher; 2nd edn; Neukirchen: Neukirchener Verlag, 1979).

Rylaarsdam, J.C., 'The Two Covenant Theologies: The Dilemmas of Christology', *JES* 9 (1972) 249-70.

Sanders, E.P., The Covenant as a Soteriological Category and the Nature of Salvation in Palestinian and Hellenistic Judaism', in *Jews, Greeks and Christians* (ed. R.G. Hammerton-Kelly and R. Scroggs; W.D. Davies Festschrift; Leiden: Brill, 1976) 11-44.

—*Paul and Palestinian Judaism* (Philadelphia: Fortress, 1977).

—*Paul, the Law, and the Jewish People* (Philadelphia: Fortress, 1983).

Schelkle, K.H., 'Das Herrenmahl', in *Rechtfertigung* (ed. J. Friedrich et al.; E. Käsemann Festschrift: Göttingen: Mohr [Siebeck], 1976) 385-402.

Schenke, H.M., 'Erwägungen zum Rätsel des Hebräerbriefes', in *Neues Testament und christliche Existenz* (eds. H.D. Betz and L. Schottroff; Tübingen: Mohr, 1973) 421-37.

Schenker, A., 'Unwiderrufliche Umkehr und neuer Bund', *Freiburger Zeitschrift für Philosophie und Theologie* 27 (1980) 93-106.

Schierse, F.J., *Verheissung und Heilsvollendung: Zur theologischen Grundfrage des Hebräerbriefes* (München: Zink, 1955).

Schreiber, R., *Der Neue Bund im Spätjudentum und Urchristentum* (unpublished dissertation; Eberhard-Karls-Universität Tübingen, 1954).

Schröger, F., 'Der Gottesdienst der Hebräerbriefgemeinde', *MTZ* 19 (1968) 161-81.

—*Der Verfasser des Hebräerbriefes als Schriftausleger* (Biblische Untersuchungen 4; Regensburg: Pustet, 1968).

—'Das hermeneutische Instrumentarium des Hebräerbriefverfassers', *TGl* 60 (1970) 344-59.

Schüssler-Fiorenza, E., 'Der Anführer und Vollender unseres Glaubens', *Gestalt und Anspruch des Neuen Testamentes* (ed. J. Schreiner; Würzburg, 1969) 262-81.

—'Cultic Language in Qumran and in the New Testament', *CBQ* 38 (1976) 159-77.

Schulz, S., 'Die Decke des Mose', *ZNW* 49 (1958) 1-20.

Schweizer, E., 'Das Herrenmahl im Neuen Testament', in *idem*, *Neotestamentica* (Zürich: Zwingli, 1963) 344-70.

Segal, A.F., 'Covenant in Rabbinic Writings', *SR* 14 (1985) 53-62.

Silva, M., Perfection and Eschatology in Hebrews', *WTJ* 39 (1976-77) 60-67.

Smith, J., *A Priest Forever* (London: Sheed & Ward, 1969).

Sowers, S.G., *The Hermeneutics of Philo and Hebrews* (Richmond: Knox, 1965).

Spicq, C., *L'Epître aux Hébreux* (EBib; 2 vols.; Paris: Gabalda, 1952).

Stadelmann, A., 'Zur Christologie des Hebräerbriefes in der neueren Diskussion', in *Theologische Berichte* (ed. J. Pfammatter and F. Furger; Zürich: Benzinger, 1973) 2.135-221.

Stone, M.E. (ed.), *Jewish Writings of the Second Temple Period*, vol. III (CRINT 2; vol. 3; Philadelphia: Fortress, 1984).

Strack, H.L., *Introduction to the Talmud and Midrash* (JPS, 1931; reprint: New York: Atheneum, 1980).

—and P. Billerbeck, *Kommentar zum Neuen Testament aus Talmud und Midrasch* (6 vols.; München: Beck, 1922-61).

Strobel, A., *Der Brief an die Hebräer* (NTD 9; 12th edn; Göttingen: Vandenhoeck & Ruprecht, 1981).

Swetnam, J., '"The Greater and More Perfect Tent". A Contribution to the Discussion of Hebrews 9, 11', *Bib* 47 (1966) 91-106.

— 'Why Was Jeremiah's New Covenant New?' *VTSup* 26 (1974) 111-15.

— *Jesus and Isaac: A Study of the Epistle to the Hebrews in the Light of the Aqedah* (Rome: Biblical Institute, 1981).

Theissen, G., *Untersuchungen zum Hebräerbrief* (Gütersloh: Mohn, 1969).

Thompson, J.W., *That Which Abides: Some Metaphysical Assumptions in the Epistle to the Hebrews* (Ph.D. Dissertation, Vanderbilt University, 1974).

—*The Beginnings of Christian Philosophy: The Epistle to the Hebrews* (Washington, D.C.: Catholic Biblical Association, 1982).

Thompson, N.H., 'The Covenant Concept in Judaism and Christianity', *ATR* 64 (1982) 502-24.

Thüsing, W., 'Lasst uns hinzutreten (Heb 1022): Zur Frage nach dem Sinn der Kulttheologie im Hebräerbrief', *BZ* 9 (1965) 1-17.

Thurén, J., *Das Lobopfer der Hebräer* (Åo: Åbo Akademi, 1973).

Thurston, R.W., 'Midrash and "Magnet" Words in the New Testament', *EvQ* 51 (1979) 22-39.

Tiede, D.L., *The Charismatic Figure as Miracle Worker* (SBLDS 1; Missoula: Scholars, 1972).

Unnik, W.C. van, 'La conception paulinienne de la nouvelle alliance', *Littérature et théologie pauliniennes* (ed. A. Descamps et al.; Desclée de Brouwer, 1960).

—'He kainē diathēkē—a Problem in the Early History of the Canon', *Studia Patristica* 4 (Berlin: Akademie, 1961) 212-27.

Vanhoye, A., *La structure littéraire de l'epître aux Hébreux* (StudNeot 1; 2nd edn; Paris, 1976).

—'Par la tente plus grande et plus parfaite ... (He 9, 11)', *Bib* 46 (1965) 1-28.

—'Le Dieu de la nouvelle alliance dans l'épître aux Hébreux', in *La notion biblique de Dieu* (ed. J. Coppens; Leuven: Leuven University Press 1976) 315-30.

Verbrugge, V.D., 'Towards a New Interpretation of Hebrews 6.4-6', *CTJ* 15 (1980) 61-73.

Vermes, G., *The Dead Sea Scrolls in English* (3rd edn; Sheffield: JSOT, 1987).

—*The Dead Sea Scrolls: Qumran in Perspective* (rev. edn; Philadelphia: Fortress, 1977).

Vielhauer, P., 'Paulus und das Alte Testament', *Studien zur Geschichte der Reformation* (ed. L. Abramowski and J.F.G. Göters; Neukirchen-Vluyn: Neukirchener Verlag, 1969) 33-62.

Vos, G., 'Hebrews, the Epistle of the Diathēkē', *PTR* 13 (1915) 587-632 and 14 (1916) 1-61.

Wagner, V., 'Der Bedeutungswandel von *berît ḥādāšâ* bei der Ausgestaltung der Abendmahlsworte', *EvT* 35 (1975) 538-44.

Westcott, B.F., *The Epistle to the Hebrews* (2nd edn; London: Macmillan, 1892).

Williamson, R., *Philo and the Epistle to the Hebrews* (ALGHJ 4; Leiden: Brill, 1970).

—'The Eucharist and the Epistle to the Hebrews', *NTS* 21 (1974-75) 300-12.

—'The Background of the Epistle to the Hebrews', *ExpTim* 87 (1976) 232-37.

—'The Incarnation of the Logos in Hebrews', *ExpTim* 94 (1983-84) 4-8.

Windisch, H., *Der Hebräerbrief* (HNT 14; 2nd edn; Tübingen: Mohr, 1931)

Wolff, C., *Jeremia im Frühjudentum und Urchristentum* (Berlin: Akademie, 1976).

Wolff, H.W., 'What is New in the New Covenant?' in *Confrontations with Prophets* (Philadelphia: Fortress, 1983) 49-62.

Woschitz, K.M., *Elpis-Hoffnung* (Wien: Herder, 1979).

Wrede, W., *Das literarische Rätsel des Hebräerbriefes* (FRLANT; Göttingen: Vandenhoeck & Ruprecht, 1906).

Yadin, Y., 'The Dead Sea Scrolls and the Epistle to the Hebrews', in *Aspects of the Dead Sea Scrolls* (Scripta Hierosolymitana 4; ed. C. Rabin and Y. Yadin; 2nd edn; Jerusalem: Magnes, 1965) 36-55.

Young, F.M., 'Temple Cult and Law in Early Christianity', *NTS* 19 (1972-73) 325-38.

Young, N.H., 'The Gospel According to Hebrews 9', *NTS* 27 (1981) 198-210.

Zimmermann, H., *Die Hohepriester-Christologie des Hebräerbriefes* (Paderborn: Schoeningh, 1964).

—*Das Bekenntnis der Hoffnung: Tradition und Redaktion im Hebräerbrief* (Köln: Hanstein, 1977).

INDEXES

INDEX OF BIBLICAL REFERENCES

OLD TESTAMENT

Ezekiel						
11.19-20	41, 133n14	36.17-28	38	*Habakkuk*	
11.19	140n34	36.26-27	41	1.5	61
13.10	45	36.26	140n34	2.4	66
16.60	133n14	*Joel*		*Zechariah*	
18.31	133n14	2.28-29	41	9.11	151n45

NEW TESTAMENT

Matthew		4.5	75	11.25	64, 73, 146 n121
3.7	159n161	4.7-8	73, 75		
26.26-29	63	4.9-16	72	11.26	82
26.28-29	85	4.19	66	15.21-22, 45-	
		4.25	144n102	49	76
Mark		5.6	73	15.51-54	79
2.22	146n116	5.10	73	15.56	78
7.4	159n161	5.14, 18-19	76		
14.22-25	63	6	117	*2 Corinthians*	
14.23b	81	7	78, 141n42,	2.14-7.4	140n27
14.24-25	85		153n70	2.14-6.10	68, 140n28
14.24	83, 147n124	9-11	72, 73, 79,	2.14-17	140n31
14.25	82, 83		90, 142n63	3	63, 68-71, 73,
14.58	136n68	9.4-5	72		79, 90, 141
		9.4	71-73		n47, 142n69
Luke		9.5	73	3.1	140n28
1.72	63	9.7-8	72	3.2-3	68
3.3	159n161	9.11	142n53	3.2	68
22.15-20	63	9.15, 16, 18	142n53	3.3	70, 75
22.28-30	146n116	9.23	142n53	3.4-18	139n26, 140
		9.30-10.13	72		n37
John		11.5, 7, 28	142n53	3.4-5	69
2.21	136n68	11.24	72	3.6	63, 73, 143
3.25	159n161	11.27	71-73, 75		n85
6.51-58	146n116	11.28	72	3.7-18	76
6.53-58	114	11.29	73, 142n53	3.7-11	69, 80
13.34	146n116	11.30, 31, 32	142n53	3.10	69, 140n37
		11.31	142n53	3.11ff.	140n37
Acts		13.8-10	143n77	3.13	70
3.25	63	13.11	77	3.14-15	77
7.8	63			3.14	64, 70, 143
7.20-40	129n31	*1 Corinthians*			n85
8.19	159n164	3.16-17	136n68	3.15-16	70
19.1-7	159n164	6.19	136n68	3.17	71
		10.14-22	82	3.17-18	70
Romans		11	147n127	4	68, 139n26
3.21-26	75	11.20	82	4.2	68
3.25	144n102	11.23-26	63	4.5-7	68
4	72	11.24	144n102	4.6	75

APOCRYPHA AND PSEUDEPIGRAPHA

QUMRAN LITERATURE

INDEX OF AUTHORS